KEEP
WHAT YOU
EARN

KEEP
WHAT YOU
EARN

**PRACTICAL STRATEGIES TO PROTECT
YOUR ASSETS FROM TAXES, LAWSUITS
AND FINANCIAL PREDATORS**

TERRY COXON

TIMES BUSINESS

RANDOM HOUSE

Library of Congress Cataloging-in-Publication Data
Coxon, Terry.
    Keep what you earn : practical strategies to protect your assests
from taxes, lawsuits and financial predators / Terry Coxon. — 1st
ed.
              p.   cm.
    Includes index.
    ISBN 0-8129-2828-8 (alk. paper)
    1. Finance, Personal.   2. Tax planning.   3. Estate planning.
4. Financial security.   I. Title.
HG179.C688   1996
332.024'01—dc20   96-2349
                                                            CIP

To Betsy,
and to Little T, Little E,
Little A, Little D
and Little B

CONTENTS

PART EIGHT
PLANNING FOR LARGE ESTATES   267

PART NINE
ACTION   293

APPENDICES

KEEP
WHAT YOU
EARN

1

FINANCIAL SOVEREIGNTY: A REACHABLE GOAL

Some investors pay little or no tax on their income and profits. Their wealth grows faster and gives them more cash to spend. This book shows how they do it, so that you can do it too.

Some families hand down large fortunes without paying gift or estate tax. What one member doesn't spend goes 100% to his heirs—with nothing lost to the tax collector. This book explains how your family can do the same.

And one advantage leads to another. Some strategies for avoiding taxes also discourage malicious lawsuits. They convert your easy-to-seize investments into wealth that would be unattractive—or even repellent—to someone thinking about suing you. Used wisely, those same techniques bring privacy, lawfully removing your affairs from the goldfish bowl of mandatory reporting.

You can gain even greater financial protection by using tax havens—countries with negligible, or no, income and estate taxes. Most tax haven governments are *in the business* of helping investors safeguard their assets, and so are inhospitable to malicious lawsuits.

FINANCIAL SOVEREIGNTY

The three benefits of careful and knowledgeable planning—tax avoidance, privacy and protection from lawsuits—add up to *financial sovereignty*. With it, you can keep what you earn, protect what you accumulate, and gain privacy for yourself and your family.

Financial sovereignty isn't free—it demands some effort and attention on your part. But the requirements are not extreme. If your investments are large enough to attract sizable tax bills or to warrant special protection from lawsuits, you probably already have done things far more difficult than the steps this book recommends.

You needn't stretch or strain to achieve financial sovereignty. You don't have to disrupt your business, or bet everything on high-risk tax shelters, or bury your wealth in illiquid investments, or tie your finances into knots or skate along the edge of the law. On the contrary, a well-thought-out financial plan *simplifies* your life. It adds to your overall safety, to your freedom to maneuver and to your peace of mind—and leaves you more time for the many good things that have nothing to do with money.

A Goal Seldom Reached

Even though financial sovereignty is a practical, reachable goal, few investors actually achieve it—or even try. The trouble begins with a peculiar dissonance.

You hear, for example, that other people avoid taxes with clever tax shelters, long after the 1986 tax law supposedly abolished shelters. But when *you* search for one, nothing looks good. The deductions are too small or too slow in coming. The underlying business ventures seem too risky or loaded down with the promoter's expenses. And more often than not, you don't understand the program well enough to commit your money without worrying.

Or you hear about wealthy people who pay no taxes at all—supposedly because they get the best legal and accounting advice. But exactly what, you wonder, do the best tax attorneys tell their wealthiest clients?

You read newspaper and magazine articles offering tax tips, angles and strategies. But most of them don't apply to you or are ideas you already use. How much tax can you save by reading another article about IRAs?

Tax planning ideas turn up in nearly everything you hear about business and investing, and although you get hundreds of pieces of advice, few of them seem to fit together. Too many of these tips are presented as cute tricks, with little explanation of the underlying principles. How can you adapt them to your circumstances without fear of spoiling the magic?

And you hear that sophisticated investors use tax havens to sidestep the U.S. tax system altogether. But when you ask your accountant about setting up a corporation in the Cayman Islands or a trust in Bermuda, he dives under his desk. When he pokes his head out, he tells you that if you go anywhere near a tax haven, you will be charged with tax evasion, or you'll be defrauded by the local scoundrels—or both.

You may be left with the sense that the tax system is incomprehensible, or nearly so. You welcome whatever tax deductions come your way, and sometimes you take the tax-saving advice your accountant or investment broker happens to offer.

But after you've exhausted these easy opportunities, you still have to write a large check to the IRS. If that's the case, learning to use tax havens and other exotic devices may seem as practical as learning to be an astronaut.

The Wall of Anxiety

We'll explore the many simple things you can do here in the United States to protect your earnings and assets.

But some of the best opportunities for financial sovereignty are found elsewhere. U.S. investors seldom exploit those opportunities, partly because of the government's attempts to neutralize tax havens.

But it isn't just the government's rules that keep American capital at home. It's worry and confusion. For most Americans, every foreign financial center is surrounded by a wall of anxiety. The wall is highest and thickest around tax and privacy havens, and it discourages Americans in ways mere tax rules cannot.

One brick in the wall is the reputation of tax and privacy havens as refuges for unsavory characters. To some extent, this reputation is deserved. The idea of holding assets privately and getting them beyond the reach of tax collectors and malicious litigants is attractive to almost everyone. And if it's attractive to you, imagine how much more it is appreciated by drug smugglers, embezzlers and nervous dictators.

But dirty money is only a tiny percentage of the wealth secreted away in haven countries, and most havens turn it away whenever they identify it. Still, there's no denying that a thief might choose one of those sunny, tax-free Caribbean islands as the best place for his own, custom-made "Keogh Plan." The comparative ease with which dirty money can be hidden in *some* havens lends a bad odor to havens in general and gives investors the sense that there's something wrong with using any haven—a feeling of guilt by association.

Another brick in the wall of anxiety is the fear of being exploited by the locals. When you first deal in a foreign country, you are an outsider, and you don't feel confident about the rules. But one thing is clear: the bankers, brokers, attorneys and all the other locals know what they are doing. If you are overcharged or receive poor service, to whom do you complain? And would anyone care? The feeling of helpless vulnerability is worse than on your first day in high school.

What about the local government? In most countries governments come and go, usually taking their policies with them. How can you know that the country's no-tax regime won't be replaced tomorrow by a U.S.-style tax-and-spend regime? Or perhaps the local government will decide simply to confiscate all assets belonging to foreigners. It can seem better to lose 40% to the reliable, predictable, due-process U.S. government than to risk losing 100% to a bunch of people with accents.

And there is the fear of those terrible, electrified quills that seem to stick out in all directions from the U.S. Internal Revenue Code. Regardless of what the tax rules say, most people feel they *must* pay taxes or they will be punished. And the punishment will be worse for the traitor who snuck away to foreign places and conspired with the financial handymen of embezzlers and dope smugglers.

Despite the easy, lawful ways for investors to benefit from tax and privacy havens, the wall of anxiety is usually enough to keep American dollars at home. The unmatchable benefits of tax and privacy havens will never be more than a pipe dream unless you learn enough about havens to understand how safe they can be. Only then will you climb over the wall.

Doing so requires more than basic, how-to instructions. Using havens is a serious matter. Your own good sense and normal spirit of caution will hold you back until you are sufficiently familiar with the principles that underlie U.S. tax rules and until you are sufficiently at home with one or more of the haven countries.

Once and for All

This book is ambitious. I want to equip you once and for all to solve your tax problems, protect your assets and achieve financial privacy.

It can't be done by giving you a mere bag of tricks. It means helping you understand the general principles of tax planning (including the government's own problems in trying to collect taxes), showing you how to coordinate tax and investment decisions and giving you a step-by-step method for designing an effective plan that protects your assets from lawsuits.

And once you learn the principles underlying effective tax planning, you'll be able to apply them even when the tax rules change—as they inevitably will.

HOW TO READ THIS BOOK

We'll cover more opportunities for tax planning and asset protection than you actually need, so don't be overwhelmed by the abundance. I know you can't use them all. But if I had left one out, it might have been one that would work especially well for you.

Some strategies I'll discuss are very simple—but not all of them. As you read through the book, don't feel you have to master every detail of every technique. What's important is to understand when the technique would be useful.

When we get to Part 7, I'll show you how to pick and choose from among all the strategies and set up a plan that is right for you. Then you may want to go back and review some topics to understand them more thoroughly—but only the ones you need for your own plan.

So don't be troubled by anything that seems too complex. It may be something you don't need. And anything you *do* need will be much simpler to understand when you see it the second time.

Much of the information in this book may be new to you, but none of it is mysterious. With it, you'll be able to screen any tax-planning or asset protection idea you encounter, you'll understand why it is likely to succeed or fail and you'll know whether it is something you can use. Most important of all, because you'll see how the tax and litigation systems work, financial planning will no longer seem so complicated. You'll have the confidence to act, and act aggressively, to keep what you earn.

What We Will Cover

Principles. The underlying principles of tax planning are explained in Part 1. We begin by looking at things from the government's point of view. You'll discover that, despite its vast power, the government's ability to levy taxes and monitor your affairs is limited by problems it can never solve. Those problems are the breeding ground for all tax-saving opportunities and are the real guarantors of privacy. Understanding them will let you act with the confidence that you aren't inviting an expensive battle with the IRS.

Reducing Risk. In Part 2 we'll look at the risk-reducing concepts of portfolio planning. Some tax-saving strategies tend to make a portfolio riskier, and they do so in ways that may not be apparent to the investor until he suffers a serious loss. The principles of portfolio planning will help you spot the economic risks that may lie hidden like stowaways in your tax plan, so you can adjust the plan to eliminate them.

Protection against Lawsuits.   Part 2 deals also with the menace of lawsuits and the comfort of privacy. Managing your investments prudently gets you nothing if your profits are taken from you. This section will help you understand why today's legal system makes it so easy to lose everything you own through one bad day in court.

Easy Tax Savings.   Part 3 deals with getting the most from simple tax planning—the more conventional devices permitted (or even encouraged) by the tax rules for keeping income off your tax return. These devices let you accumulate and reinvest income free of current tax and without much additional effort.

Protection Through Trusts and Partnerships.   Part 4 explains two kinds of "imaginary persons"—trusts and partnerships—that can help you reduce taxes and protect your wealth.

Estate Planning.   Part 5 deals with estate planning. Tax rates run from 37% on estate values over $600,000 to a top rate of 55% on estate values over $3 million. Unless you protect your estate, your heirs could lose more than half of it. And with the generation-skipping tax, up to 80% of what you leave to your grandchildren could be lost to tax.

The government could turn out to be your biggest heir. But with the right plan it's possible to disinherit the government. And a well thought out estate plan can go even further—to create powerful structures that help your heirs keep what *they* earn.

(The more complex estate-planning topics are set aside in Part 8. The techniques explained there can push even the largest estate toward a zero estate tax bill. But you're not likely to need those techniques if your net worth is under $1 million, or under $2 million for a married couple—in which case you can safely skip over Part 8.)

Havens.   Part 6 covers lawful strategies for using tax and privacy havens. The opportunities range from convenient, prepackaged programs that are practical for almost any investor to elaborate plans suitable only for large portfolios.

You needn't send all your money, or even most of it, to a haven country. Placing just a small portion of your wealth outside the United States may enable you to protect all of it.

Part 6 also explores specific havens: countries that invite investors to operate privately, tax free or both. Each haven has its own advantages and disadvantages; each is a wise choice for some investors but a poor choice for others.

Your Own Plan. Part 7 shows how to use what you've learned to design and execute a specific, detailed, concrete plan for achieving financial sovereignty:

- how to select the tax-planning and privacy techniques that are best for you
- how to place your investment portfolio beyond the reach of lawsuits
- how to ease into changes in your financial life without creating new worries

Action. Part 9 shows you how to get things done, and it provides the most important element of all: how to get started.

RULES FOR YOU

I realize that you may wonder how it can be possible to escape the high taxes and exhaustive reports the government seems to demand. After all, the government makes the rules, and it enforces them with an almost vengeful fervor.

The answer, as you'll see, is that *privacy and tax avoidance are part of the rules.* By telling you what you must report, the rules tell you what you can keep silent—as well as what leads to a high tax bill and what does not.

It may strike you as fantastic that you can shield your assets from lawsuits when the courts are so enthusiastic about inventing new grounds for people to sue you. But even though the rules seem to be stacked against you, there still *are* rules. Understand them, and your property can be safe.

You don't have to be rich to use the rules to your advantage. Granted, having more money makes it easier to bear the overhead (such as legal and accounting costs) of thorough financial planning. But a better understanding of the tax and litigation systems will help almost anyone keep more of what he earns. Whatever your circumstances, there are techniques in this book that you'll think were developed with you in mind.

Rules for the Real World

The "income tax" is not really a tax on income, nor is the "estate tax" really a tax on estates. Each is a tax levied for not knowing the rules and for not planning your investments properly. And a court judgment is not really a blank check on your property; it is only a blank check on the property you leave exposed. It's up to you to arrange things so that the rules tell you "No tax. No reports. Nothing that can be seized." ⚷

PART ONE

PRINCIPLES OF TAX PLANNING

You might spend hour upon hour learning tax-planning tricks and be no better off. You could collect an impressive catalog of techniques but still not know which of them to use or how to assemble them into a coherent plan that is right for you. And no box of ready-made tax-planning tools can prepare you for what is sure to come—constant change in the rules.

A tax professional, on the other hand, isn't bothered by changes in the rules. Even if the entire Internal Revenue Code were replaced tomorrow, so that all his planning techniques became obsolete, he would soon be back at work, because he knows more than mere technique. He understands the underlying economic and political principles—factors no government can escape—that constrain *any* tax system and always point toward money-saving opportunities for the alert.

Part 1's introduction to those inescapable factors will equip you to judge the reasonableness and plausibility of the tax advice you receive from any source—from professionals, from the financial press, and even from know-it-alls at cocktail parties. It will give you the courage to act, because you will understand why, by the logic of the tax rules, a given technique should work. And it will help you understand how some tax strategies can lead to dangerous disputes with the IRS, while others protect both your money and your sleep.

2

THE TAX COLLECTOR'S PUZZLE

Year after year, despite decades of tinkering, refinement and reform, the government continues to wrestle with an insoluble puzzle. The puzzle will keep troubling the government for as long as there is an income tax. No new plan of tax reform will make it go away.

Understanding the puzzle is central to your job of tax planning. Every tax-saving strategy under present law—or under *any* conceivable law— stems from this one, unanswerable question: *how can the government accurately measure the income it wants to tax?*

The revenue authorities take the puzzle seriously. If the government is careless in defining the "income" it taxes, it will produce results unwanted by the very politicians whose purposes are served by an income tax.

Poorly conceived tax rules allow some industries to understate their income, while forcing others to pay taxes on income they haven't really earned. The industries that are hurt tend to shrink; their products become comparatively scarce and expensive. And, with their shrunken incomes, those industries may generate less tax revenue than if the government had treated them more evenhandedly.

And tax rules that mismeasure income feed public resentment, since some people pay more tax than others, whose true incomes are greater. Every sign that the tax laws are flawed—that they don't measure income accurately—increases public resistance to high rates of taxation. If resistance grows too great, people in government whose careers and conceits are fed by public spending might eventually wind up with fewer billions at their disposal.

The government doesn't want that to happen. So it keeps trying, year after year, to reform the tax system, to devise rules that measure income accurately. Yet it never seems to succeed. *It never will.*

WHAT IS INCOME?

True income is the flow of economic value—anything that adds to the total value of what you own. But economic value is not always susceptible to accurate, objective measurement, in the way a rock can be weighed on a scale or a roasting turkey's temperature can be taken with a thermometer. Economic value is subjective. It depends on what people want and feel and believe, and no instrument can measure such things unless it can read minds and hearts.

Diamonds are more plentiful than rubies; yet diamonds, carat for carat, are worth more. Why are the white stones more valuable than the red? Nothing about their objective, physical nature will give you the answer, because it is hidden in the tastes and preferences of the people who buy diamonds and rubies. Even if those people were eager to explain themselves, they couldn't tell you just *how much* they prefer diamonds. And even if their answers were precise when given, they wouldn't mean much for long, since human preferences are constantly changing.

Human wants are limitless, but there are clear limits to what, at any moment, people are able to do and have. Economic values arise from the compromises people make between their vast, shifting desires and their limited opportunities to satisfy them. Because those values refuse to stand up, stand still and let themselves be measured, the tax collector will always lose the game of hide-and-go-seek that income plays with him.

A Simple Case

It might seem easy to measure the income of someone who simply earns a salary. If he doesn't invest in tax shelters or have money held in trust, if he doesn't even have a home mortgage or an Individual Retirement Account, then it might seem that his true economic income is his salary—no more and no less.

But look a little closer and you find that an individual incurs costs and expenses in earning a salary. He has to pay for transportation to and from work. He may spend money on clothes he wouldn't otherwise buy and on lunches that would cost less at home. And he may have spent thousands of dollars acquiring the skills and knowledge he uses in his work.

Ideal, precise rules for measuring his income would, somehow, take all these and other costs into account. The rules would deduct the cost of commuting (unless he enjoys traveling about town early in the morning and late in the afternoon). They would deduct the cost of the clothes he wouldn't otherwise buy (to the extent it exceeds the cost of the clothes he would buy anyway). They would deduct the difference between the cost of eating lunch at work and the cost of eating lunch at home (unless he would eat out anyway). And each year these ideal rules would deduct a portion of the cost of his education (unless he didn't learn anything useful in school or had enough fun to offset the cost).

The Internal Revenue Service employs over 96,000 people. If they were expert at mental telepathy, they might be able to measure incomes accurately. But because IRS agents can't read minds, the government gives them arbitrary rules to follow: no deductions are allowed for commuting expenses, for clothing that is suitable for wearing outside of work, for lunches that aren't part of "business entertainment" or for the cost of acquiring the skills a job requires (although you *can* deduct the cost of improving your skills).

But these arbitrary rules raise questions of their own. How do you distinguish between (nondeductible) commuting and (deductible) business travel if, for example, the taxpayer makes a business-related stop on his way to work? How do you determine what clothing is suitable for wearing outside of work? How business-like does a lunch have to be to qualify as "business entertainment"? Can a business lunch be so entertaining that it's not deductible? And how do you distinguish *acquiring* a job skill from *improving* a job skill?

These unanswerables do not by themselves provide any special tax-saving opportunities, but they illustrate the one idea underlying all income tax planning: *even in the simplest cases, income is impossible to measure precisely.*

A BIGGER PROBLEM

The government's job is even more difficult when it tries to measure the income of a business.

A large part of the Internal Revenue Code amounts to a formula for calculating a business's net taxable income. This is where the discrepancies between the government's rules and economic reality are greatest—which is why tax shelters usually are organized around business ventures.

Just watching the cash register won't tell you whether a business is making a profit. To compute its income precisely, you must know the value of everything the business owned and owed on the first day of the year, and compare those amounts with everything it owned and owed on the last day of the year. The difference between the two, plus anything paid out to the owners, would be the business's true net income. But no one, least of all the government, can collect all this information.

To begin with, what is the market value, on any day, of the equipment the business owns? You can look at the books the business keeps, but they're only a formality—numbers calculated according to the government's rules. They say nothing about the actual wear and tear, nothing about the machinery's actual resale value or replacement cost, and nothing about its present or future usefulness.

Nor do the government's rules consider the business's goodwill and reputation—assets not even the owner can evaluate with much confidence. Any change in their worth during the year is part of profit or loss, but goes undetected by the tax rules.

The government is no more successful at measuring business liabilities. The rules simply ignore the effect of inflation and interest rate changes on the value of outstanding debts. But any decrease in the value of debt adds to true economic profit—and is invisible to the IRS.

No Help from Taxpayers

And, of course, the IRS does not have the taxpayers' willing cooperation in measuring income. Most taxpayers do what the rules demand, but almost no one tries to make the IRS's job easier.

The government is aware of the public's reluctance to cooperate, and constant skirmishing ensues. Taxpayers or their advisors find a way to reduce taxes. The government responds by changing the rules. But since the rules can never be perfect, taxpayers inevitably find opportunities in the new rules—to which the government responds by writing still more rules.

As the game proceeds, year after year, the rules become more complicated. When I began writing this book, the Internal Revenue Code was 1,648 pages long. By the time I finished writing, it had grown to 1,739 pages.

Tug of War

Adding to the tax collector's predicament is the nature of government itself.

The government is not a single person with a single mind. It is thousands of people, each with his own likes, dislikes, superstitions and objectives. It's no surprise that the rules they produce add up to a patchwork of inconsistent opinions, compromised purposes and contradictory effects.

In many cases the distortions in the tax rules are deliberate. Their purpose is to subsidize politically favored industries by understating the income of taxpayers who invest in them.

GIFT AND ESTATE TAX

The government has trouble enough taxing income. Its problems are even greater in taxing gifts and estates.

In trying to measure your income, the government has a reliable point of reference: it knows that you and everyone else ordinarily pursues his own financial interest. When you sell something (your services, an investment or anything else), you seek the highest price, while the potential buyers are shopping for the lowest price. And when you buy something, you want to buy cheaply, while all the potential sellers are trying to get as much as possible. Transactions occur when the buyer and seller find a price each is willing to accept. Their agreement reveals to the tax collector the value they place on what is being traded.

But gifts are another matter. By their nature, gifts transcend simple financial self-interest. You don't bargain when you make a gift; you bestow—without having to reveal to anyone the gift's true value. This leaves the gift tax collector to decide for himself whether the value you report is correct.

The tax collector has no problem if you give money or publicly traded stocks or bonds, since the gift's value is apparent. He knows that a dollar is worth a dollar, and he can find the current value of a publicly traded stock or bond in the newspaper.

But some things are harder to appraise. The value of a building or of a rare coin, for example, allows a range of reasonable estimates—appraisals the tax collector cannot easily dispute. This gives you latitude to declare a value that produces the tax result you want. If you give to a charitable organization, you can select a figure that's high but reasonable, for the sake of a large income tax deduction. If the gift is to a friend or family member, you can select a value that's low but still reasonable, to minimize gift tax.

Other gifts—such as a gift of raw land, a closely held business or privately issued securities—are even harder to appraise. The range of reasonable estimates and the opportunities for tax planning may be quite large. And some gifts, such as a business opportunity you provide to a friend or relative, are impossible to appraise—and may be virtually invisible.

The tax collector faces the same problems in appraising the estates of deceased individuals. Thus a well-planned estate may include some hard-to-value assets, so that the estate's executor may reasonably assign a low value to them.

OPPORTUNITY ZONE

Between economic reality and the *description* of economic reality incorporated in the tax rules, between true income and the government's *definition* of taxable income, between the true value of a gift and its reasonably *stated* value, is a gap—wide in places—where all tax planning takes place.

In most cases the government's description of an economic event is defective in one or more of three areas: valuation, recipient and timing.

Valuation.   What value was gained or lost? Most tax shelters depend primarily on this point. The tax rules may overstate the value of the shelter's expenses—depreciation, operating expense, or something else. Or the rules may overstate the value of the assets the shelter purchases. Strategies for shifting wealth to your children and grandchildren also rely on the tax rules' inability to value assets correctly.

Recipient.   Who received income? In the real world, only breathing, flesh-and-blood individuals receive income. The stylized world of the tax rules, on the other hand, is populated by corporations, trusts, associations, and other imaginary persons. The tax rules pretend those imaginary people receive income—and in some cases permit the real people behind them to pay little or no tax, as we'll see.

Timing.   When is income received? Value you earn in one year may not appear on your tax return until many years later. In the meantime you can invest all of it for additional income and profit. The simplest strategies delay the reporting of investment earnings for only a year or two. But by tacking delay upon delay, you can use for many years a large fund of money that otherwise would have gone immediately to the tax collector. And by tailoring certain strategies to feed money into tax havens, you can turn temporary delay into permanent avoidance.

No Tricks

The art of tax avoidance is often thought of as a bag of tricks. It isn't.

A trick relies on deception and carries the risk of being discovered. You have no way to evaluate most of the tax tricks you hear about, no way to judge which of them would go undetected—and you have good reason to fear the consequences of being caught. So tax avoidance may seem a dangerous game, one you would be foolish to play.

In truth, there are no tricks to tax planning. There is the imaginary world implied by the government's rules, and there is the world as it really is. Tax planning plays on the differences between the two, following the government's rules at every step.

Don't Look Now

In Part 3, we'll begin looking at specific ways for you to exploit those differences. But I hope you don't skip ahead to "the good stuff." The techniques explained in this book will be far more useful if you first take the time to examine the principles that underlie them. ⌐☞

3

WORDS AT PLAY

Words have meanings. But few words have meanings that are absolutely precise.

Except for *and, not, or* and other logical terms, words don't have clean, sharp boundaries. Even words with hard centers may have a good bit of fuzz around the edge. What, for example, is the difference between a bench and a pew? Is it possible to define *bench* and *pew* precisely enough to eliminate all possible arguments over whether any particular piece of furniture is one or the other?

It is the lawmaker's task to weave words, with all their fuzziness, into rules that aren't fuzzy. His job isn't easy.

Readers ordinarily try to understand what an author means. But those who are governed use their wits to *mis*understand the lawmaker's words. While they want to know the intended meaning, their keenest interest is to find a meaning that suits them.

To deal with this problem, the lawmaker may overlay one word or phrase upon others having similar or contrasting meanings. You seldom see anything in a statute as simple as "Fraud is illegal." Instead you'll find something like, "It shall be illegal to obtain any money or other property or claim upon property by means of any fraud, deception, misrepresentation or untruthful statement."

TAXPAYER'S OPPORTUNITY

This technique (which is partly responsible for the strange tone of most lawyerly documents) can yield a statement whose meaning is more precise than its component words. But because of the imprecision inherent in human language, no effort or artistry can purge a statement of all ambiguity. In the imprecision that remains after the lawmaker has done his best—in the residual fuzz—lies the taxpayer's opportunity.

The tax rules try to classify each payment you make or receive, to produce the "right" tax consequences. Much tax planning involves altering the complexion of a transaction just enough so that it fits within the meaning of one word rather than another. And much bad tax planning fails because the taxpayer has stretched a word too far.

Cat Tax

Suppose, for example, that your hometown imposes a tax of $100 on owners of cats, but no tax at all on owners of dogs. Obviously, you'd prefer that the city tax collector think of your pet as a dog—even if neither its mother nor its father was ever known to be one.

Name your pet "Rover" if you like, but if it hunts mice, walks on fences and says "meow," don't expect the tax collector to believe it is anything but a cat. You'll have to pay the tax, and perhaps a fine, if you try to pass the animal off as a dog just by calling it one.

The attempt would fail because the animal has so few doglike characteristics and so many catlike ones. But if in addition to being called a dog, your pet is large (as cats go), and if it is an unusual breed (such as a calico collie), and if you keep it so well fed that no one ever sees it chasing a mouse, and if you trim its claws to keep it from climbing fences, and if you train it to say "bow-wow" or even "meow-wow," you might save yourself $100.

TAX TERMS

Following is a small sampling of terms that have led to tugs-of-war between taxpayers and the government. All of them show up in everyday conversation, and you might suppose their meanings are clear. But, as we'll see, they leave plenty of room for argument.

Some of the terms will appear again, later in the book. But for now, take them simply as examples of how the word game is played.

Employee versus *Contractor*

You're an *employee* if the person who pays for your work also controls and supervises it. Otherwise, you're a *contractor*.

The distinction can be critical for a business seeking the special tax benefits of a "qualified" pension plan (discussed in Chapter 13). Misclassifying workers can increase the cost of the plan, interfere with valuable tax deductions and even make the plan ineligible for favorable tax treatment. Erroneously calling an employee a *contractor* can lead to bills for years of unpaid Social Security taxes and other payroll levies.

Factors arguing that a worker is an employee are:

- He is required to work at a particular place during particular hours.

- He is required to follow the instructions of the business that pays him.

- He is paid for his time, not for what he produces.

Factors arguing that a worker is a contractor are:

- None or few of the *employee* factors are present.

- The worker provides his own tools, equipment, workplace and insurance.

- The worker provides services to other businesses (i.e., he has other customers).

No one of these factors is decisive. If a worker looks partly like a contractor and partly like an employee, his customer *may* be free to choose what to call him. In other cases a little rearranging may be sufficient to transform an employee into a contractor, or vice versa.

Investment Expense

To be an *investment expense,* a payment must be reasonably necessary for conserving investments, collecting income, or making trades. If you own $5,000 worth of stock in Nestlé Corporation, the cost of a trip to Switzerland to visit the company headquarters is not an investment expense, because it is not reasonably necessary, since you couldn't expect to increase your investment income or profits by enough to pay for the trip.

Business Expense

To be a *business expense,* a payment must be an ordinary and necessary cost of doing business.

To claim such a deduction, you must be in a business, doing something for profit. Don't think you can deduct the cost of dinner on the basis that you eat dinner for a living—unless you earn money as a restaurant critic.

The IRS sometimes suspects that a taxpayer is calling his hobby a business to make the costs deductible. Horse ranches are a notorious example. But if an activity, however pleasant, shows a profit during any two of the most recent five years, the courts will presume the activity is a business. This shifts the burden to the IRS to demonstrate that the activity is a hobby.

On the other hand, if you do something consistently unprofitable, it's up to you to prove it's a business. Facts that would argue in your favor are:

- You keep business-like records and accounts.
- You hire employees or consultants with experience in the activity.
- You advertise or otherwise try to promote sales.
- The activity is of a kind in which prolonged losses are common but sometimes lead to very large profits.
- Only a deranged person would do it for fun.

If an activity is a *business,* then its "ordinary and necessary" expenses are deductible. The "ordinary and necessary" provision lets the IRS disallow expenses it finds bizarre (such as fees paid to a psychic) but which it cannot easily prove are unrelated to a business.

Gift

For tax purposes, a *gift* is a transfer you make gratuitously—for the benefit of the recipient and without any agreement, understanding or obligation that the recipient provide something in return.

The tax collector may have trouble determining whether a transfer is a gift. To begin with, his concept of a gift doesn't quite match what gifts ordinarily involve.

In truth, you seldom make a gift without expecting *something* in return. A parent makes a hundred gifts a day to a small child. While the parent doesn't expect Junior to respond by writing a check, the parent does expect Junior to say "thank you" and even to perform valuable services, such as cleaning his room. And parents who give large sums to their children or grandchildren also expect the recipients to say "thank you," to remember birthdays and other family celebrations and to show up for Christmas dinner at least every third year.

Almost anyone who receives a gift knows that such tokens are anticipated and that the flow of gifts is likely to slacken if the tokens are not forthcoming. Thus, in the ordinary course of things, something is given and something *is* expected in return. While the reciprocity is not as clear cut and obvious as with, say, selling a house through an escrow, it is just as real.

For tax purposes, the primary characteristic of a gift is the giver's "detached and disinterested generosity." Such a motive is indicated by:

- *Closeness of relationship.* Transfers between parents and children *look* like gifts. Transfers between complete strangers *don't* look like gifts. Transfers between cousins or between friends of long standing *may* look like gifts, especially if there is no apparent business relationship.

- *Absence of something given in return.* If the recipient of a supposed "gift" makes a "gift" of comparable value to his benefactor at about the same time, the two transfers will look like a trade. But if the transfers are, say, a year or more apart, and if the fair market values are substantially different, they may appear to be gifts.

- *Differences in circumstances.* Valuable gifts ordinarily are made to someone who is less wealthy. But there are exceptions, such as gifts by very old grandparents to wealthier descendants and gifts to charitable organizations.

Option

A taxpayer may liquidate an investment indirectly, by selling someone an option to buy the investment. The tax advantage can be huge. (Using options to save taxes is discussed in Chapter 15, "Managing Capital Gains.") But what exactly is an option *under the tax rules?*

An option gives the holder the right to do something without being obligated to do it. A call option, for example, gives the holder the right to buy something (such as certain shares of stock) at a specified price (called the *striking price*) until a specified expiration date. It will be profitable for the holder to *exercise the call option* (use his right to buy the stock) only if the stock's open-market price rises above the striking price.

To be an option for *tax purposes*, a contract must entail a substantial degree of uncertainty at the time it is made about whether the option holder will eventually exercise it.

If General Motors stock is trading at $50 per share, the right to purchase a share for $50 at any time during the coming six months is clearly an option for tax purposes—since the option may or may not be exercised, depending on whether the price of GM is above or below $50 six months from now. But the right to buy GM stock for $2 per share during the coming 30 days would not be an option for tax purposes. The possibility the holder would forgo exercising his right is too remote, since there's so little likelihood of GM falling from $50 to less than $2 in just 30 days.

DOUBLE TALK

You may find some of these distinctions a bit hazy if this is the first time you've scrutinized the meanings of tax terms.

But don't worry. They will be explained more thoroughly later, as they are needed. The purpose here is simply to alert you that words can be stretched—but only so far without snapping. ⚿

4

WHERE THE TAX RULES COME FROM

You don't have to memorize all the details of this chapter. You're not back in civics class, and there won't be a quiz. What's important to remember is simply that there are rules and that there are some consistency and stability to them.

To be sure, the rules are complex, which can leave you feeling you're playing a no-win game on a court with trapdoors, trip wires and a wet marble floor. Discouraged and demoralized, you might give up and let the government win by default.

But in fact you *can* win the game. There is no rule saying, "Pay whatever tax you are told to." Despite their vastness and complexity, the rules are finite, and the ways in which they can change are limited and constrained. Thus the rules leave open the opportunity to devise a plan of tax avoidance you can count on to work.

STRUCTURE OF RULES

"The rules" aren't simply a long list of instructions. There is a hierarchy to them. Some rules are, in effect, the children of others; they exist only through the operation of their parent rules. When conflicts emerge, the rules at one level yield to those at a higher level. What's more, "the rules" include rules for making and changing the rules. Generally, the most junior rules are the most easily changed.

At the top of the hierarchy is the U.S. Constitution. Below it are tax laws, Treasury Regulations, Revenue Rulings and Private Rulings.

U.S. CONSTITUTION

The present regime of income taxation was authorized in 1913 by ratification of the Sixteenth Amendment to the Constitution.[1]

The Congress shall have the power to lay and collect taxes on income, from whatever source derived, without apportionment among the several States, and without regard to any census or enumeration.

Few provisions of the Constitution have been upheld with more vigor.

TAX LAWS

Second in the hierarchy of rules are the tax laws passed by Congress.

Nine months after ratification of the Sixteenth Amendment, Congress enacted the Tariff Act of October 3, 1913. It was six pages long and taxed income at rates up to 6%. The Tariff Act was followed by more income tax measures. Each one formally repealed its predecessor and stood as a complete, "new" law, although, typically, the new law would repeat provisions of earlier laws.

The pattern of repeal-and-replace continued until the Internal Revenue Code of 1939, which was written in a format that left room for later changes. The 1939 Code remained in force for 15 years, evolving through an accumulation of amendments. Then it was replaced by the Internal Revenue Code of 1954, which was concocted out of the provisions of the 1939 Code, plus some new material.

As with the 1939 Code, many provisions of the 1954 Code stood unchanged year after year. But more provisions were added, including those of six major "tax reforms" passed by Congress.

In 1986 most of the accumulated provisions of the 1954 Code were reenacted into law, along with still more provisions, as the Internal Revenue Code of 1986.

Take a Look

If you've never actually seen the Internal Revenue Code, you might browse through it the next time you visit an attorney or accountant. Or bet-

---

[1] The first U.S. tax on income was levied by Congress in 1864 to help finance the Civil War, and was repealed soon after. A second income tax was enacted in 1894, but was declared unconstitutional by the Supreme Court in 1895.

ter yet, buy a copy. (Ordering information appears in Chapter 35, "Where to Get Help.")

You needn't become a student of the Code to plan your affairs successfully, but you should invest a little effort once in a while to read a few paragraphs on topics that interest you. Mark anything you don't understand, and ask a tax advisor to explain it. This exercise is worthwhile—not so much for the particular bits of information you acquire as for avoiding the feeling of bewilderment that paralyzes many taxpayers.

Bad Joke

When you open the book, which is nearly 2,000 pages long, you probably will wonder, "How can anyone read all this stuff?" The answer is that almost no one can. I'm not sure that any one person ever has read the entire Code—certainly not the congressmen and senators who voted it into law.

It's a little chilling, and a bit laughable, to think you can go to jail for disobeying a law that was pasted together over a period of 45 years by congressional staff assistants and Government Printing Office typesetters. On the other hand, the mere size of the Code assures that no one can understand it completely and that it will be full of surprises and tax-saving opportunities.

Like any other federal law, the Internal Revenue Code is subject to review by the federal courts. In principle, any part of it could be found unconstitutional. In practice, however, this has happened only rarely. Legal controversies about taxes are seldom about the Code's validity; they are about its meaning.

Structure of the Code

The Internal Revenue Code is divided into ten subtitles. They are:

Subtitle A. Income taxes

Subtitle B. Estate and gift taxes

Subtitle C. Employment taxes

Subtitle D. Miscellaneous excise taxes

Subtitle E. Alcohol, tobacco, and certain other excise taxes

Subtitle F. Procedure and administration

Subtitle G. The Joint Committee on Taxation

Subtitle H. Financing of presidential election campaigns

Subtitle I. Trust fund code

Subtitle J. Coal industry health benefits

Subtitles A and B contain most of the material that affects your personal tax planning and account for about 60% of the entire Code. Subtitle F sets out the procedures for enforcing the Code and settling disputes between taxpayers and the IRS (a topic we'll cover in the next chapter).

Subtitle I was added in 1977. It originally dealt solely with the Black Lung Disability Trust Fund and took up 2½ pages. Why this particular disease, of all the maladies a U.S. citizen might suffer, was enshrined in its own subtitle is a mystery to me. But the mystery hints more than a little at what motivates congressmen in making and amending tax laws.

Each of the subtitles is divided into chapters, with 59 chapters in all. The chapters are further divided into subchapters, parts and subparts.[2] Finally, each subpart is made up of one or more sections.

Code Sections

There are a total of 1,680 sections. They are numbered sequentially, but with some gaps, from Section 1 (the very beginning of Subtitle A) to Sec. 9722 (the very end of Subtitle J). They range in length from a few lines to a few pages. Sec. 42, which deals with the low-income housing credit, is 20 pages long.

It is by section number that passages in the Code usually are cited in prospectuses, trust documents, professional opinions and other legal writing.

Most sections are arranged on the page in outline, or skeletal, format. The conventions for citing a passage in the Code are keyed to that format and can let you refer to as little as a single sub-sub-clause of a particular section. "Sec. 1246(a)(2)(B)(ii)(II)," for example, points to a 14-word sub-sub-clause in a section two pages long.[3]

---

[2] For example, you may have heard of a Subchapter S corporation, which is a corporation that qualifies for special tax treatment under Subchapter S (Election of Certain Small Business Corporations as to Taxable Status) of Chapter 1 (Normal Taxes and Surtaxes) of Subtitle A (Income Taxes).

[3] In particular, it points to Section 1246, Subsection (a), Paragraph (2), Clause (B), Subclause (ii), Sub-sub-clause (II).

TREASURY REGULATIONS

At the third level in the hierarchy of tax rules are the Regulations issued by the Secretary of the Treasury.

The Internal Revenue Code, in numerous places, authorizes the Secretary of the Treasury to issue Regulations to flesh out the Code's more general rules. Section 7805 gives him additional, wide authority: ". . . the Secretary shall prescribe all needful rules and regulations for the enforcement of this title. . . ."

Unless a court finds that a Treasury Regulation contradicts the Code or other federal law, the Regulation has the force of law. Most Regulations leave little room for argument, because the Code gives the Secretary so much room for making Regulations. But Regulations *are* thrown out by the courts now and then, and the Treasury itself has altered Regulations when it had second thoughts about their defensibility or when it decided that the revenue at stake was too small for the burden imposed on the public.

There are 2,645 Treasury Regulations, including "Temporary Regulations" that may persist longer than DDT. Each Regulation has a number relating it to a particular Code section. Regulation 1.1247-2, for example, refers to the second Regulation dealing with Code Section 1247. The "1." indicates an income tax Regulation. Regulations dealing with gift or estate tax are numbered beginning with "2."

In researching a difficult tax question, your adviser probably will go first to the Code and then to the Regulations. The Regulations are more definite and specific than the Code and may tell him how to shape a particular transaction to get the best tax results.

REVENUE RULINGS

Fourth in the hierarchy of tax rules are Revenue Rulings.

A Revenue Ruling states the official IRS position on a particular question. Unlike a Regulation, a Ruling is not an extension of the Code. It does not have the force of law. Rather, it states what the IRS believes to be the correct interpretation of the law.

Typically a Revenue Ruling describes a hypothetical transaction and then explains its tax consequences by citing relevant provisions of the Code and the Regulations. If you ask your attorney or accountant about the tax results of a transaction you are considering, he probably will search through the Revenue Rulings for something similar.

If your tax advisor finds a ruling contrary to what you want, you will have to decide whether to:

1. alter the transaction in some way to improve the results,

2. proceed with the transaction and accept the unwanted tax consequences, or

3. proceed with the transaction and disregard (implicitly contradicting) the Ruling when you prepare your tax return.

Challenging a Revenue Ruling is no small matter. In most cases, a Revenue Ruling has been thought out carefully by the IRS and reflects a position the IRS is prepared to defend in court.

So, in most cases, (1) or (2) is the wisest choice, since it's usually foolish to pick a fight, even if you think you can win. And it often is possible to alter a transaction, perhaps only slightly, to avoid a Revenue Ruling you don't like.

But sometimes it makes sense to contradict a Revenue Ruling. Now and then the IRS issues a Ruling that most tax experts agree is incorrect and probably can be beaten in court. Or your tax advisor may conclude that, while the Ruling might be correct, there is a substantial possibility that the courts would decide otherwise.

In any such case, you might choose to disregard the Ruling, in the hope that:

■ you won't be audited; or

■ if you *are* audited, the auditor won't notice that your return contradicts the Ruling; or

■ if the auditor does challenge you on the point, you will prevail in Tax Court or on appeal to a higher court.

PRIVATE RULINGS

At the bottom of the hierarchy of tax rules are Private Rulings. If you are uncertain about the tax consequences of a particular transaction, you can ask the Treasury for a Private Ruling, which will apply only to you.

Private Rulings (also called *Letter Rulings*) can be inspected at the IRS office in Washington, D.C. (with the taxpayer's name removed). They also are published by a number of professional tax services. Even though a Private

Ruling applies only to the taxpayer who requested it, tax professionals examine private rulings for new ideas and for clues to IRS thinking.

COURT DECISIONS

Decisions of the Tax Court and other federal courts can throw out Treasury Regulations and Revenue Rulings. Such decisions, in effect, force the IRS to rewrite Regulations and Rulings, and they may answer questions on which the Regulations and Rulings are silent or unclear.

But the IRS doesn't give up easily. When a court rejects its interpretation of the law by ruling in a taxpayer's favor, the IRS may persist in applying the interpretation to other taxpayers. So bold is the IRS in this regard that it publishes a list of court decisions in which it has decided not to "acquiesce"—making it the only government agency that conducts its own program of civil disobedience.

Even when the IRS does formally give up, it takes its time in rewriting any Regulations or Rulings that have been overturned. It may leave them on the books for years—either neglecting to apply them or losing whenever it tries to. Thus a diligent tax professional doesn't stop with the Regulations and Rulings. He examines the decisions of the tax court and the higher federal courts for indications that certain Regulations or Rulings have gotten a poor reception.

HOW THE RULES ARE CHANGED

The tax rules shift constantly, especially those at the bottom of the hierarchy. The Treasury and the IRS issue dozens of new Regulations and Rulings each month, and "tax reform acts" are an almost annual event. Indeed, part of the job of tax planning is to allow for changes in the rules.

Changing the Constitution

Every now and then a member of Congress proposes to amend the Constitution to limit or abolish the federal government's power to levy an income tax. None of these proposals gets very far, but if one is ever ratified by the states, you are sure to hear about it.

Changing the Code

According to the Constitution, revenue bills must originate in the House of Representatives, and they usually do, although some begin in the Senate as amendments to bills sent from the House. Aside from this formality, tax laws are passed by Congress and signed by the president, just like any other law. All changes in tax law for at least the next few years are likely to be enacted as amendments to the Internal Revenue Code of 1986.

The Constitution seems to prohibit ex post facto laws—laws that apply to events occurring before they were enacted. However, the Supreme Court has ruled that this prohibition applies only to criminal statutes, and Congress accordingly claims the power to change tax laws retroactively.

Nonetheless, Congress usually limits the application of a new law to transactions begun on or after the law's effective date. Under a *grandfather clause,* earlier transactions go untouched.

Some tax bills are written to be effective as of the date submitted to Congress. Even this limited retroactivity can be a problem for you. A proposed law can be left waiting in Congress for as long as two years (the length of a Congressional session). Meanwhile, you simply don't know what the rules are. Thus a mere proposal in Congress can force you to alter your plans.

Changing Regulations

The Secretary of the Treasury can alter regulations at any time without prior notice.

Normally, each new regulation is published in the *Federal Register* as a *Proposed Regulation.* Depending on the comments the Treasury receives from the public and on its further consideration, the Treasury may:

- adopt the Proposed Regulation as a (final) Regulation; or
- withdraw it; or
- publish a new Proposed Regulation; or
- let the proposal float in limbo—possibly for years.

There often is a long delay between enactment of a Code provision by Congress and issuance of Regulations by the Treasury. Nonetheless, a new Regulation may be given the same effective date as its related Code section. In other words, Regulations can be very retroactive.

A Proposed Regulation can continue as such for many years, without being stamped "final." As of January 1994, the Treasury still had not issued complete final Regulations for the Tax Reform Act of 1984 or for the Tax Equity and Fiscal Responsibility Act of 1983.

Changing Revenue Rulings

The Internal Revenue Service can alter, withdraw or add a Ruling at any time without notice.

Because Rulings are only the opinion of the IRS about the meaning of the Code and are not themselves part of the law, changes in Rulings are not, strictly speaking, retroactive. They are new explanations of what the IRS currently believes was true all along.

Changing Private Rulings

Although it rarely happens, the Internal Revenue Service can withdraw a Private Ruling at any time by sending the taxpayer a letter. However, the Private Ruling would continue to apply to transactions the taxpayer had already completed, provided the taxpayer hadn't obtained the Ruling through fraud or misrepresentation.

STABILITY

Since the government can and does change the rules, even retroactively, you may wonder how tax planning is possible. The answer is that the government has more than you to worry about.

A tax proposal before Congress *might* be enacted retroactively. But many congressmen and much of the public will oppose a measure simply because it is retroactive. So most tax measures aren't, because it is easier to get them passed that way.

A tax proposal might be written to apply in the future to transactions, investments, contracts or other arrangements begun before the proposal was made. But usually a proposal isn't retroactive even in this sense, since at least some of the people who would oppose it will acquiesce if their particular transactions are left undisturbed, or grandfathered.

The Treasury could change a Regulation just to catch you—but it probably won't. The same Regulations apply to everyone. A change designed to catch you on one point might let other taxpayers escape on some other point. And the resentment, ill will and potential political consequences are much less for changes that aren't retroactive.

It's true that the IRS can alter a Revenue Ruling at will. But when you are being audited or are facing an IRS appeals officer, you aren't dealing with the entire Internal Revenue Service. You're dealing with an individual for whom Revenue Rulings are his employer's stated policy. He would be insubordinate not to follow them.

Please Send Money

The rules can and do change, but the people who make the changes are deliberate. Their purpose is to collect money, not to attract hate mail. They know that the less irritating the rules are, the more money they will collect. So they try hard not to stir up any more resentment than is absolutely necessary to take in $1 trillion or so each year. ⚭

5

HOW THE RULES ARE ENFORCED

At other times and in other places, taxation was far simpler than it is for us. Soldiers came to your house and took what they wanted. If you resisted, they put an axe in your head.

Modern IRS procedures are less brutal, but every tax system, including our own, relies on the threat of bloody violence. If you fail to pay what the IRS claims you owe, and if you then disregard or exhaust all means for legally protesting the assessment and still refuse to pay, government agents will try to take your property. If they cannot seize enough by confiscating your bank accounts or intercepting your wages, they will auction off your home and your personal possessions. If you resist by staying in your home or by hiding your possessions, they will put you in jail. If you resist being put in jail, they will hurt you or even may kill you. You also may be put in jail if you fail to make certain reports to the IRS or if you lie to it.

Most people fear the IRS—and with good reason. It can do terrible things to you. But despite its considerable powers, the IRS operates within a somewhat settled legal system. Constrained by the law, the tax collector is more like a dangerous robot than a reckless vandal; his violence is programmed, not random. If you understand the robot's programming, you can *safely* avoid high taxes.

NASTY ENTERPRISE

A second, ironic factor works to protect you. The objective of the IRS is to collect money. Its success at this can easily be measured, as can the revenue generated by the individual auditors and other IRS employees you someday may deal with. It is almost as though the IRS and its staff were a business oriented toward profit.

Most other government agencies don't have measurable objectives, which is why they are so troublesome. A building inspector's job, for example, is to protect the public from unsafe buildings. But his effectiveness is hard to gauge; no one can determine how much safer we are (if at all) because he has zealously enforced the building code. So he's free to act on prejudice, malice, or whimsy, and to torment builders over the smallest infraction.

But an IRS agent is looking for dollars-and-cents results. His personal advancement depends on how much additional revenue he brings in, not on how much grief he causes. As a result, unless he believes you are easily intimidated (and especially if your attorney or accountant seems ill-prepared), he won't waste his time pursuing a weak claim—because he can collect more by working on someone else.

REPORTING

The heart of the IRS enforcement system is reporting. With but a few exceptions, you are required to report all your income.

To discourage you from omitting anything, the tax system requires every business you deal with to report everything it pays you. Corporations must report the interest and dividends they pay. Employers must report wages and salaries. Businesses that hire you as an independent contractor must report the fees they pay.

In addition, the tax system neatly recruits all of us as paid informers—by allowing *deductions*.

Deductions reduce your tax bill, so you gladly declare them—and thereby report the income of the people to whom you made the deductible payments. Your payment for medical expenses, for example, is your doctor's income. He knows he must report the income because you may deduct the payment.

The same is true for *your* income. Anything you don't report might be listed, as a deduction, on the return of the person who paid you.

Of course, not all the reports the law demands are actually made. But you don't know which payments you receive will go unreported, which makes it dangerous not to report every dollar yourself.

Other events, that are not payments of income, also must be reported. Brokers must report their customers' sales, regardless of profitability.

Mutual funds must report redemptions by their shareholders. Partnerships with any gross income must file tax returns, even though partnerships don't pay income tax. And you must make reports if you have $10,000 or more in a foreign bank account, if you own 5% or more of a foreign corporation, or if you transfer property to a foreign trust—even if no tax is owed.

PROCESSING YOUR TAX RETURN

Within a few days after the IRS receives your tax return, a clerk will enter the information into the IRS computer system. If there is an error in your arithmetic, the computer will adjust your tax bill down or up and send you either a refund or a notice demanding more money.

Later, perhaps months later, the computer will calculate your return's *audit score*, which estimates the probability you have shortchanged the tax collector by enough to warrant an audit.

The formula for computing audit scores is secret. But the accumulated experience of tax professionals, combined with a little reflection about what might make a return look fishy, indicates that the following contribute to a high score.

- *Reporting failures.* The computer attempts to match the income you report in your return with the payments to you reported by others.[1] If the computer finds something you omitted, your audit score goes up. The bigger the missing payment, the bigger the increase.

- *High total income.* The extra tax the IRS can collect from an individual earning a million dollars a year may be worth a few hours of audit time even if the flaws in his return are tiny in relation to his income.

- *High deduction ratio.* Some taxpayers' deductions equal 70% or 80% of their income. A taxpayer's deductions could even exceed his income if he has a bad year. But the higher the ratio of deductions to income, the greater the chance some of the deductions are invalid.

---

[1] Payment matching obviously is a big job, since it means sorting through billions of separate reports. But a large fraction of reported payments are in fact matched to individual tax returns, and the fraction is growing.

- *Cash business.* A business that runs on cash (rather than checks or credit cards) seems to beg its owner to underreport his income—especially if customers won't be claiming deductions for their purchases. Vending machine operators, for example, may think it's safe not to count a few dimes.

- *Business losses.* If your return shows large business losses, perhaps you contrived the business for tax purposes. An audit may reveal invalid deductions.

- *"Shady" occupations.* Doctors, dentists, independent contractors and the self-employed have a bad reputation with the IRS for not reporting all their income.

- *Office in the home.* The rules for deducting the expense of an office in the home are so extreme and implausible that many taxpayers assume the IRS won't enforce them strictly. It will, and it regards any such deductions with suspicion.

- *Business travel and entertainment.* Travel and entertainment deductions must be well documented as to cost and business purpose, and the documentation must include receipts. The IRS knows that many people don't bother to collect receipts and keep proper records.

- *Interest payments to related parties.* Paying interest to your child or your own corporation raises the possibility that you are improperly shifting income to someone in a lower tax bracket. More audit points.

- *Death.* Rather than kick you when you are down, the IRS will wait until you are dead—when you can't help in preparing a correct return or in defending past returns. The tax return your executor files for the last year of your life has an especially good chance of being audited, and it may trigger an audit for the two preceding years.

After your audit score has been assigned, the IRS will enter you in a lottery. The higher your score, the greater your chance of "winning."

If you do win, an IRS employee will examine your return to decide whether you should be audited. And you may be audited even if you don't win the lottery—if you are a notorious criminal (who understandably would be shy about reporting his income) or if the IRS found large deficiencies in a previous year's return.

The IRS audits about one million returns of all types each year. Depending on your gross income, your current chance of an audit is roughly as follows.

Income Range	Chance of Audit
$10,000 or less	less than 1%
$10,000–$25,000	1%
$25,000–$50,000	2%
$50,000 and over	4%

Types of Audit

If you are picked, you may undergo an office audit or a field audit.

An office audit usually is just a request for proof that you actually made certain payments and made them for the purpose you claim. For example, if you claim a deduction for mortgage interest, the auditor may ask to see your canceled checks and a statement from the lender. The audit may be handled by mail, or you may be required to visit a local IRS office.

The IRS will conduct a field audit if it intends to examine a large volume of records. The audit takes place at the office of your attorney or accountant, or—if you don't object, at your own office or home.

In either type of audit, the auditor isn't interested in making arbitrary claims, nor is he trying to make you miserable. Instead, he wants to confirm or eliminate his suspicion that something is wrong with your return—that you didn't report all your income or that some of your deductions are invalid.

Although you won't enjoy the audit, you can take some comfort from the auditor's situation. He is working against the clock, trying to make his time pay. He won't trouble you much over any item he believes you can substantiate, and he may be receptive to your defense of the return. If nothing is wrong, he would like to discover this quickly, rather than waste hours on work that yields nothing.

If the auditor concludes you owe more tax, he will propose a settlement. If you agree, you pay the additional tax and the matter ends there—unless the IRS later discovers evidence of tax fraud, or unless you simply don't have the money.

If You Disagree

Rather than accept the proposed settlement, you can appeal to the auditor's supervisor or to the Appeals Division of the IRS. The supervisor or the appeals officer is as much your adversary as the auditor himself. But on close calls you may reach a better settlement with him, since he generally is more knowledgeable and more concerned about the costs and difficulties of litigation.

Compared to court proceedings, all of this is informal. It is a kind of negotiation. You needn't testify under oath, file briefs, or call anyone "Your Honor." Your accountant probably can provide all the help you need.

If you cannot settle the matter, the IRS will send you a *statutory notice of deficiency* by registered or certified mail. You then have three choices.

- Pay the amount demanded and give up.
- Pay the amount demanded and sue for a refund.
- Refuse to pay, and file a petition for review in Tax Court.

A tax court petition must be filed within 90 days of the date of the notice of deficiency. If you miss the deadline, you are left with only the first two choices, both of which require paying the assessment immediately. Neither the IRS nor the Tax Court will bend this strict and inflexible rule. (There also is a rule that the IRS must file an answer to your Tax Court petition within 60 days. That rule, however, is neither strict nor inflexible, and is often ignored.)

TALK TO THE JUDGE

The Tax Court is a panel of 19 judges headed by a chief judge. It also includes 13 special trial judges, who may hear small cases, and six semiretired senior judges, who may hear cases of any size. Tax Court proceedings are conducted from time to time in most large cities.

When you file a petition in Tax Court, it is assigned a docket number, and your case is scheduled for a trial-setting conference to be held within one to two *years*. If by that time you haven't settled with the IRS, a Tax Court judge will begin your trial, usually within two weeks. More than 90% of all Tax Court cases are settled before trial, without the judge actually hearing the case.

If there is to be a trial, the judge first will review a trial memorandum summarizing the written arguments submitted by your attorney and by the IRS. Shortly after the trial, each side will file a *trial brief* and then a *reply brief*. Then, after another six months to a year, the judge will render his decision.

It generally takes three to four years from filing a petition to receiving a decision. The Tax Court rules completely in the taxpayer's favor about 4% of the time and completely against the taxpayer about 50% of the time. In the rest of the cases, the Tax Court tells the taxpayer and the IRS to split the difference.

District Courts and Claims Court

Rather than petition the Tax Court, you can pay the tax and sue for a refund, either in a Federal District Court or in the U.S. Claims Court. Your choice will be guided by three considerations.

First, in District Court you can demand a jury trial, which, depending on the case, might be to your advantage.

Second, District Court judges generally are not experts on tax matters. They may be open to arguments of fairness and equity that carry little weight with judges in Claims Court or Tax Court.

Third, while there is only one Claims Court (located in Washington, D.C.), there are 95 District Courts. You can insist that your suit be heard in the District court for your place of residence.

The various District Courts sometimes render different decisions on similar questions. If past decisions show that *your* District Court is likely to be friendly or unfriendly to your position, you would choose between District Court and the Claims Court accordingly.

The District Courts and the Claims Court together hear about 1,400 tax cases per year. It generally takes one to two years from filing a suit to receiving a decision. The District and Claims Courts rule completely in favor of the taxpayer about 15% of the time and completely in favor of the IRS about 75% of the time.

Appeals

You may appeal the findings of the Tax Court, the District Court, or the Claims Court, in each instance to a U.S. Circuit Court of Appeals. (Each District Court and the Claims Court belong to one of 12 judicial *circuits*.)

Waiting time in the Circuit Appeals Court is about one to three years. It hears about 400 tax cases per year and rules completely in favor of the taxpayer about 10% of the time and completely in favor of the IRS about 85% of the time.

Last, if you're a hard-core litigation buff, you can appeal the findings of the Circuit Appeals Court to the U.S. Supreme Court. The Supreme Court accepts very few tax cases—and those few generally involve questions of law on which the Circuit Appeals Courts have rendered conflicting decisions, or they deal with questions of judicial procedure.

The IRS has the same rights of appeal as you. Thus, the entire procedure continues until one side either gives up or exhausts its opportunities for appeal.

Philadelphia Is Nicer

Except for a few eccentric personalities, no taxpayer wants to have anything to do with this process.

Tax litigation is expensive. It may cost only a few hundred dollars of your accountant's time to see you through an audit of your personal return. But going to Tax Court over a simple matter will cost at least a few thousand dollars in legal fees—much more if the case is complex. Costs increase as you climb the ladder of appeal. To litigate a moderately complex matter through to the Supreme Court might cost $500,000.

And the whole process is disagreeable. Even if you win, victory is more like getting over a disease than claiming a trophy.

Since resisting the IRS is so unattractive, what prevents the IRS from bullying you and everyone else?

One factor is political. The public will tolerate high taxes more readily if it believes there are consistent rules. So congressmen and senior Treasury officials know their lives will be more pleasant, and their careers more secure, if they hold the IRS staff to the law.

A second factor is cost. Congress gives the IRS a limited budget to work with. The IRS can't afford enough auditors and litigators to deal with all the taxpayers who would resist if it behaved too arbitrarily.

A third factor is the burden on the courts. There currently is a backlog of about 40,000 cases—over a years' worth—before the Tax Court. A taxpayer with even a very weak case can delay matters simply by filing a petition. The IRS wants to shrink this opportunity for delay by reducing the backlog of cases.

A fourth factor is the risk of litigation. The IRS benefits from the uncertainty surrounding some tax questions. It prefers to have those questions remain unanswered, rather than take the chance that a court will establish a precedent favorable to taxpayers.

INTEREST AND PENALTIES

If the IRS bills you for additional tax, it will automatically assess interest to compensate the government for the "loan" you took by not paying your taxes on time. The interest is not tax deductible.[2]

The IRS also may assess civil penalties, to punish you for breaking the rules. There is a laundry list of such penalties (see the box on page 45). Additional interest, on the penalties themselves, will be charged from the date the penalties are imposed to the date you pay them.

The IRS makes civil penalty assessments at its own discretion, without a hearing or other proceeding. To contest a civil penalty, you go to an IRS appeals officer and then to court, just as though you were contesting your tax bill.

TAX FRAUD

The procedures and penalties discussed so far are civil matters: the government claims you owe a bill and attempts to collect it. If you plan poorly, if you are gullible and purchase ill-conceived tax shelters, if you fail to keep proper records, or if you are wishful in interpreting the rules, you may pay heavily in civil penalties and interest—but you won't go to jail. The only way to incur a criminal penalty (prison) is to be convicted, in a trial, of tax fraud.

The essential ingredient of tax fraud is intentional deception. A few examples are:

- Failing to report income, especially if you appear to have concealed the income by not depositing it into your customary bank account

- Claiming depreciation or other deductions for purchases not actually made

- Claiming depreciation or other deductions for assets that don't exist or that you don't own

- Using counterfeit or forged receipts or contracts

---

[2] The interest rate is adjusted quarterly and equals the short-term *Applicable Federal Rate* (an official index of yields on U.S. Treasury bills and Treasury bonds) plus three percentage points.

CIVIL PENALTIES

Failure to file. The penalty for failing to file a return when due is 5% per month of the tax involved, up to a maximum of 25% (five months' worth of tardiness).

Failure to pay. The penalty for failure to pay the amount of tax shown on the return is ½% per month of the unpaid amount, but not more than 25% altogether.

Negligence. "Negligence" means carelessness or disregard of the rules in preparing your tax return. The penalty is 20% of the underpayment.

Substantial underpayment. The substantial underpayment penalty may be imposed if the tax you declare on your return is less than 90% of the tax the IRS claims you owe. The penalty is 10% of the underpayment.

Substantial overvaluation. The substantial overvaluation penalty may be imposed if you exaggerate the value of an asset by 50% or more. (An overvaluation might reduce your tax bill by, for example, increasing deductions for depreciation or charitable contributions.) The penalty is 10 to 30% of the resulting understatement of tax, depending on the extent of the overvaluation. For overvaluations of property contributed to charity, however, the penalty is always 30%.

Tax fraud. The civil penalty for tax fraud is 75% of the underpayment. The nature of tax fraud and the possible criminal penalties are explained nearby.

■ Backdating contracts or other documents to an earlier year

■ Failing to file a return

Notice that, except for failing to file a return, each of these actions involves a lie. In failing to report income, for example, the lie is the taxpayer's signed statement on Form 1040 that the return is "true, correct and complete."

Criminal Penalties

Prosecuting an individual for tax fraud is expensive and time consuming—and hard work for government employees, few of whom chose government employment because they were looking for action. So even if the IRS decides you have committed tax fraud, it may simply impose a civil penalty, because it can do so without the time, effort and risk of a criminal trial.

Criminal prosecution is likely to be considered only if one or more of the following factors is present.

- The evidence of criminality is strong and clear, so that a jury probably would say "Guilty."
- The taxpayer can be presented to the jury as a drug dealer, pornographer, crime boss or condescending sybarite who deserves to go to jail for *something*.
- The taxpayer is a prominent and respected person, so that his conviction would be a well-publicized reminder to us all not to trifle with the IRS.[3]
- The taxpayer has offended the wrong government official.

Prosecutions for tax fraud take place in district court, and the defendant has the customary right to a jury trial. Given the complexity of the Internal Revenue Code and the mountain of records often needed to calculate a person's tax bill, it's hard to prove "beyond a reasonable doubt" that a taxpayer's errors were intentional. More often than not, the defendant's lawyer argues that, although his client erred by keeping poor records or by relying on mistaken advice, he did not *intentionally* violate the rules.

TAX RISK

Tax risk is the possibility the IRS won't accept your return as you filed it and that, as a consequence, you will:

- Suffer the worry and inconvenience of an audit; or
- Have to pay additional tax, penalties, or interest; or
- Be subject to criminal prosecution.

---

[3] Indictments of prominent persons are most likely to be announced in the first quarter of the year, to remind taxpayers who are preparing their returns of what is at stake.

Although tax risk has its own distinctive emotional flavor, it is in fact only one more kind of financial risk. Just as you can't be sure what an investment's profit or loss will be, you can't be sure what a transaction's tax consequences will be—although some investments and tax ploys are far more reliable than others.

It won't do any good to say you want absolute safety in tax planning, because *no* strategy can eliminate tax risk entirely. Even if you send the government every dollar you earn, you still face the risk of being audited—since the IRS might wonder whether you're holding something back.

But the IRS doesn't strike wholly, or even chiefly, at random—and when it does strike, the consequences for the unlucky target depend primarily on what he has done. Thus, while you can't eliminate tax risk, you can control the level of risk by your choice of tax-saving devices.

Weighing Risk

Because tax risk is *risk*, you can deal with it best by applying the same methods you apply to investment decisions.

In making any decision, you compare the risk with the possible reward. An opportunity for large tax savings that adds only a small amount of tax risk is attractive. If, for example, a given tax-planning technique would reduce your tax bill by one half and increase your risk of audit by 1%, you probably should use it.

On the other hand, there are hazards you won't expose yourself to, no matter how great the possible advantage. For nearly all of us, no tax savings, however great, is worth the risk of going to jail—just as no potential investment profit, however great, would tempt many of us to risk losing everything.

But most decisions about risk depend on who is deciding. To be acceptable, a risk must be acceptable to *you*. Some opportunities for tax savings and some opportunities for investment profit are reasonable bets for other people, but are too risky for you to live with.

Diversification in Tax Planning

Diversification reduces overall risk in tax planning, just as it does in investing. It is unwise to rely, year after year, on only one tax-saving technique, no matter how sure and simple it may appear. Even with the least controversial technique, you might misunderstand its scope, you might not apply it properly, or the rules might change.

Tax-exempt municipal bonds, for example, may look like a foolproof device for reducing taxes. But even with them, things can go wrong. The municipal bonds *you* buy might turn out not to be tax exempt, because of some flaw in the way they were issued. Or you might encounter wrinkles in the Internal Revenue Code that make part of your profit taxable. Or there might be changes in the rules that you don't hear about, until your accountant prepares your tax return.

Attitudes Toward Risk and Opportunity

The following describes six levels of tax risk and tax-saving opportunity, starting with the least risky (and the most highly taxed). Try to locate yourself. At what level are you now? Do you want to stay there? Or would you like to move to a different level?

Level 1: Passive.   The Passive taxpayer faces the lowest possible degree of tax risk—and pays heavily for his comfort.

The Passive taxpayer claims only the least controversial and least exceptionable deductions: personal exemptions for himself, his spouse and his minor children; mortgage interest and property taxes on his residence; state and local income taxes; small cash contributions to church and charity (for which he has receipts or canceled checks); and contributions to IRAs for himself and his spouse. Except for the IRAs and for the pension plan provided by his employer (to whom he is unrelated), the Passive taxpayer makes no effort to defer taxes.

A Passive taxpayer isn't likely to be audited. If he is, the inconvenience is brief, involving nothing more than a request for receipts and canceled checks.

Level 2: Plain Vanilla.   The Plain Vanilla taxpayer is as cautious as the passive taxpayer, but he works harder to reduce his tax bill.

The Plain Vanilla taxpayer may invest in simple tax shelters such as rental property (which he doesn't try to use as a vacation house) with a cash down payment of at least 10%. If he's self-employed, he contributes to a defined-contribution Keogh or corporate pension plan sponsored by a bank, mutual fund, or other financial institution. If he works for his own corporation, he pays himself a fixed monthly salary. He may buy tax-exempt bonds or deferred annuities.

The Plain Vanilla taxpayer pays much less tax than the Passive taxpayer. His risk of audit is a little higher, but an audit wouldn't be much more than a nuisance, since nothing he does is controversial or needs to be executed with special care.

Level 3: Thorough.   The Thorough taxpayer wants to protect his large income from taxes, but he doesn't want to face a substantially greater risk of penalties than the Passive or Plain Vanilla taxpayer. He uses all the techniques they do and others, including strategies explained in this book. He limits himself to methods that *in principle* are not questionable—although he understands that some, such as sales of long-term options, require careful execution.

The thorough taxpayer faces a greater risk of audit. But unless he has been sloppy, an audit should not lead to any additional tax, interest, or penalties.

Level 4: Combatant.   The Combatant uses techniques that attract and provoke auditors but that probably can stand up in court. He hopes not to be audited. But he is ready to fight it out if necessary, and he expects to win—although he knows there is some risk of losing.

Level 5: Gambler.   The Gambler's tax strategies probably wouldn't stand up in court, but they are difficult to call fraudulent. He's gambling that he won't be audited—because if he is and then loses in court, he faces the substantial understatement penalty plus interest. But he is careful to protect himself against criminal prosecution—by preparing an interpretation of the Internal Revenue Code that hasn't yet been tested in the courts, by limiting himself to techniques that permit some reasonable doubt about whether he intended to break the law, or by obtaining an opinion from his lawyer that his return is correct.

Level 6: Fraudulent.   The Fraudulent taxpayer doesn't bother with tax planning. He relies on sham transactions, bogus receipts and conceal-ment of income to reduce his tax bill. If he reads this book at all, he does so in the prison library.

Finding the Right Level

Some Passive or Plain Vanilla taxpayers investigate tax planning because they are tired of paying so much. They may want to move up the lad-der to Level 3 (Thorough), but because they are not willing to take large risks, they won't go any higher.

Others have long been at Level 3 and do not wish to bear even the small risk of moving to Level 4 (Combatant). They study tax planning, searching for additional Level-3 techniques to cut their tax bills further or to gain more flexibility with their investments without paying more tax.

Still other taxpayers have been at Level 4 or higher and are tired of worrying. They are searching for ways to *reduce* tax risk without paying a great deal more in taxes.

Chapter 1 held out the possibility of a low tax bill. How much risk must you bear in order to achieve that goal? Not much. Level 3 is high enough for almost anyone.

Even Level 3 doesn't expose you to any significant risk of a tax assessment or penalties. (This is not a book for financial daredevils.) All Level 3 requires is that you think and plan and act carefully; it requires you to be thorough.

In the remainder of the book, we'll look primarily at tax-planning techniques that belong at Levels 2 and 3. Nothing we will discuss, except to warn against it, will be higher than Level 3. ⌐

PART TWO

PLANNING FOR SAFETY AND PROFIT

All the world's ambulance chasers wish you well in your efforts at tax planning. The more you save, the more you can accumulate for them to take.

And what you don't lose to the ambulance chasers, you may lose to the investment markets—if, even briefly, you fail to be ready for the surprises they spring on investors.

So, if you want to keep what you earn, you need a plan to protect against lawsuits. You also need to balance your investment portfolio carefully, to be ready at all times for unforeseen inflation, unforeseen stock market declines, unforeseen real estate slumps and other unexpected market troubles.

Protection against malicious lawsuits and market risks are not mere add-ons. They are not goals to pursue *after* you avoid taxes. They are goals to pursue *as* you avoid taxes—so that what you do to reduce one problem doesn't increase your vulnerability to another.

Reconciling the three objectives—lower taxes, less market risk and protection against lawsuits—is tricky. Some of the conflicts may not become obvious until it is too late. This part explains the conflicts now, so that you won't have to discover them through painful experience.

6

PORTFOLIO PLANNING

The obvious way to make investment and tax decisions is one at a time.

Should you buy stock in Xcorp? Well, look at its balance sheet and check its earnings history. Any problems? Any new products? How is the price behaving? Get all the information—and if you like what you see, buy the stock with whatever cash you haven't committed to something else.

Should you buy U.S. Treasury bonds? They're free of default risk, and pay interest with absolute reliability every six months. If you want more income, maybe you should buy some.

Is your tax bill too high? Set up a pension plan, or at least get an IRA.

Do you still need deductions? Maybe you should invest in real estate. Start shopping for an attractively priced property.

Making decisions in this fashion, one at a time, as questions comes up, is the straightforward, common-sense way to do things.

The Route to Better Decisions

But you will make better investment decisions, and you will make better tax decisions, if you make them together—as elements of a comprehensive financial plan. An overall plan increases profit, reduces risk and lets you adapt easily to changing circumstances. And such a plan may eliminate the disadvantages of some tax-saving devices.

Coordinating dozens of decisions, some of which are difficult enough to make one by one, may seem impossibly complex. It needn't be. In Part 7, we'll see how you can design a fully coordinated investment and tax plan simply by making decisions *in the right order*. In this chapter, we'll prepare for the task by examining the basic principles of portfolio planning.

DECISIONS AND RISK

Investment literature often speaks about objectives, such as income, growth, or safety.[1] But in fact all investors have the same, sole objective: they want more. And whether they call it more income, more profit, more capital or more of something else, what they all want is more money. Even the investor whose says his goal is "safety" means he wants to retain more of his money.

But wants are not choices. You have to decide what steps you will take to get more—even though every decision carries the risk of being a mistake.

Understanding Risk

Risk is a subtle concept. It doesn't mean loss. It means the *possibility* of loss. Reducing risk means shrinking that possibility—leaving fewer opportunities for failure, fewer ways for bad luck to hurt you.

Nearly all investors say they dislike risk and want less of it, but what they really dislike and wish to avoid is loss. Hikers say they want to avoid rattlesnakes. What they really want to avoid are rattlesnake bites.

Having quieter surroundings or fewer germs or less clutter is certain to reduce the problem of noise or sickness or disorder. But having less risk might *not* reduce your losses. Even if you are as cautious as you can be, you still might be very unlucky—just as the most careful hiker *might* get bitten.

Promoters of speculative investments sometimes ask whether you are willing to bear high risk in return for a high reward. The question is nonsensical. If an investment actually does yield a high reward, it carries no risk at all. A better question is whether you are willing to bear high risk in return for the *possibility* of high reward.

When an investment has run its course, you are left with a profit or a loss. You are never left with risk. That trickster, risk, isn't real in the sense that profit and loss are real. Risk isn't dollars and cents; it is the shadow cast by what you don't know when you make decisions.

---

[1] In most cases, the writer is thinking of the investor's temperament, rather than his objective.

Understanding Liquidity

Investors also want liquidity, which is the ability to make changes quickly and at little cost. Liquidity allows you to adjust to new information, to new personal circumstances, and to changes of heart.

The desire for liquidity is an echo of risk. Because you don't know for sure where today's decisions will lead, you need the freedom to make changes as you go along.

One aspect of that freedom is market liquidity—the ability to buy or sell an investment on short notice and with little trading cost. A house, for example, has poor market liquidity. The costs of arranging a sale—brokerage, advertising and closing costs—are high. And if you had to sell on, say, two weeks' notice, you probably would receive much less than if you could spend six months finding a buyer.

Nearly all publicly traded stocks are more liquid than any real estate, but even among stocks the degree of liquidity varies. Stocks of small companies, on which brokers generally charge high commissions and fees, tend to be less liquid than stocks of large companies.

A second aspect of the freedom to make changes is tax liquidity—the ability to change investments without upsetting your tax plan. An IRA, for example, affords almost complete tax liquidity, letting you switch from one investment to another without paying tax on profits or undoing past deductions. The tax liquidity of stocks or bonds you own directly is much lower, because selling might increase your tax bill.

HARD-TO-SWALLOW PRINCIPLES

The principles of portfolio planning show how to reduce risk and increase liquidity without weakening your chance for profit. Not all the principles are obvious, common-sense ideas. Some may run counter to your intuition, and almost no one responds to them by saying, "Of course." But, familiar or not, the principles are true, and investors who disregard them forsake a large advantage.

The basic axiom of portfolio planning is that *only the portfolio's net result is important.* The result for any one investment is unimportant. Thus no matter how many losing investments you make or how big some of your losses may be, if your portfolio is profitable overall, it is a success.

This basic axiom is self-evident, but the implications and associated principles are not. Following are five hard-to-swallow (HTS) principles of portfolio planning.

HTS Principle #1—There Are No Safe Investments. Some investors recoil at the thought of risk, and they resolve to purchase only safe investments. But there are no safe investments. None. Every investment, considered in isolation, exposes you to the chance of serious loss. There are no exceptions.

U.S. Treasury bills might seem absolutely risk-free. A T-bill is an unconditional obligation of the U.S. government, and there has never been a default. A T-bill's short term to maturity (no more than one year) prevents large price declines, even when interest rates rise sharply. T-bills are what people buy when they want absolute safety.

But the safety of U.S. Treasury bills is incomplete. T-bills are sorely exposed to loss of purchasing power, since the unpredictable course of inflation makes it impossible to say what the dollars a T-bill pays will be worth when the bill matures.

If you hold T-bills for a brief period, you can reasonably disregard this uncertainty. But if you use them as a long-term, one-asset investment program (buying new bills as the old ones mature), the uncertainty becomes a grave risk. You're betting that interest rates will outrun inflation rates, which seldom happens during long periods of high inflation. If you lose the bet, your purchasing power will shrivel.

Treasury bills are safer than money in the bank, but they aren't safe from inflation.

Almost every investment has fans—who, because of unexamined assumptions or the investment's familiarity or its past success, think the investment is safe. But everyone's favorite investment is vulnerable to something.

HTS Principle #2—Risky Investments Can Reduce Risk. The desire for safety is no reason to shun risky investments. An investment that, by itself, is extremely chancy can reduce a portfolio's overall risk—if it faces *different* hazards than the rest of the portfolio.

Gold, for instance, is a risky investment. Its price has dropped as much as 50% in a single year. From its high in 1980 to its low in 1985, it fell 65%. Yet, because gold profits from the adversities that injure most other investments, it can reduce a portfolio's overall risk.

An investor who is wedded to U.S. Treasury bills, for example, could increase his safety by investing a small portion of his portfolio (say, 10% or 15%) in gold bullion. If inflation rises to high levels, the price of gold probably will multiply many times over. Its gains could make up for all the purchasing power the T-bills lose.

And if there is no inflation, the loss on gold should be more than offset by the interest earned on the T-bills.

HTS Principle #3—Borrowers Needn't Be Debtors. Most investors feel instinctively that borrowing is risky. Borrowing *can* be risky, but in some circumstances it reduces risk.

If most of your portfolio is tied up in fixed-dollar assets you can't liquidate—such as a pension plan that promises to pay a fixed number of dollars (without a cost-of-living clause) or life insurance or annuities—you are, like the T-bill investor, badly exposed to the risk of higher inflation. Borrowing can reduce that risk.

First, you can use the borrowed funds to buy real estate, precious metals and other investments that profit from inflation.

Second, the dollars you owe will offset the inflation risk of a similar amount of your fixed-dollar assets. Inflation that reduces the purchasing power of the assets also will reduce the purchasing power burden of the debt.

So long as you don't borrow more than your fixed-dollar investments are worth, you're not exposed to the risk of being a net debtor.

HTS Principle #4—Illiquid Investments Need Not Impair a Portfolio's Liquidity. Your portfolio can be liquid even if many of its investments are not.

Suppose 25% of each of your investments were locked inside a vault that couldn't be opened for five years. Would your portfolio be 25% illiquid? Not necessarily. The liquidity of your other assets would give you effective control of the entire portfolio. You could reduce your holdings of any particular kind of investment by up to 75%, which is a limit a conservative investor probably wouldn't want to exceed. And you would be free to spend up to 75% of your investment assets, which is more than you probably would want to spend in any five-year period.[2]

HTS Principle #5—Investment Income Makes You Poorer. "Income" is how the tax collector keeps score. The greater your income, the more you lose to income tax. But appreciation—the increase in an asset's market value—goes untaxed until the appreciated asset is sold.

---

[2] Even if you wanted to eliminate an investment, you probably could offset the locked-up 25% with short sales (sales of borrowed investments) or other techniques available through many investment brokers.

In the investment markets there's generally a trade-off between income and appreciation. Investments that promise high income offer little prospect for appreciation, while most growth investments are stingy with current income.

A tax-exempt investor, such as a pension fund, should choose investments for maximum total return—income plus appreciation. A $100 investment that yields nothing but appreciates to $112 gives a tax-exempt investor a profit of $12. So does an investment whose price stays fixed at $100 and yields $12 in dividends.

A tax-paying investor, on the other hand, should choose investments for their total *after-tax* return—income plus appreciation, net of tax. Because income is taxed each year, while appreciation isn't taxed until an investment is sold, a dollar of appreciation is worth more to a tax-paying investor than a dollar of income. For the tax-paying investor, appreciation is a prince; income is a frog.

The fact that you live off your investments doesn't exempt you from this principle. If your investments are appreciating, you can tap that profit (while preserving capital) by making small, periodic sales. And much of the cash you withdraw may be a tax-free return of capital, leaving you with a lower tax bill and more money to spend.

So if you think you "need" income, think again.

MAKE ROOM FOR TAX-PLANNING SUCCESS

The government tolerates many tax-planning devices because risk and illiquidity discourage taxpayers from using them. Careful portfolio planning softens those disadvantages, letting you enjoy a low tax bill without sacrificing prudence and convenience.

The few tax-shelter investments still available (discussed in Appendix C) depend on prosperity or rising inflation for their profits. So they're safe to use only if your portfolio includes other investments that profit from tight money and hard times.

Some tax-deferral devices (discussed in Part 3) accommodate almost any type of investment, so they don't force you to take extra risks. But certain of them are illiquid; they tie up your capital, perhaps for long periods. You can reduce that disadvantage to a mere nuisance by including *some* assets in your portfolio that are easy and cheap to liquidate.

THE ART OF PORTFOLIO PLANNING

Portfolio planning is the art of combining investments to reduce overall risk, increase profit, and improve liquidity.

Portfolio planning tells you nothing about how much risk you should bear. That question depends on your own skills, circumstances, attitudes and emotional makeup. But whatever your attitude toward risk, thoughtful planning will increase the level of profit you can reasonably hope to achieve. Or, to put it the other way around, whatever level of profit you hope to achieve, the principles of portfolio planning can show you the least risky way to pursue it.

Genuine Diversification

"Diversify" is standard advice for investors who want to reduce risk. But investors seldom follow the advice effectively. Too often, they confuse diversification with proliferation.

You won't diversify your portfolio simply by piling one investment on top of another. A portfolio of stock in 20 different companies, for example, is hardly diversified at all; it is one big bet on the stock market.

You can diversify your holdings only by combining investments that face different risks. But how do you do that?

A common thread running through investment uncertainty is inflation. Does the future hold higher or lower inflation, and how rapidly will inflation shift from one level to another? Most investments will be affected in dramatic and systematic ways by the answers to those questions. Thus, the starting point in planning a diversified portfolio is to categorize investments by how they tend to be helped or hurt by inflation.

Three Categories

Rising inflation is beneficial for:

- commodities of all kinds, especially precious metals, and most especially gold;
- real estate;
- foreign currencies; and
- stocks of real estate and natural resource companies.

Rising inflation is harmful for fixed-dollar investments, especially long-term, fixed-rate bonds and mortgages. Except in its early stages, it is harmful for stocks and for business in general.

Gradually declining inflation is beneficial for:

- Common stocks
- Private businesses
- Long-term bonds and mortgages
- U.S. Treasury bills and other money market investments
- Cash-value life insurance, annuities, and pension plans that promise to pay a fixed number of dollars

Gradually declining inflation is harmful for most investments that profit from inflation, although it can be good for commodities other than gold and for the stocks of real estate and natural resource companies.

Rapidly declining inflation is beneficial for:

- U.S. Treasury bonds and the highest-grade corporate bonds
- Well-secured mortgages
- U.S. Treasury bills
- Deposits at conservatively run financial institutions
- Annuities and pension plans that promise to pay a fixed number of dollars, but only if they are funded or secured by one or more of the four items just listed

Rapidly declining inflation is harmful for nearly every other type of conventional investment, because it often is accompanied by widespread bankruptcies and bank failures, and because it carries the threat of a general financial crisis and deflationary depression.

No matter how many investments it has, a portfolio is truly diversified only if it includes substantial amounts from *each* of the three inflation-related categories. Depending on how you expect inflation to behave, you may want to give one category a larger share than another. And if you are adventurous, you may want to shift money from one category to another from time to time, as you foresee imminent twists and turns in inflation's path. But if you leave any one of the three categories empty, you leave your portfolio in a risky state—no matter how wide the variety of investments in the other two categories.

Finer Diversification

The three categories refer to the general tendency of investments to behave in certain ways. But investments don't always do what they *tend* to do. Any investment can surprise you. The only way to prepare for those surprises is to diversify *within* each of the three categories.

Rising Inflation. If inflation rises rapidly or gets bad enough to disrupt normal economic activity—or if there is even a fear of such disruption—many so-called inflation hedges will be hurt. Real estate would be particularly vulnerable. But the disruption would be extremely profitable for gold. Thus, a portfolio's inflation hedges should include gold.

Ideally, other inflation hedges should be included as well, since large-scale government sales of bullion or other events we cannot now imagine might temporarily suppress the price of gold.

Gradually Declining Inflation. Gradually declining inflation is healthy for most businesses, which is why it tends to help the stock market. But an individual business or stock—or even a particular industry—might do poorly despite general prosperity. So, to be ready for prosperity, a portfolio should have interests in a number of different industries, whether in the form of marketable stocks, stock warrants, or broadly based mutual funds.

Rapidly Declining Inflation. High-grade debt instruments (bonds and other IOUs safe from default) become more valuable when inflation declines rapidly—since interest rates tend to fall, with some delay, along with inflation rates. Yields on Treasury bills and other short-term instruments would be substantially above the rate of inflation. Long-term Treasury bonds would show big profits.[3]

But rapidly declining inflation usually is traumatic. Many debtors are unable to honor their obligations, and uncertainty clouds the standing of bond issuers who previously had high credit ratings. Consequently, a portfolio isn't truly prepared for rapidly declining inflation unless a large portion of its fixed-dollar assets is in U.S. Treasury securities. Other dollar assets can be included, such as well-secured mortgages or high-grade bonds, but no single such investment should amount to more than 2% or so of the total portfolio.

BOGUS TAX PLANNING

Ideas may be presented to you as tax planning, when in fact they are only investment recommendations. Reduce your taxes by buying real estate,

---

[3] Prices of existing bonds generally rise when interest rates decline.

you may be told—or eliminate taxes altogether by drilling for oil and gas. The tax benefits may be real, but the investment's profitability might not be.

If you actually could foresee which investments will be winners and which will be losers, you wouldn't need to bother with tax planning, since such foresight would bring unlimited profits. Even after paying tax at say, a 90% rate, 10% would remain, and 10% of infinity is still infinity.

To deserve the name, a "tax plan" should be workable even if you intend to handle all your capital conservatively, never trying to outguess the markets and never taking on business risks.

What would a no-forecast investment program look like?

Permanent Portfolio

Investment advisor Harry Browne has written extensively about a "permanent portfolio"—a collection of investments designed to protect and increase purchasing power regardless of what the future holds. A permanent portfolio is meant to succeed through prosperity, inflation, depression, good times, bad times, war, and peace. And it must do the job without requiring you (or anyone else) to forecast the twists and turns of the investment markets. A permanent portfolio operates with no foresight at all.

To be assured of a source of profit in any and all circumstances, a permanent portfolio relies on investment categories that are particularly volatile, so that any one of them has the power to carry the entire portfolio. And, to eliminate the need for timing, each category's share of the portfolio is fixed.

The basic permanent portfolio devised by Mr. Browne is a paragon of simplicity. It is shown in the box below. The "gold" is real gold (bullion or

THE PERMANENT PORTFOLIO

Investment Category	Share of Portfolio
Gold	25%
Leveraged stocks	25%
U.S. Treasury bonds	25%
U.S. Treasury bills	25%

coins), not gold mining stocks. This is the investment most profitable during times of high inflation or other extreme difficulties.

The "leveraged stocks" are a broad selection of highly volatile stocks or mutual funds that invest in such stocks. During times of prosperity, they should *outperform* a rising market.

The "U.S. Treasury bonds" are long-term bonds—25 to 30 years. Such issues can appreciate dramatically when interest rates fall.

The "U.S. Treasury bills," the one nonvolatile investment, are short-term issues that will hold their principal value even when interest rates are rising sharply. They are a cash reserve that would survive even a collapse of the banking system.

You set up a permanent portfolio by buying the appropriate investments. Then, at least annually, you buy or sell, as needed, to keep your actual holdings in each category at 25%. These periodic adjustments offset the effect of changes in investment prices, which otherwise would leave you overinvested in some categories and underinvested in others.

The chart below shows a 25-year history of such a permanent portfolio, together with the price history of gold, stocks and bonds. The portfolio did a remarkable job of preserving capital and achieving a steady gain. Its average rate of return was 7.8% per year, and it showed a loss in only two years (5.6% and 1.0%). In 1987, the year of the stock market crash, the portfolio

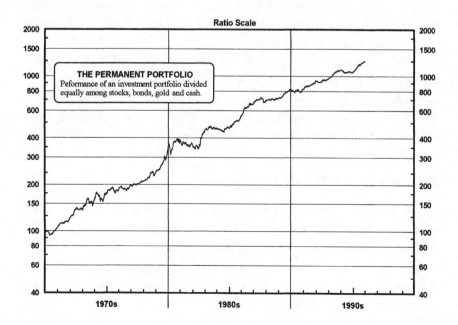

Ratio Scale

THE PERMANENT PORTFOLIO
Peformance of an investment portfolio divided
equally among stocks, bonds, gold and cash.

1970s   1980s   1990s

gained 5.8%. And on October 17 of that year, the day the stock market lost 17%, the portfolio declined only 3%.

There is nothing magical about the percentages in Mr. Browne's simple permanent portfolio. A permanent portfolio with different percentages or more categories might work even better. But any plan to achieve the stability and security of a permanent portfolio must satisfy two strict requirements. First, for any imaginable economic circumstance, the portfolio must contain one or more investments that should be especially profitable. Second, the portfolio must be committed to holding a fixed percentage in each investment, so that you never miss a profit because a bull market has caught you by surprise.

A mutual fund, the Permanent Portfolio Fund, was organized in 1982 for investors who want a convenient way to apply the permanent portfolio strategy. Information on the fund can be found in Chapter 35, "Where to Get Help."

Tax on a Permanent Portfolio

Some of the investments in the simple permanent portfolio make tax planning easy. Gold produces no income at all, and volatile stocks tend to have low dividend yields.

It might seem like shrewd tax planning to restrict the portfolio to precious metals and low-yield stocks. It isn't. The tax savings would require a dangerous bet—that there will be no periods of tight money, rapidly declining inflation or outright deflation.

The investments that protect the portfolio against such risks happen to be the source of most of its potential tax burden—the interest-earning Treasury bills and Treasury bonds. Possible substitutes, such as corporate bonds, money market funds, bank CDs and most other fixed-dollar assets, would present the same tax problem.

PLANNING CONFLICT

A safe portfolio's need for fixed-dollar investments (to allow for the day when most other investments will be losing money) presents a fundamental conflict between portfolio planning and tax planning. Investment choices that reduce taxable income tend to increase the portfolio's vulnerability to tight money, severe recession, and deflation. Investment choices that protect against those hazards tend to increase the tax bill.

The conflict will be present whether your portfolio is guided by the permanent portfolio concept or by some other principle. But the conflict is only a tendency, not an absolute. There are ways to resolve it, and we will examine many of them in the chapters that follow. They can come close to eliminating income tax on your portfolio, no matter how conservative your investment strategy.

The Test

You may decide to use the permanent portfolio concept or some other safe strategy to handle a portion of your assets—the part you don't want to risk losing. The rest of your assets would be available, if you wish, for deliberate risktaking and speculation—to shoot for especially high profits.

But even if you decide not to establish a permanent portfolio, you can apply the concept to test any tax plan you may be offered. If the plan can reduce the taxes of a permanent portfolio, then it has merit. But if the plan won't work with a permanent portfolio, or if it requires the economy to avoid tight money and hard times or to behave in any other particular way, or if it assumes you will jump nimbly and infallibly from winning investment to winning investment, then it is not a tax plan at all. It is an investment plan, and it is one that invites you to play a risky game. ⌐╍

7

THE MENACE
OF LAWSUITS

Today a single misstep can cost you everything. An error in judgment, a moment of inattention, an ill-chosen word, even a remote and innocent involvement in some mishap can place everything you own at the disposal of a state or federal court. There someone would explain how badly you had treated him and would plead for the judge to shake you by the heels until your last nickel clinks on the floor.

The threat of litigation was not always the terror it has become. In years gone by, the willingness of the courts to award damages was limited by narrow and well-established standards.

Courts, legislatures and the public seemed to understand the danger of inviting the legal system to right every wrong and soothe every hurt. They knew that too much courtroom justice would be unhealthy. It would invite disagreements and discourage people from settling the unavoidable ones privately, it would train everyone to nurture his grievances and exaggerate his hurts, and it would place the fear of litigation at the center of every relationship. Courts intent on perfect justice would turn us all into adversaries.

MODERN TIMES

Times have changed. Today's courts are more eager to do good, as they see it, and less wary of the harm their efforts might produce.

The essence of a lawsuit is the plaintiff's attempt to harness the coercive power of government for his own purpose. The plaintiff's arguments are not academic. He is asking the court to direct local police, state sheriffs, federal marshals and the government's other organs of enforcement to compel the defendant to do as the plaintiff demands. Thus litigation involves not just the courts but all of government. The "litigation explosion"—as it has been called, is just one more path by which government grows.

Modern Thoughts

The central, if unspoken, premise of modern thinking is that human affairs are inherently manageable. Despite the chaos and surprises of history—peace, famine, invention, strife, revolution, progress and disaster—despite the intricacy of society's web of relationships and despite the confusion of motives that propel human action—despite all this, modern thinking finds the world limitlessly susceptible to improvement. The troubles and mysteries of life are only so many problems waiting for experts to solve. All that's needed is for the intelligent and well-intentioned to grasp the power to get the job done. And that power lies in government.

Those who share the modern view fully will find it difficult to say "No" to any plan for government to make things better. They hope that, freed from the narrow and parochial interests of private individuals, the government's impartial administrators will run the plan with rational precision and will use the power of the state to assure that everyone cooperates.

The obvious tardiness, inefficiency and perversity of most government activity do nothing to discourage this attitude. Every government failure is counted as a valuable lesson—another step down the learning curve, a necessary cost of making government more effective. Complaints about poor results are taken as proof that government needs more money and more power.

Modern Courts

Within the legal system, the modern view struggles against traditional principles that for centuries restrained litigants, attorneys, and the courts themselves. Courts once saw themselves as a device for cooperation between private parties, who could rely upon them to enforce private agreements. And they were an alternative, and hence a deterrent, to private vengeance. Serving those purposes well was task enough for any institution. To attempt more would require wisdom and foresight judges knew they didn't have.

Modern courts are more ambitious. Judges consider themselves part of the wise few and are sure they have the power to accomplish good—to bring justice and fairness to an unjust, unfair world. Such a judge believes that the consequences of his enlightened actions can be whatever he wants them to be—if only he will act. When traditional legal principles get in the way, he talks around them or pushes them aside.

Beware. The judge who acts so ambitiously—whether out of enthusiasm for the good he hopes to do, or because of the legal philosophy he has embraced, or because legislation and higher courts have urged him in that direction—is a one-man taxing authority. Of course, he calls the court's demands "judgments," not "taxes," but they are taxes nonetheless—money confiscated from unwilling citizens by the force of government. Thus asset protection isn't something to undertake in addition to tax planning. It is *part* of tax planning—the part that guards against ad hoc taxes (judgments) imposed by courts.

FALLEN BARRIERS

The litigation explosion was set off by removing traditional barriers to litigation and pushing out the limits of what a plaintiff can hope to win.

Standards of Liability

By traditional common-law standards, a person could not be found liable unless he knew, or reasonably should have known, that his actions or omissions were likely to be harmful.

In today's courts, a person may be found liable for failing to know what *no one* knew or even imagined. The Johns Manville Company, for example, was driven into bankruptcy by suits from persons made sick by inhaling asbestos the company had manufactured and sold decades earlier. That the dangers of airborne asbestos were unknown at the time the material was sold did nothing to protect Manville, which was forced to pay billions in claims. Under the Manville doctrine no manufacturer will ever be free of legal liability—because a product's harmful effect may be discovered only decades after the last of the product has been sold.

Weakening the standard of liability seems attractive if you open your imagination to the good the courts can do. The new standard gives every customer an open-ended insurance policy against any harm that might be traced to the products he buys.

But the same standard means that no manufacturer can ever really own anything, because all its assets are permanently up for grabs. No degree of care, and no passage of time, can protect a manufacturer from claims by customers or anyone else affected by its products. The result of this uncertainty will be fewer products available to us and higher prices for those that are left.

Deep-Pockets Theory

Some mishaps are the work of more than one person. In traditional legal theory, only the person who was the proximate, or immediate, cause of a mishap could be held responsible. Now a tragedy's smallest bit player can be forced to pay for the entire production.

Under the doctrine of "joint and several liability," *any* party found negligent to *any* degree may be held liable for *all* the damage. Thus blame is not allocated so much by fault as by wealth. If some of the liable parties are broke, the others can be forced to pay the entire bill—even if their parts in the mishap are incidental.

At age 92, Louella Wilson lent her grandnephew, John, money for the down payment on a car. John hit another car and was sued for damages. Mrs. Wilson was sued, too, on the grounds that she was negligent to finance her grandnephew's car purchase. The plaintiff won the suit and was awarded $950,000. Since John lacked the means to pay, Mrs. Wilson was ordered to pay the entire award.

Punitive Damages

A court may do more than compensate the plaintiff for his suffering. It may award additional, *punitive* damages to punish the defendant and warn others not to imitate his errors. Statutes governing some types of complaints specify how large punitive damages can be. Or a court may decide on its own to impose a large judgment to "send a message" to the defendant and other potential wrongdoers.

Traditional practice hesitated to grant punitive damages, generally allowing them only if a defendant had acted with malice, causing harm intentionally.

Modern courts are more liberal. They may award punitive damages simply because it seems like a good way to protect society from future wrongdoing. But this leaves civil defendants with less protection than criminals —who can draw comfort from the higher standard of proof required for a criminal prosecution, who know the maximum possible penalty before they act, and who never have to face a prosecutor who is hoping to share in a large award.

Professional Liability

If the world is inherently manageable, then when bad things happen, someone must be at fault—and the victim's attorney will be ready to explain who it is. If a professional is involved in the mishap, he's probably the one.

Giving birth, for example, is a difficult and hazardous project. Much can go wrong, possibly leaving the parents with a child who is retarded, deformed, or dead. This is the kind of hard fact that modern thinking wants to deny. If grieving parents can persuade a court that their family's misfortune was due in some way—even a small way—to a doctor's error, the doctor and the hospital that let him practice may have to pay for the child's care and the parents' grief. By presenting the child and his parents sympathetically, an attorney may persuade a jury that it was "negligent" for the doctor to forgo a laboratory test for a 1-in-10,000,000 possibility, or to be clumsy in applying a new medical technique or to fail to think quickly or inventively enough in an emergency.

Professionals don't always succeed at what they try, nor should they be expected to. A professional usually is called in precisely because a problem is so difficult. His job is to make the best of the situation handed to him, not to make miracles.

But a judge or juror who sees the world as inherently manageable will find it hard not to blame a professional. It is the professional who possesses the knowledge and skill that makes the world manageable. If things have gone badly, so the judge or juror would reason, the professional *must* be at fault.

Wider Net

Traditional practice discouraged litigation. While society preferred it to dueling with pistols or breaking the legs of delinquent debtors, litigation was seen as a costly process that, if not checked, would breed acrimony and uncertainty. But in the modern view, litigation is a source of good and so should be encouraged.

Until recently, attorneys in most states were prohibited from advertising. The advertising of legal services, it was feared, would tend to turn small disputes into big lawsuits, as ambulance chasers tutored their clients in the variety of things to complain about. Then "progressive" forces (most of whose members had no previous experience as defenders of the free market) found the ban on advertising to be an obnoxious violation of free-market principles—because it deprived the public of an ample supply of litigation. They insisted that consumers would be better served if law firms were allowed to advertise and compete for business—the business of making government grow.

Fifty years ago class-action suits were rare. Now if an attorney can find a single individual with a $10 grievance that arguably is shared by one million other sufferers, he can seek the court's permission to sue for $10 million on behalf of them all. And with punitive damages, the $10 grievance might support a $50-million suit. The attorney doesn't have to know or care whether any sizable fraction of the one million actually feel aggrieved.

Some states will now permit anyone to file a civil suit on behalf of the state's entire population, as though he were the attorney general of the state. Opening the door to such "private attorneys general" assures that no grievance will go to waste merely because the actual attorney general—who might be held back by a fear of being seen as a public nuisance, appearing neurotically contentious, or seeming to favor one group at the expense of another—will not pursue it.

Only the Beginning

This brief review doesn't cover all the ingredients of the litigation explosion. There's much more to it. But the factors discussed here point to two conclusions for anyone hoping to protect his assets.

First, *anyone's grievance, complaint, disappointment, or endorphin deficit could turn into a lawsuit against you.*

Second, *it is not so much wrongdoing that makes you the target of a lawsuit as it is the ability to pay a judgment.* If you have enough money to be worth fighting over and you have been seen in a vicinity where something bad has happened, today's courts will welcome any argument that the bill for setting things right should be sent to you.

RULES OF THE GAME

A lawsuit is a war.

In ordinary business dealings, both sides expect to benefit. A transaction occurs only because both sides want it. But in a lawsuit, what one side wins, the other side must lose—and more. It is impossible for both parties to go home happy.

Because of this, people behave differently in lawsuits than they do in business transactions. A spirit of fairness, a reasonable disposition or an attitude of goodwill count for nothing. Even your fiercest business competitor will treat you better than will your antagonist in a lawsuit. Your competitor knows that one day you might be a customer or a supplier or a partner. He hopes you will refer business you don't want or can't handle. And he would like to have a reputation for fair dealing. A plaintiff in a lawsuit, on the other hand, has only one objective: to pound you into submission.

Order of Battle

A lawsuit against you begins when your antagonist, the plaintiff, files a written complaint with a court. The complaint will allege that you (and possibly others) have done certain bad things that hurt the plaintiff, and it will ask the court to force you to pay compensation or "damages."

It can make exciting reading. The description of your bad acts will be extravagant and so will the amount of damages claimed. Only history's worst villains have actually reached the depths of wickedness in which you will be said to dwell, and only the greatest thieves among them would be able to pay the damage award being sought.

The legal system does little to discourage a plaintiff from overstating the harm he has suffered. The courts won't penalize him for crying too loudly, and his complaint isn't subject to slander or libel laws. The rules of the game generally let the plaintiff inflate his allegations for free. Adding more allegations is free, too.

The extravagance can pay off. The plaintiff's lawyer knows the suit may take many years to settle, so he tries to draw the complaint broadly enough to cover misdeeds that might come to light only as the suit proceeds—to protect against any statute of limitations. The claim for damages may be fabulous because the plaintiff's attorney doesn't know how much the court might be willing to award, and because it takes no more effort to ask for $10,000,000 than to ask for $100,000.

It also costs very little for the plaintiff to add names to a lawsuit, so you may be just one of many defendants. And you may be only an afterthought.

Even a lawsuit that arises from grievous wrongdoing can entangle the blameless. The plaintiff's lawyer may include you as a defendant if your name was mentioned by witnesses or if it appears in any document he examines, even though he has no reason to believe you're at fault. He knows you might be frightened into a settlement (the proceeds of which could finance the suit against other defendants), or you might be bullied into giving useful information or testimony—and that the chance to get an award against you could be lost if he lets a statute of limitations run out.

Before the lawsuit can proceed, you must be formally served with the complaint. You may be served by someone handing you a copy of the complaint, or by signing for a piece of registered mail without wondering what sort of scorpion the envelope might contain. If you don't respond to the court within a certain time (20 days in federal district court, 30 days in most state courts), the court may enter a judgment against you. You could lose by default.

Assuming you do respond, a period of dickering may ensue. The plaintiff may ask for something—money, information, testimony—as the price for dropping the suit or dropping you from it. The dickering may go on for weeks, months or years—or it may not occur at all.

Discovery

The plaintiff has the right of "discovery"—which forces you to answer questions posed by his attorney in the presence of a court stenographer and to open your files and records to the plaintiff. The transcripts of the discovery proceedings and any records uncovered can be used against you at the trial.

In principle the information demanded must be reasonably relevant to the lawsuit. But this principle may do little to restrain the plaintiff's digging, since almost anything might turn out to be relevant—especially in light of all the other information obtained through discovery.

Next there will be one or more status conferences, at which the judge reviews the case's progress with attorneys for both sides. Then there will be a trial-setting conference, which sets the date for the trial and establishes a schedule for the filing of written briefs by both sides. Later the judge will hear and rule on pretrial motions, and then, finally, the trial will begin. The longest civil jury trial in U.S. history ran for three years. It was expensive.

The outcome of the suit will be decided by a jury, unless both sides have waived a jury trial. Generally, for the plaintiff to win, it is sufficient for a simple majority of the jury to determine that a preponderance of the evidence supports his claims. In some states and for some findings, higher standards may be required, such as a two-thirds majority or "clear and convincing proof." But the standards are always much less strict than for a criminal conviction, which ordinarily requires a unanimous finding of guilt beyond a reasonable doubt.

If you lose the suit, the jury or the judge will determine the amount of the award. The person who has won the suit then becomes your "judgment creditor."

Seizing Property

If you don't pay the award immediately, your judgment creditor may begin searching for your property.[1] He also may ask the court for a creditor's examination, at which you would be compelled to disclose the existence and whereabouts of your property.

A U.S. marshal (if you lost in federal court) or one or more county sheriffs (if you lost in state court) will seize any of your property the judgment creditor locates. The exact procedures differ from state to state, but, generally, movable property will be taken away. If your house is seized, it will be padlocked, and you will be evicted. For property transferable by signed documents, such as real estate and registered securities, the court will issue orders in lieu of the usual paperwork.

As your property is seized, it will be sold at public auctions conducted by a U.S. marshal or county sheriff. The proceeds will be paid to your judgment creditor.

Speak Up

Because a lawsuit is not itself a criminal proceeding, your Fifth-Amendment right to remain silent generally does not apply. Failure to answer questions during discovery, during the trial itself or at a creditor's examination could result in fines or imprisonment for contempt of court. False statements would subject you to prosecution for perjury.

However, you could invoke the Fifth Amendment if answering a particular question would expose you to prosecution for a crime. For example, if you had embezzled and hidden $100,000, the Fifth Amendment would allow you to refuse to answer a question such as, "Have you hidden any money?" It is an odd result, but committing a crime can protect you from paying judgments.

---

[1] Private agencies, akin to detective agencies, can be hired to ferret out your assets.

Striking Back

You don't have to remain on the defensive in a lawsuit. You can file a suit against the plaintiffs or other defendants, alleging *they* are the bad actors. And if you win the initial suit, you can sue the plaintiffs for malicious prosecution, claiming they knew there was no reasonable basis for their allegations.

Even if you successfully defend yourself against a lawsuit, you may lose heavily. Legal expenses alone can be many thousands of dollars—and possibly many hundreds of thousands. You can have years of misery and worry. Your reputation may be destroyed. And through it all, you will find it difficult to carry on with your ordinary business because of the distraction and uncertainty and because the lawsuit will raise doubts about your integrity in the minds of people you deal with.

As a rule, the only way to win is not to be sued in the first place or to get yourself dropped from the suit quickly if you are sued.

PROTECTION

As in any war, the best protection is to make yourself an unattractive target. You will be safe if potential litigants know you're prepared to fight back or if they see little chance of actually collecting on a judgment. Doubly safe is the individual who is ready to defend against a lawsuit and also is seen to own nothing that can be seized to pay a judgment.

Liability Insurance

The conventional protection is to purchase liability insurance, such as professional malpractice insurance, homeowner's and driver's accident liability insurance and product liability insurance. A liability policy will reimburse you, up to a stated limit, if you are forced to pay a judgment for a loss covered by the policy.

The policy may require the insurer to pay your legal expenses up to a stated limit. Even without such a provision, your insurer probably will want to support your defense (and control the way it is conducted), in order to avoid paying a large judgment. The common arrangement is for a policy to cover, up to a certain limit, the total cost of both the legal defense and the settlement or damages—so that each dollar spent on defense reduces the amount available to pay the plaintiff.

An insurance policy is a great comfort if you are sued, but it has a mixed effect on your risk of getting sued. On the one hand, potential litigants are discouraged by the thought that you can fight back and send the bill to your insurer. On the other hand, your insurance may whet their appetite, since they know your insurer will pay a judgment promptly if you lose. Thus liability insurance can be a lightning rod for litigation.

Fear of attracting lawsuits has led some professionals to shun all insurance and "go naked"—carrying no liability insurance at all—rather than pay high malpractice premiums to build up a jackpot for potential litigants. Using some of the techniques referred to later in this chapter and explained later in the book, they transfer assets to others, keeping nothing that would be attractive to litigants. Thus prepared, they can tell all potential tormentors there is nothing to be gained by suing.

Going naked can work. But you may find the strategy too daring for comfort.

If you decide to carry liability insurance, I suggest you get a policy that covers the likely cost of defending against a lawsuit—but not enough to pay a large judgment. Such a policy is a cannon your enemies cannot hope to convert into a cash register.

NO SPOILS

With or without liability insurance, you will be safe only if you arrange your affairs to eliminate the prizes that attract lawsuits. You must wrap up your assets so that they are beyond the reach of court judgments—as though you were going naked. If you are thorough, no one will want to sue you, since winning a suit wouldn't mean winning any money.

Transfer Assets

What you don't own can't be seized to satisfy a judgment. You can lose your own house in a lawsuit, but you can't lose your neighbor's house.

One way to get property out of your hands is to give it away—to a family member or to someone else. A valid gift places the property beyond the reach of your judgment creditors.

Giving property away to protect it from potential creditors may seem like shooting your dog to keep it from being stolen. But it isn't. You probably will give away most of what you have sooner or later—supporting children and a spouse, making gifts to grandchildren and others, and dispensing other property through your will. As a rule, if you make those gifts before you are sued or run into other difficulties, your creditors cannot reverse them— which is a strong reason for giving now.

Giving away property doesn't have to mean giving up all the benefits of ownership. You can give away stock in a corporation you continue to control or interests in a partnership you manage. Or your gifts may be to trusts that operate under your influence and for your purposes.

There even are ways to assure that "gifts" are used for your own personal welfare. You can protect assets from potential creditors by transferring them to a trust that treats you as the primary beneficiary.

UGLY WEALTH

Some types of property are difficult and expensive for a creditor to seize. Others may be easy to reach but difficult to liquidate. Some assets are pro- grammed to deteriorate or even self-destruct if they fall into the wrong hands. Still others may be valueless to a third party and even threaten him with a tax bill. Some assets are hard for a potential litigant to appraise (to determine whether they're worth going after). And some types of property are protected from creditors by state or federal law.

To a potential litigant, any such property is "ugly wealth." If that's all you own, you're not an attractive target for a lawsuit. And if you are sued or threatened with a suit, the ugliness of your wealth should make it easy to negotiate a quick and inexpensive settlement.

Cash on deposit with a local bank is easy for a judgment creditor to seize. But money someone has agreed to pay you in the far future is difficult to seize. It is even more difficult if your debtor is in a foreign country. Mat- ters are still worse for your creditor if the foreign country won't honor judg- ments from other jurisdictions. And if it is difficult for outsiders to evaluate the debt (to determine how much can be squeezed out of it), a would-be judgment creditor won't know whether the effort of squeezing you would be worthwhile.

Marketable securities are nearly as attractive to a judgment creditor as cash. They are easy to find, evaluate, seize and liquidate.

Privately issued securities, on the other hand, can be unattractive. First, there is the problem of valuation. Are the securities worth the cost of press- ing a lawsuit? The question may be impossible to answer. And if an outsider can't evaluate the securities, who would bother to bid on them at a creditor's auction?

Securities can be designed to leave little value for an outsider. For example, a family member or a family trust, partnership or corporation may have the right of first refusal to purchase the securities, making it difficult to attract bids from others. Or the terms of the securities may provide that the issuing partnership or corporation can redeem them at a fixed price if they are offered for sale.

Some assets—such as a personal residence, pensions and some types of personal property—are legally exempt from the claims of broad categories of creditors. A local attorney can tell you what kinds of property are protected in your state. It's worth finding out about. Such property is an appetite depressant for potential litigants and a comfort for you.

EARTHQUAKE SAFETY

A lawsuit is much like an earthquake. There may be rumblings beforehand, but when it strikes, it strikes as a shock. Then it is too late to prepare. The damage has been done.

When a process server hands you the stack of papers you hoped never to see, it will be too late to use the asset-protection strategies that are easiest and most effective. The best strategies will work only if you apply them early. So to safeguard yourself and your family from lawsuits, you must safeguard them *now*. Succeeding chapters will show you how. ⚷

8

FINANCIAL PRIVACY IN AMERICA

This is a short chapter, for the same reason a chapter on skiing in Guatemala would be short. There isn't much financial privacy in the United States to talk about.

Americans generally don't place much value on their own financial privacy, nor do they have a great deal of respect for the financial privacy of others. A desire for privacy is seen as a bit fishy ("What are you trying to hide?"), so efforts to protect your own may attract the very attention you want to avoid. In financial matters, there are few modest eyes in America; almost no one feels uncomfortable viewing the financial affairs of others.

THIS IS YOUR LIFE

The ordinary course of life and business in the United States tends to put your finances on display. If you travel, you need a credit card to check into a hotel. (Have you ever tried registering without a credit card? It can be done, but the janitor will show you to your room.) So the credit card company will have a record of your stay.

All other purchases you make with the credit card will be recorded in the same file. Thus, anyone who learns your account number (such as store clerks who handle your card) has the address of a storehouse of information—including your Social Security number, the data you gave the credit card company about your other credit cards, and where you keep your bank account. And anyone with access to your bank records can identify all your credit cards from the checks you write to pay the bills.

Even if you wore a mask and made every purchase with cash, tax reporting still would leave you with few secrets. Every business that pays you more than $600 of income must file a report, as must any broker who handles a sale for you. Even if no one else knows about your income, the Internal Revenue Service almost certainly will.

Government regulation undermines your privacy in other ways. For example, because the government pretends to protect you from unscrupulous investment professionals, it asserts the right to examine the records of your stockbroker and your investment advisor. Of course, those records list all your investment transactions.

DECLINE OF PRIVACY

Although the U.S. government recognizes no right to financial privacy, your loss of privacy is not yet complete. The details of your financial affairs still are scattered among the separate computer and noncomputer files of different government agencies. And additional information about you potentially available from third parties requires time and effort to ask for and process.

But year by year the IRS and other government agencies keep grinding away at the problem, and they gradually are getting better and better at organizing and compiling personal information. It hasn't happened yet, but eventually all the information you report *and all the information about you that others report* will be fully collated and monitored continuously by IRS computers—available to government employees at the touch of a button.[1]

Government agencies aren't the only ones watching. Every purchase you make by check or credit card is recorded in the computer of a store, bank, or credit card company. This information is valuable to many businesses and is often sold or traded. Middlemen—such as market research organizations, credit bureaus, and list brokers—assemble personal financial information and sell it to the ultimate users, such as banks and other lenders, mail-order merchants and companies designing new products and testing new marketing strategies.

The trafficking in information about your personal financial affairs may seem a petty annoyance—a mild case of bad manners. That's all it would be, if the information were used solely for commercial purposes. But it doesn't

---

[1] Of course, the government has assured us that your personal information will never fall into the wrong hands or be misused.

stop there. The story of your financial life can be bought by anyone—including someone considering a lawsuit against you. With it he can reconstruct your financial history, estimate your net worth (which tells him how much trouble and expense a suit might be worth), and identify the specific assets to be seized if he wins.

MODEST STEPS

There are a few steps you can take within the U.S. to preserve a modest degree of financial privacy, if you are willing to go to the trouble.

1. Limit your use of credit cards and checks. Don't carry more cash than you are comfortable with, but when it's not inconvenient, pay with $20 and $50 bills. Even a modest effort in this regard will make it much harder for someone to piece together the story of your financial life.

2. Keep your checking account at a bank outside the county where you live. This won't make the account invisible. If someone is interested, he'll find it, but an out-of-county account will slow him down.

3. Change banks every few years.

4. Use a non-interest-earning checking account, so you won't have to give a Social Security number.[2]

5. Use a money market fund for checking, so that no one can dig through your records without digging through the fund's records.

A BIGGER STEP

Not very exciting, is it?

Your only practical hope of substantial privacy is to move part of your financial life to a country where privacy is respected by law, tradition and business necessity. That may seem, at first glance, to be enormously inconvenient. But it's not. Some of your financial affairs can be exported very easily, and you don't have to have everything overseas to gain privacy. Chapter 22, "Foreign Financial Services," and the rest of Part 6 show you how. ⚿

---

[2] You probably will be asked for your Social Security number, but the bank is not required to obtain it for a non-interest-earning account.

PART THREE

GETTING THE MOST FROM SIMPLE TAX PLANNING

You should begin cutting taxes with the simplest, most conventional techniques. You may need more sophisticated methods as well, but first you should milk all the advantage possible from what is plain and ordinary.

You probably have some acquaintance with the tax-planning techniques covered in this part. (What a happy life you must lead if you have never heard of life insurance.) I hope to add to what you already know by explaining how to gain the maximum advantage from each tax-planning tool, how to minimize the cost of using it and how to judge whether it is worth using at all.

9

THE VALUE OF TAX DEFERRAL

The prisoner stood before the king, who spoke. "You are a thief. You have stolen from rich and poor alike. You are a hundred thieves, who has stolen every day of his life. I condemn you to death."

"Your Majesty, I am past all opportunity for dissembling. I cannot deny the truth of your judgment nor the justice of the penalty. I plead only that I might atone for my crimes by working a wonder full of honor and glory for your Kingdom."

The prisoner paused for as long as he dared. The King's counselors, ever cautious, searched the King's face for clues to the advice he might want. The High Counselor was about to speak, but, seeing the King's eyes widen slightly, held back.

The prisoner continued. "Stay the executioner's hand for a single year, and I will teach Your Majesty's royal steed to speak. He will greet ambassadors, scold ministers and dispute with scholars. Having worked this wonder, I will beg Your Majesty for mercy. But should I fail, I will go to my death without complaint."

The King consented, and the prisoner was led back to his cell, where his cellmate listened in astonishment to the story. "But a horse can't talk! What will you do when the year is up?"

"In exchange for nothing I have gained a year of life and a year of possibilities. Perhaps the King will grow foolish and forgiving. Perhaps he will die, and the new king will not care about me. Perhaps the prison will be broken open in a battle. Perhaps something neither you nor I can imagine will save me. And maybe the horse will speak."

The Prisoner in Cell 1040

The King proposed to confiscate the prisoner's life. The U.S. government proposes to confiscate large chunks of your wealth. For the prisoner, delay was the next best thing to escape. It can be the same for you.

Even if you eventually must pay a tax, mere delay is a victory. And the longer the delay, the greater the victory, since money you hold back from the tax collector today is yours to profit from until tomorrow. Even when tomorrow comes and you must pay the tax, you still get to keep the extra earnings.

And the tax you delay might never be paid in full—or at all—because:

- Tax rates may decline, even if only temporarily.

- Later years may bring losses or deductions that reduce the tax liability.

- Potential tax liabilities may disappear when you die.

- You may find a way to divert income from the U.S. tax system.

- Or the horse may speak: the tax rules might change in ways that are particularly favorable to you—in ways you can't even imagine now.

THE TIME VALUE OF TAX DEFERRAL

Income you earn in one year is *tax deferred* if you don't have to report it on your tax return until a later year. Deferral sends your tax bill into the future—possibly the far future—leaving more cash at your disposal in the meantime. So long as the deferral continues, you can earn extra returns by investing money that otherwise would have gone to the tax collector.

Tax deferral doesn't postpone the financial benefit of your income. It postpones only the tax consequences.

Measure the Advantage

Suppose, for example, you're in a 30% tax bracket, and you deposit $1,000 in a regular savings account earning 5%. One year later you'll receive $50 in interest. After allowing for $15 of income tax, you'll have $35 to keep—an after-tax return of only 3.5%.

If you leave the money on deposit, withdrawing just enough each year to pay the tax bill, the results will be as shown in the following table.

Regular Savings Account (5% Return) with Current Taxation

Year	Income Before Tax	Income After Tax	Account Balance
1	$50	$35	$1,035
2	52	37	1,072
10	68	48	1,411
20	96	67	1,990
30	136	95	2,807

Suppose instead that you could put your savings in a "Special Account," whose income isn't taxed until you withdraw it. How great would the advantage be?

It would be considerable, especially if you leave your money in the Special Account for a long time, as the next table demonstrates.

Special Account (5% Return) with Tax Deferral Compared with Regular Account

Year	Income Before Tax	Income After Tax	Special Account Balance	Special Account's Advantage
1	$50	$50	$1,050	$15, or 43%
2	53	53	1,103	$31, or 43%
10	78	78	1,629	$218, or 53%
20	126	126	2,653	$663, or 67%
30	206	206	4,322	$1,515, or 84%

As the table shows, the Special Account grows much faster than a regular account. By the tenth year, for example, the Special Account has $218 more than the regular account—an earnings advantage of 53%.

The table also shows how the advantage of tax deferral accelerates with time. After 20 years, the Special Account's advantage is 67%.

Why do the benefits of tax deferral accelerate over time? The acceleration comes from unleashing the full power of compound interest. Unhindered by taxation, the Special Account compounds at the full rate of 5% per year, rather than the 3½% after-tax rate of a regular account.

A Second Look

The tables may seem to overstate the Special Account's advantage. Although a much bigger pot of money accumulates inside the Special Account, tax must be paid on those earnings before they can be spent—so the advantage of deferring tax for 10 or 20 years might not be nearly so great as the tables suggest.

But you're not likely to accumulate money for decades and then spend it all at once. More likely, you'll spend it over many years. In that case tax deferral can continue long after you have finished accumulating wealth, so that more of the accumulated wealth keeps generating income for you.

When you invest for "the future," it probably is a future of many years' duration, perhaps beginning the day you retire. Your goal is to maximize the amount of spendable cash you can withdraw from your investments, *year after year,* once the future has arrived. The Special Account, even with its potential tax liability, will hold more capital when you want to start spending. If your capital is, say, 30% larger because of tax deferral, you will be able to spend 30% more each year without touching the capital.

Or perhaps you already have more wealth than you'll ever need to spend on yourself. In that case, tax deferral can continue for a very long time, possibly late into the lifetimes of your heirs—so long that its advantages will dwarf the taxes they may eventually have to pay.

And if tax deferral continues for the rest of your life, the tax you delayed might never be paid, since some potential tax liabilities disappear at death.

THE THREE DIMENSIONS OF TAX DEFERRAL

Time is the first dimension affecting the value of tax deferral. The longer deferral continues, the more you benefit.

The second dimension is *interest rates.* The higher interest rates go, the more profitable tax deferral becomes.

The following table again compares a regular savings account with a Special Account—but at an interest rate of 10% rather than 5%. Great as the Special Account's earnings advantage is when the return is 5%, it is even greater at 10%.

The third dimension of tax deferral's power is *tax rates.* Not surprisingly, the higher tax rates go, the greater the payoff for deferring the taxes on your investment returns.

Comparison of Regular Savings Account
(10% Return) and Special Account

Year	Regular Account	Special Account	Special Account's Earning Advantage
1	$1,070	$1,100	$30, or 43%
2	1,145	1,210	$65, or 45%
10	1,967	2,594	$627, or 65%
20	3,870	6,727	$2,857, or 99%
30	7,612	17,449	$9,837, or 149%

A PORTFOLIO POINT OF VIEW

Tightening your belt for 20 or 30 years while you wait for tax benefits to ripen isn't an exciting proposition. But you don't have to tighten your belt at all to benefit from tax deferral. You can defer taxes even if you are spending all your earnings.

To have the benefit of tax deferral "for free," look to your portfolio for spendable cash—not to particular investments. Don't take money from the investments that earned it. Instead, draw on the investments, regardless of their earnings, that can give you cash without triggering taxable income. The result will be more cash to spend now, without dipping into capital, or more cash to spend later, without having to postpone even one dollar of spending.

More Cash Later . . .

Suppose you have $1,000 in a tax-deferred Special Account and $1,000 in a regular savings account, each earning 5%. The total earnings, before tax, are $100 per year.

Let's assume you want to spend the entire $100 each year. If you view the two accounts separately, you'll withdraw $50 per year from each (so that the entire $100 is taxable income), pay $30 in tax, and have $70 per year to spend. But you would be wasting the tax-deferral power of the Special Account.

Instead, withdraw enough each year from the regular account to have $70 of after-tax, spendable cash. Don't touch the Special Account. In the first year, for example, you would need to withdraw only $85—enough to put $70 in your pocket after paying $15 in taxes on the regular account's $50 of income.

The regular account would shrink by $35 in the first year (it earned $50 and you withdrew $85). But the Special Account would increase by the entire $50 it earned, so your overall portfolio would be gaining value. By the end of the 20th year, the regular account would be nearly exhausted, but the Special Account would have grown to $2,653—enough to pay you *$90* per year after tax and still keep growing.

Withdraw spending money from your portfolio's most lightly taxed source of cash—rather than from the investments that have earned the money—and you'll be able both to spend all your investment earnings *and* continue to defer taxes.

. . . Or More Cash Now

Tax deferral also can give you more cash to spend *starting right now.*

To change the example slightly, suppose you want to spend the maximum amount possible for 20 years, but without dipping into your $2,000. By withdrawing money from the regular account and letting the Special Account grow, you could spend $86 per year for 20 years—a 23% increase. At the end of the 20 years, the regular account would be exhausted—but the balance in the Special Account would have grown to slightly more than $2,000.

TAX DEFERRAL AND PORTFOLIO SAFETY

Tax deferral does more than just reduce your current tax bill. It removes the need to consider tax consequences when you decide how much of your portfolio to allocate to each investment category (fixed-dollar assets, equities, gold, etc.)—and thereby resolves the conflict between tax avoidance and portfolio safety.

As explained in Chapter 6, the conflict is greatest with bonds, money market investments and other "fixed-dollar" assets. Your portfolio will be vulnerable to downturns in the economy unless it includes healthy portions of such investments. But the interest they generate normally is fully and immediately taxable. Thus the tax cost of holding fixed-dollar investments can make portfolio safety seem like an expensive luxury. Tax deferral makes the luxury affordable.

Inflation Protection

The reward for wrapping fixed-dollar investments in a program of tax deferral is greatest during times of inflation.

Inflation means that the purchasing power of a dollar is shrinking. Interest rates normally rise along with inflation, to compensate holders of fixed-dollar investments for the continuing shrinkage in the purchasing power of their principal. But after the bite of current taxes, the extra yield is too little to offset inflation completely. The erosion of purchasing power slows but doesn't stop.

Tax deferral cures the problem. It stops the erosion of purchasing power by capturing the full benefit of higher interest rates. And by so doing, it eliminates the cost of keeping your portfolio ready for the sharp declines in stock, real estate and gold prices that normally come when, inevitably, inflation winds down.

FINDING SPECIAL ACCOUNTS

No one advertises a "Special Account," but many arrangements provide the tax deferral of a Special Account—such as pension plans, annuities, life insurance, deferred-payment sales and tax-efficient mutual funds. Some can even make tax deferral permanent—that is, turn tax deferral into *tax elimination.*

Costs

Tax deferral isn't free. Each method carries some disadvantage—such as complexity, investment limitations, or low liquidity. And each involves administrative and promotional expenses, whether as explicit fees or through reduced rates of return.

Tax deferral will bring you a big *net* benefit only if you keep the costs under control—which you can do.

The disadvantage of complexity diminishes, the more you understand the principles of tax planning (which is one reason for asking you to read Parts 1 and 2). The disadvantages of illiquidity and restricted investment choice should disappear almost entirely if you make decisions for your portfolio as a whole, rather than one investment at a time (as discussed in Chapter 6, "Portfolio Planning"). And administrative and promotional expense can be limited by careful shopping—finding tax-deferral mechanisms that are low in cost—with the guidelines given in later chapters.

Opportunities

You can enjoy the benefits of tax deferral even if you need to spend all your investment return each year. You can defer taxes without deferring spending.

Don't pass up any low-cost opportunity for deferring taxes, even if it runs for just a year or two. Another year may bring another opportunity. And by tacking one short period of deferral onto another and then another and another, you can achieve the big payoff that comes with long-term deferral.

Don't pass up a chance to defer taxes simply because you can't see where it leads or what you will do when it has run its course. It leads to tomorrow, and when tomorrow comes, you will know more than you do now. ☞

10

EASY TAX PLANNING WITH MUTUAL FUNDS

Mutual funds can cut taxes as easily and cleanly as scissors cut paper.

By choosing the right funds, you can defer ordinary income, allow it to compound free of current tax, and transform it into capital gain. In some situations, you can even use a mutual fund to turn taxable income into tax-free cash. And you can exploit this tax-planning power while enjoying the convenience and simplicity that make mutual funds so popular.

MUTUAL FUND INVESTING

A mutual fund is a company that creates and sells as many shares of its own stock as investors want to buy. It buys back the same shares (redeems them) whenever a shareholder wants to cash out.

With the money it receives from selling shares to investors, a mutual fund purchases stocks, bonds, money market instruments (such as commercial paper and U.S. Treasury bills) or other investments. Most funds specialize in a single type of investment.

A mutual fund allows an investor with even modest capital to diversify widely and to avoid numerous administrative chores, which are performed by the fund's management. If a fund's investments are successful, each shareholder profits through increases in the redemption value of his shares and/or by receiving dividends and distributions paid out of the fund's earnings.

Investors buy and redeem shares each day at a price that reflects the current value of the fund's assets. The fund adds up the market value of its investments, subtracts any debts, and divides the net amount by the number of shares outstanding. The result is the fund's *net asset value* for the day—the price you must pay to purchase shares from the fund (plus, in some cases, a commission), and the price the fund will pay if you choose to redeem your shares.

Because you can redeem on any business day, you always have access to your share of the fund's net assets, including any earnings that have accumulated inside the fund.

Taxation of Fund

A mutual fund is subject to tax as a corporation. However, if a fund passes certain tests (having to do primarily with the nature of its income and assets), it receives a tax deduction for money it distributes to shareholders. Thus, by distributing all its income and profits each year, a mutual fund escapes corporate income tax altogether. Shareholders, of course, are subject to tax on the distributions they receive.

At first glance, the rules seem to invite a mutual fund to serve as a conduit, merely passing the tax liability for its activities on to its shareholders. In many cases this is exactly what happens—but not always.

OUCH! A DIVIDEND

Most funds, as a matter of policy, pay out all their ordinary income and short-term capital gains as taxable dividends. Money market funds generally pay such dividends every day. Funds that invest in stocks and bonds ordinarily pay dividends every three months and distribute any long-term capital gains once per year.

Paying the maximum possible dividend allows a fund to boast of its high yield and usually elicits applause from shareholders and financial writers. A dividend check looks good, feels good and smells good. But in fact a dividend from a mutual fund is an injury. It gives the shareholder nothing he didn't already have—except a tax bill.

Since a dividend is paid out of fund assets, it reduces the redemption value of fund shares by an equal amount. If a mutual fund pays a dividend of $1 per share, the redemption value of its shares goes down by the same $1. Thus a dividend delivers *no economic benefit* to shareholders. Nonetheless, shareholders must *pay tax* on the dividend.

TAX-EFFICIENT FUNDS

A few "tax-efficient funds," on the other hand, pay dividends only once a year and only in the *minimum* amount needed for them to avoid corporate income tax. The dividend generally is only a modest fraction—on the order of one third—of the fund's actual income per share. The rest (the other two thirds) is added to the redemption value of each investor's shares.

Carrying out a minimum-dividend policy demands complex bookkeeping by the fund. But the policy provides valuable tax advantages to you.[1]

Tax-efficient mutual funds are particularly advantageous for investing in fixed-dollar assets, such as bonds, U.S. Treasury bills, and CDs. All or most of the return from such investments is interest—and subject to current tax unless you do something to protect it. Thus fixed-dollar investments especially need the protection afforded by a tax-efficient fund.

With a tax-efficient fund, you can invest in fixed-dollar investments and defer tax on two thirds or so of the return—the portion the fund adds to the redemption value of your shares. This allows your return to compound much faster, for more rapid accumulation of wealth—and without effort, complexity or additional expense on your part.

A tax-efficient fund is less important, but still helpful, for investments in stocks and other growth assets.

Long-Term Investors—Faster Compounding

A tax-efficient fund translates part of its income into increases in the redemption value of your shares. Neither you nor the fund is subject to immediate tax on this increase. You are taxed on your profit, generally as a capital gain, only when you redeem your shares. If you redeem only some of your shares, tax deferral continues for the rest.

Income Investors—More Spendable Cash

Even if you want to spend your investment return each year, you can benefit from a tax-efficient fund's low dividend policy. Most of your annual return will come to you as a tax-free return of capital, giving you more spendable, after-tax cash.

---

[1] A mutual fund must distribute all of its net income as dividends in order to avoid corporate income tax. A tax-efficient fund minimizes the taxable, per-share dividends it must pay by counting a portion of each redemption payment it makes during the year as a "dividend."

Suppose, for example, that you are in a 28% tax bracket and that you want to generate spendable cash by using a mutual fund that invests in short-term corporate bonds. If you invest $50,000 in an ordinary bond fund yielding 6%, your return will be $3,000 per year. But after paying taxes, you would have only $2,160 left to spend.

Suppose, instead, that you use a tax-efficient fund earning the same 6% total return—and that the fund pays only one third of its income (2%) as taxable dividends and adds the rest (4%) to the redemption value of your shares. If the price is $50 per share on the day you buy, you get 1,000 shares. One year later you will receive $1 per share in dividends ($1,000), and the redemption value of each share will have risen, by $2, to $52 (appreciation of $2,000).

If you want to spend the $2,000 of appreciation, simply redeem $2,000 worth of shares (38.46 shares). This would bring to $3,000 the total cash you have collected. But you could keep most of that $3,000, because most of it would be a tax-free return of capital. Only the $1,000 in dividends and $77 in capital gain ($2 on each share redeemed) would be taxable—a total of $1,077 in *taxable* income, instead of $3,000.

More Spendable Cash with a Tax-Efficient Mutual Fund

Shares redeemed	38.46
Redemption price per share	$52
Capital gain per share	$2
Capital gain	$77
Dividends	$1,000
Total taxable amount	$1,077
Tax @ 28%	$302
After-tax, spendable cash	$2,698

The tax-efficient fund's first-year cash advantage over an ordinary bond fund would be $538 ($2,698 versus $2,160). That's 25% more spendable cash without dipping into capital.

Capital-Loss Investors—Tax-Free Cash

On your tax return, you can apply a capital loss from one investment to offset a capital gain on another investment, so that the gain goes untaxed. However, you can't use a capital loss to offset more than $3,000 of ordinary income per year. So if you do have a sizable capital loss, a dollar of capital gain is much more valuable than a dollar of interest or dividends—since the dollar of capital gain is effectively tax free.

You can earn capital gains on successful investments in stocks, real estate, foreign currencies, and commodities. So if you have a capital loss, you will find such investments especially attractive—if you are willing to bear the risks they involve.

Money market instruments and short-term bonds, on the other hand, carry negligible price risk. But such investments normally earn ordinary income, not capital gains. However, a tax-efficient fund holding such investments can generate capital gains for you. Simply purchase shares in the fund and then redeem them just before the annual dividend is paid. *All* your return will be capital gain. And if you have enough offsetting capital losses, all your return will be tax free.

You can reinvest in the same fund (at the reduced, after-dividend price) immediately after dividend day and hold your shares for another year of low-risk appreciation, until the next dividend day. You can continue the process until you have used up all your capital losses.

All Investors—Disappearing Tax Liability

If you do not redeem all your shares in a tax-efficient mutual fund during your lifetime, the income you have deferred will never be subject to income tax. The potential tax liability will evaporate.

The shares you haven't redeemed will pass to your estate and then to your heirs. Under rules that apply to most inherited investments, your heirs will get a fresh start. Their "cost" for the shares (for computing capital gain) would be the shares' value on the date you died—no matter what you paid for them. Thus the heirs will pay no income tax on profits you deferred during your lifetime, whether they keep the shares or redeem them immediately.

LIFE ON MARS

A thoughtfully managed mutual fund is a powerful and easy-to-use tax-planning tool. But the management of most funds seem to believe their shareholders live on Mars, where there is no income tax. Fortunately, some funds care about your tax problems. A short list of tax-efficient funds appears in Chapter 35, "Where to Get Help," and there may be others that I haven't found, but which your own efforts might uncover. ⌐

11

DEFERRED ANNUITIES

Special provisions in the Internal Revenue Code make it easy for insurance companies to reduce your taxes.

With the right kind of insurance policy, you can accumulate interest or other investment earnings without current tax—even though the insurance company gets a tax deduction for the money it sets aside for you each year. Since the insurance company can deliver tax benefits without incurring tax liabilities of its own, it can pay you a full, competitive rate of return.

For tax planning, the most important insurance products are deferred annuities (explained in this chapter) and cash-value life insurance (explained in the next chapter).

Don't let the names mislead you. *Annuity* may sound like a lifetime income, but it also is a powerful device for deferring tax on interest or other investment profits. *Life insurance* may sound like protection for your dependents, but it also is a way to defer or *eliminate* tax on investment earnings—including earnings you spend during your lifetime.

LIFETIME ANNUITIES

The basic form of annuity is the *lifetime* annuity. It is a promise by an insurance company to pay you a fixed amount of money each year for the rest of your life, in return for a premium you pay in advance.[1]

---

[1] The buyer of an annuity, the owner of the annuity, and the annuitant (the person whose lifespan limits the payments from the annuity) needn't be the same person—but usually are.

A lifetime annuity protects against living so long that you run out of money. No matter how old you get, it keeps paying. Of course, any investment will keep paying forever if you spend no more than it earns. But a lifetime annuity can pay more, because when you die the company will keep whatever capital remains.

For example, suppose you can earn 8% per year by investing in bonds. If you're sixty-five years old, an insurance company might pay you 12% per year on a lifetime annuity, depending on its estimate of how long you are likely to live.

An insurance company loses money on annuity buyers who live longer than expected. But it makes the money back on annuity buyers who die early.

Tax Treatment of Lifetime Annuity

Initially the payments you receive from a lifetime annuity are partly taxable and partly tax free. You calculate the tax-free portion by prorating your investment over the number of years you expect to live (as indicated by an actuarial table).

This split continues until the tax-free payments equal your initial investment. Then, if you live longer than the actuarial table predicted, all further payments are fully taxable.

For example, suppose you invest $100,000 in an annuity and begin receiving payments immediately. If an actuarial table says you have 25 years to live, the first $4,000 you receive each year (⅟₂₅ of the premium) would be tax-free, and the rest would be taxable. This split would continue for 25 years, after which all further payments would be fully taxable.

Notice that you are taxed only on payments you receive. If you received no payment, there would be no tax.[2]

DEFERRED ANNUITIES AND TAX DEFERRAL

A lifetime annuity offers no income tax advantages. A *deferred annuity* does.

---

[2] For the annuity tax rules, a lifetime income is a series of substantially equal payments that run for your lifetime or for a period at least as long as your life expectancy.

With a deferred annuity, you postpone the lifetime income. Until it starts, the insurance company simply credits your contract with interest each year—which isn't taxable so long as you let it accumulate.[3]

And there is no need ever to start taking a lifetime income. Instead, you can withdraw all or part of the annuity's value whenever you want. Thus a deferred annuity is, in effect, a tax-deferred savings account—just like the "Special Account" discussed in Chapter 9. You put money into the deferred annuity, the interest compounds, and you pay tax only when you take the money out.[4]

TAXATION OF WITHDRAWALS

Money you withdraw from a deferred annuity (before starting a lifetime income) is taxable to the extent of the annuity's accumulated earnings. Any further withdrawal would be a tax-free return of capital.

Suppose, for example, that you purchase an annuity for $10,000, and after eight years its value has grown to $18,000. Withdrawals up to $8,000 would be fully taxable. Withdrawals beyond $8,000 would be tax free. If you withdraw the entire $18,000, $8,000 would be taxable and $10,000 would be tax free.

If you make a withdrawal before age 59½, the taxable portion is subject to a 10% penalty tax, in addition to the regular income tax.[5]

Loans

You cannot avoid tax by borrowing against a deferred annuity. If you use it as collateral to borrow from the insurance company or anyone else, the loan proceeds are taxed as though they were a withdrawal.

Exchanges and Investment Character

You can exchange one annuity contract for another, even with a different company, without incurring tax. This makes a deferred annuity a good investment, in addition to being a valuable tax-planning tool.

---

[3] To defer tax, the annuity must be owned by a natural (flesh-and-blood) person or by a grantor trust (explained in Chapter 16, "Trusts"). A corporation, partnership, or nongrantor trust that owns a deferred annuity must pay tax on the earnings each year.

[4] If you tell the insurance company to begin paying a lifetime income, the annual amount will depend on your age at the time and on the annuity's accumulated balance.

[5] The penalty doesn't apply if you're completely disabled or if you die and the withdrawal is made by your survivors.

Because you are free to make withdrawals and exchanges whenever you want, the insurance company knows it can keep your money only if it keeps paying a competitive interest rate. Thus a deferred annuity is effectively a floating-rate (adjustable-rate) fixed-dollar investment. The interest rate will tend to fluctuate along with rates on CDs and short-term bonds.

VARIABLE ANNUITIES

A variable annuity is a special type of deferred annuity. Instead of interest, the annuity's earnings are determined by the performance of a particular investment, such as a mutual fund sponsored by the insurance company.

Some variable annuities let you choose from a series of investments— usually including a money market fund, a stock market fund and a long-term bond fund. You can switch from one investment to another whenever you want.

The tax rules just explained for withdrawals, loans and exchanges apply here as well. Withdrawals and loans are taxable, up to the amount of the annuity's accumulated earnings. An exchange of one annuity contract for another is tax free.

Switching a variable annuity from one investment to another also is tax free, making the annuity a good place for speculative capital. And for the wealth you want to manage conservatively, a variable annuity lets you adjust your holdings from time to time, to maintain balance and diversification, without incurring taxes.

Life Insurance Element

A variable annuity, unlike a simple, interest-earning annuity, contains an element of life insurance. If you die, the insurance company will pay your beneficiaries at least what you paid for the annuity, even if the underlying investment has been a loser.

Suppose, for example, that you put $50,000 into a variable annuity that invests in shares of a stock market mutual fund. One year later a weak stock market has reduced the shares' value to $40,000. Despite the loss, if you happen to get ground into the pavement by an A&P truck, the insurance company will pay your beneficiaries the full $50,000 you invested. It is as though your $10,000 stock market loss had turned into a $10,000 life insurance policy.

SHOPPING FOR DEFERRED ANNUITIES

Insurance companies usually add features and options to dress up their products, but most of the extras are of little value or significance. When you shop for a deferred annuity, look past the distractions.

The four points to consider in evaluating simple, interest-earning deferred annuities are interest rate, sales commission, withdrawal charges and the insurance company's financial strength.

Interest Rate

A deferred annuity's interest rate changes from time to time. It usually is somewhat less than you could earn on other secure, fixed-dollar investments with an adjustable interest rate. The difference is the insurance company's charge for tax shelter. You want to make sure the charge isn't too high. But if you ask an insurance company how it determines the interest rate for deferred annuities, the answer probably will be long and coy. You'll hear about . . .

- *Minimum interest rate.* Every deferred annuity promises that the interest rate won't go below a certain minimum—which often is too low to matter.

- *Starting rate.* Some annuities start out with a rate that is fetchingly high. The rate may even be labeled "guaranteed" or "minimum." But it applies only for the first few years. It's a teaser rate that tells nothing about what you'll be earning a year or two later, when the teasing stops.

- *Historical rate.* Many insurance companies will tell you what their annuities have earned in the past. This can help you compare companies—*if* you obtain the right details. Ask the company what rates it paid to annuity holders generally, excluding introductory, teaser rates. And ask for year-by-year figures, rather than an average of several years. An average may hide more than it shows.

- *Indexed rate.* Ideally, the interest rate should be tied to an index of open-market rates, such as the yield on bank CDs or Treasury bills. Indexing makes it easy for you to compare one company with another, and it assures that the annuity that's generous today won't be stingy tomorrow. But most annuities are not explicitly tied to a rate index.

Remember that you can always switch annuities later. So you don't have to be certain a particular annuity will always be best. And your freedom to switch means the insurer must continue to pay a competitive rate, no matter what the contract says.

Sales Commission

Most annuities are *no-load* investments—you pay no explicit sales charge. A few companies do impose a sales charge of 4% or so, which may be worth paying if the other terms are favorable. If you expect to hold a deferred annuity for, say, 20 years, a 4% sales charge reduces your return by just 0.2% per year.[6]

Withdrawal Charges

If a deferred annuity has no sales charge, or if it has a high initial interest rate, there probably will be a charge for "early" withdrawals—usually according to a sliding scale. For example, the company might charge 6% on withdrawals in the first year, 5% on withdrawals in the second year, and so on until withdrawals become free after the sixth year.

Withdrawal charges usually are limited to the contract's earnings, so you'll recover your original investment even if you cash in the next day.

As will be explained on page 106, a deferred annuity probably is a wise investment only if you plan to hold it at least 15 years, which would be long enough to avoid all withdrawal charges. Thus withdrawal charges are the least significant of the four considerations.

Financial Strength

An annuity is a promise. It is worthless if the insurance company can't keep the promise.

Several publications rate insurance companies for financial strength. Information about them appears in Chapter 35, "Where to Get Help."

Stick to the companies that appear strongest. But, even then, don't let yourself become too vulnerable. Don't put more than 15% of your total

---

[6] A company that doesn't charge commissions still incurs costs in selling it annuities. Its customers bear those costs one way or another—usually by receiving a slightly reduced interest rate. Thus, if an annuity is held for many years, there may be no significant difference in return between one with a sales charge and one without it.

assets into any single insurance company. Diversify, just as though you were buying stocks or bonds.

SHOPPING FOR VARIABLE ANNUITIES

Variable annuities are subject to the same kinds of sales commissions and early withdrawal charges as simple, interest-earning deferred annuities. But rates of return, expenses and financial strength must be analyzed differently for variable annuities.

Investment Performance

The return on a variable annuity will depend on the future performance of its underlying investments—and also on your own future investment decisions, if the annuity lets you switch from one investment to another.

Most companies offering variable annuities portray their investment managers as wizards who can outperform the markets with their eyes closed. Don't believe it. Every investment's future performance—and every investment *manager's* future performance—will differ from the past. So disregard the earnings records some insurance companies brag about. The return on the variable annuity *you* buy will depend primarily on what the markets do—not on what the insurance company does.

Variable Expenses

If a variable annuity's return lags behind the underlying investment, it's because of the annuity's expenses—the recurring fees and other costs associated with the annuity. The expenses are charged regardless of performance, and they reduce your net return.

The primary recurring expenses of a variable annuity are:

- *Policy fee.* This is what the insurance company charges for giving you a piece of paper with the word *annuity* written on it. The annual charge may range from 0.1% to 1.0% of the annuity's value.

- *Mortality fee.* This is what the company charges for the life insurance element—to cover the risk that you might die with your annuity investment in a loss position. The annual charge may range from 0.25% to 0.55% of the annuity's value.

■ *Investment expenses.* These usually are the expenses of the mutual fund in which the annuity invests. The annual burden may range from 0.15% to 1.5% of the annuity's value. (This rate may be the same as for the policy fee, leaving the casual reader with the impression of just one fee when in fact there are two.)

Notice how widely these expenses vary. For some annuities, the total annual charges (year after year) exceed 2.5% of the annuity's value. For others, the total charges are less than 1.0% per year. Careful shopping can improve your net return considerably.

Information on discount insurance brokers and particular variable annuity programs appears in Chapter 35, "Where to Get Help."

Variable Promise

A variable annuity is tied to a specific pool of investments. The insurance company owns the investments, but earmarks them as belonging to variable annuities. So, even if the company goes broke, you still should receive what you've been promised—your share of the underlying investment pool. The segregated investments would have to be stolen for this promise to be broken.

Nonetheless the insurance company's bankruptcy could mean delay in getting your money, along with the anxiety that would cause. And if a variable annuity were in a loss position, the life insurance element might not be paid. Thus a company's financial stability is an important consideration even for a variable annuity—but much less important than for an interest-earning annuity.

Annuity Strategies

Depending on the alternatives available to you, a deferred annuity may be the best way to shelter a portion of your interest earnings. And a variable annuity can let you switch from one investment to another while deferring tax on your profits.

But annuities have certain costs and disadvantages—including possible withdrawal charges and/or commissions, continuing expenses or interest rate concessions to the insurance company, and the rough tax treatment afforded withdrawals before age 59½. As is often the case, however, the negatives can be reduced by thoughtful planning.

Investing the Right Amount

First, make sure you won't need to make an early withdrawal. A deferred annuity's primary advantage is tax-deferred compounding. Given time, tax deferral will more than offset an annuity's subpar before-tax yield. But if you liquidate too soon (if there hasn't been enough time for tax-deferred compounding to do its work), the annuity will prove, in retrospect, to have been a mistake. So limit your investment in a deferred annuity to what you know you won't need for at least 15 years.

Second, to avoid the 10% withdrawal penalty, don't invest any money you might need before age 59½.

A rule of thumb is to put no more than one third of your total budget for any investment category in deferred annuities.

Multiple Contracts

For greater tax liquidity—freedom to make changes without triggering taxes—split your annuity budget among two or more separate contracts. For example, if you decide to invest $60,000 in deferred annuities, you might purchase three annuities for $20,000 each, instead of a single annuity for $60,000.

Suppose a few years later: (*a*) the value of each annuity has grown to $30,000 ($20,000 in capital plus $10,000 in earnings), and (*b*) you need to withdraw $25,000. If you withdraw the entire $25,000 from just one of the annuities, only $10,000 will be taxable, while the other $15,000 will be a tax-free return of capital.

Had you instead put your $60,000 in a single annuity and let it grow to $90,000, the entire $25,000 withdrawal would come from earnings and thus would be taxable.

If you buy more than one contract from the same insurance company in the same year, the IRS will treat them as a single contract. So to effectively split your annuity investment for tax purposes, buy the contracts in different years or from different companies. ⚿

12

LIFE
INSURANCE AS
AN INVESTMENT

You can continue to breathe normally and still profit from life insurance.

Life insurance, as conceived in the eighteenth century, was meant to protect a family against the premature death of its breadwinner. In exchange for a small payment each year, the insurance company promised to pay the breadwinner's family a large death benefit if disaster struck.

It took only a little tinkering to transform this simple plan into an investment. By charging somewhat more each year than needed to cover the risk of early mortality, the insurance company could establish a kind of "savings account" inside the policy. And by lending or investing the extra premium, the company could earn enough to pay interest on the savings account. The account would grow. Eventually it could be tapped to keep the policy going, without further payments from the policyholder, and the policyholder would be free to withdraw money from the savings account whenever he wished.

200 Years to Get It Right

For approximately 200 years, life insurance was an investment—but not a *good* investment. Interest rates on fixed-dollar investments generally were low, and the rates paid by insurance companies were even lower.

The high inflation of the 1970s forced life insurance to change for the better.

Interest paid on life insurance was not taxable. But interest rates on bonds, U.S. Treasury bills, certificates of deposit and other fixed-dollar investments were rising to keep pace with rising inflation, making the low rates on life insurance more and more conspicuous. Eventually insurance companies had to raise their rates to competitive levels in order to keep their policyholders and attract new ones.

Other changes were made. The higher interest rates boosted the value of the tax deferral that life insurance provided, so insurance companies reshaped their policies to emphasize investment uses. The savings account, which had been a mere add-on, became the center of the policy. Death benefits were minimized—so that a bigger share of each premium dollar could go into the savings account, instead of being spent on charges for the risk of early mortality.

"Life insurance" had become a tax-sheltered savings account with a minimum of pure life insurance attached to it. It could be a good investment even for someone who had no family to protect.

BASIC TAX RULES

The tax rules on life insurance are no longer so extravagantly favorable as they once were, but life insurance still is an easy source of some extraordinary advantages.

A life insurance policy, like a deferred annuity, lets you accumulate interest without current tax. But life insurance can do more—it can eliminate the income's taxability altogether. Benefits paid when the insured person dies are tax exempt. And even while you're living, cash withdrawals from *certain kinds* of policies are tax free. In the worst case, withdrawals from a life insurance policy are taxed no more harshly than withdrawals from a deferred annuity.

For the Living

It is the opportunity to accumulate, and then withdraw, interest earnings—perhaps tax free—that makes life insurance an attractive investment.

There are limits to using life insurance to generate tax-free cash for yourself. You can't consume *all* of a policy's value during your lifetime without poisoning the tax benefits, but you can consume much of it. And because of the tax advantages, the right kind of life insurance may give you nearly as much spendable, after-tax cash as a fully taxable investment—so that the benefits your survivors collect are, in a sense, close to free.

Pure Risk Contract

The tax rules governing life insurance are complex. The essential elements and the opportunities they provide will be easier to understand if we first look at a simple, model policy—which I'll call a *risk contract*. The provisions of a risk contract are these:

- *Pay and name.*   On the first day of the year, you pay the insurance company a certain amount of money (the *premium*), and you name a beneficiary.

- *Die and win.*   If you die during the year, the insurance company pays a certain amount—say, $100,000—to the beneficiary.

- *Live and lose.*   If you don't die during the year, the insurance company pays nothing to you, to the beneficiary or to anyone else—ever.

An insurance company profits from selling risk contracts if it takes in more money from all its customers than it has to pay to the beneficiaries of those who "die and win."

The insurance company bases the premium on the likelihood, in its estimation, that you will not live out the year. That likelihood depends primarily on your age, but also on your sex and the apparent state of your health. For example, for a $100,000 risk contract, the premium for a thirty-year-old male in normal health must be at least $173—since a standard mortality table shows that out of every 100,000 thirty-year-old males, 173 are likely to die during the year.[1]

The risk contract is the basic building block of *all* life insurance. Every policy you hear about, from as many life insurance salesmen as you can stand to listen to, is strung together out of one-year risk contracts.

CASH-VALUE POLICIES

A cash-value life insurance policy links a series of one-year risk contracts to an interest-earning "savings account." Both the size of the risk contracts and the balance in the savings account change from one year to the next. But together they always equal a fixed death benefit, such as $100,000. Thus if the savings account grows, the size of the risk contract shrinks.

---

[1] In practice an insurance premium also allows for the insurance company's administrative and selling costs, the return the company expects to earn on its premium-financed investments and what it believes potential customers are willing to pay.

Deaths per Year per 100,000 Persons and Minimum Cost of a $100,000 Risk Contract at Various Ages

	MALES		FEMALES	
Age	Deaths per 100,000 Persons	Minimum Cost of $100,000 Risk Contract	Deaths per 100,000 Persons	Minimum Cost of $100,000 Risk Contract
21	191	$191	107	$107
30	173	$173	135	$135
40	302	$302	242	$242
50	671	$671	496	$496
60	1,608	$1,608	847	$847
70	3,951	$3,951	2,211	$2,211
80	9,884	$9,884	6,599	$6,599
90	22,177	$22,177	19,075	$19,075
98	65,798	$65,798	66,585	$66,585

Hypothetical Cash Value Life Insurance with a Death Benefit of $100,000, Purchased with a Single Premium of $30,000

Year	Savings Account	Risk Contract	Death Benefit
1	$30,000	$70,000	$100,000
2	$32,000	$68,000	$100,000
3	$34,000	$66,000	$100,000
4	$37,000	$63,000	$100,000
5	$40,000	$60,000	$100,000
6	$43,000	$57,000	$100,000

You can purchase a cash-value policy in any of several ways.

- Make just one large payment (*single-premium life*).
- Make fixed annual payments for a few years (such as *seven-pay life*).
- Make fixed annual payments for many years (*whole life*).
- Pay premiums from time to time but not on a fixed schedule or in fixed amounts (*universal life* or *flexible life*).

With any cash-value policy, part of the first year's premium pays for the first year's risk contract, and the rest goes into the savings account. In each succeeding year, the insurance company credits the savings account with interest and with any additional premiums you pay, and charges the savings account for that year's risk contract.

Grow or Dwindle

Where this process leads depends on how much is in the savings account when you stop paying premiums.

If the account is big enough, it will earn more than enough interest to pay for that year's risk contract. And, as the account continues to grow, the risk contract will become smaller each year, and hence less costly—so that even less of the savings account's interest will be needed to pay for the risk contract. Such a policy is "paid up." It requires no further premiums from you, and it gains value as time passes.

On the other hand, if you stop paying premiums before the savings account is big enough, each risk contract will cost more than the savings account earns, and so the account will dwindle. If the savings account reaches zero before you die, the policy will lapse (come to an end), and your beneficiaries will receive nothing.

Policy Loans

You can withdraw money from the savings account at any time by taking a loan from the insurance company. The loan is tax free if certain requirements are met. Otherwise, all or part of the loan is taxable—as explained in this chapter under "Seven-Pay Test for Tax-Free Borrowing" and "Possible Tax on Policy Lapse."

Depending on the terms of the policy, the interest rate may be comparable to what you would pay on a well-secured mortgage. Or the insurance company might charge a very low, or even zero, interest rate, but stop paying interest on an equal amount of the policy's savings account. Either way, your net borrowing cost—the interest rate the company charges on the loan, less the rate it pays on the savings account—will be low to nil.

There's no obligation to repay a policy loan. If you die while the loan is outstanding, the insurance company simply deducts the loan balance before paying your beneficiaries. You don't even have to make interest payments. The insurance company simply adds the unpaid interest to the loan balance each year.

Loans and Lapses

If you don't make interest payments, the loan balance will grow, but so will the savings account. However, the loan balance may grow somewhat faster, because its interest rate may be higher and because the savings account's growth is held back by charges for each year's risk contract.

This process might continue indefinitely. But if the loan balance catches up with the amount in the savings account, the insurance company will use the savings account to pay off the loan, and the policy will lapse.

How much of the savings account can you borrow without flirting with a policy lapse? The answer depends primarily on the policy's net borrowing cost and on your age. As a rule of thumb, if the net borrowing cost is low (1% or less), and you are at least 65 years old, you can borrow as much as three quarters of the savings account on a paid-up policy and be confident the policy will never lapse—even if you make no interest payments. If you're older, you can borrow a larger portion.

Tax-Free Exchanges

You can exchange a life insurance policy for a new one, even with a different company, without incurring tax on the old policy's accumulated earnings. You can even make a tax-free exchange of a life insurance policy for an annuity.

COLD WATER

The insurance industry maintains a large and powerful lobby in Washington. One of its missions is to protect the favorable tax treatment afforded life insurance, and it has done an excellent job. But Congress, to keep from losing too much revenue, has imposed a number of rules that discourage investors from using life insurance primarily to earn tax-deferred or tax-exempt income.

To Qualify

To qualify as life insurance, a policy must be worth substantially more if you are dead than if you are alive. To put it differently, the policy's risk contract must always be at least some minimum size in relation to the savings account. The practical effect is that charges for each year's risk contract will be at least 1% or so of the balance in the savings account.[2]

If a policy does satisfy the Internal Revenue Code's definition of life insurance, it provides the basic tax advantages described in this chapter. The policy's earnings are tax deferred, and money paid to your beneficiaries is tax exempt.

Seven-Pay Test for Tax-Free Borrowing

A life insurance loan is tax free if you have paid for the policy no more rapidly than with seven equal annual premiums.

A *seven-pay policy* (with seven equal annual premiums) obviously passes the test. So does a whole life policy. And so does a flexible life policy if you don't pay too much during the first seven years. But a *single-premium policy* fails the test.

If a policy fails the seven-pay test, loans are treated in the same way as withdrawals from a deferred annuity—that is, loans up to the full amount of the policy's net earnings are taxable. The taxable portion is subject to a 10% penalty tax if you haven't reached age 59½.

Possible Tax on Policy Lapse

You don't have to repay a policy loan, so if you borrow more than you paid in premiums, you are withdrawing a profit. That "tax-free" profit will become taxable, even if the policy satisfies the seven-pay test, if you ever let the policy lapse—that is, if you ever let the loan balance outgrow the savings account.

The lapse of a policy that satisfies the seven-pay test would be painful if you had withdrawn a large profit through tax-free borrowing. The profit, which you might have spent years ago, would be income on your current tax return. You would have a tax bill to pay.

The need to keep a policy from lapsing restrains you from withdrawing all the profit tax free. You must leave enough to let the savings account stay ahead of the loan balance.

---

[2] The savings account must not exceed the single premium that would make the policy paid up. Thus the insurance company must bear at least a minimum amount of risk, for which it will charge you each year, that it may have to pay the portion of the death benefit not covered by the savings account.

SHOPPING FOR LIFE INSURANCE

Even the simplest life insurance policies are difficult to compare. The frills, features and doodahs that many companies attach can make shopping for life insurance even more difficult.

Profitability

Life insurance generally involves no explicit sales or withdrawal charges. But, as with deferred annuities, a policy's profitability depends on the interest rate the insurance company pays.

Insurance companies—even companies that have always paid competitive rates—play the same peekaboo games with interest rates on life insurance as they do with rates on deferred annuities. The picture is further clouded by the annual charges for a policy's risk contracts, which will differ from company to company.

The past provides the most useful, simple indication of the potential profitability of a cash-value life insurance policy. For each policy you consider, ask the company what the cash value (the savings account balance) would be today if you had bought the policy ten years ago. The greater the value today, relative to the premiums paid, the more profitable the policy is likely to be in the future.

Loan Costs

Also give close consideration to the policy's loan terms, unless you're sure you'll never want to borrow.

It is the *net cost*—the difference between the interest rate you pay on a loan and the interest rate the insurance company would pay on the policy's savings account—that matters. If the policy is earning 8% and the cost of a loan is 10%, then the net cost is 2%.

Some companies let you borrow at a *zero* net cost, charging no more on the loan than they pay on the savings account.

VARIABLE LIFE INSURANCE

Variable life is a special type of cash-value life insurance. As with a variable annuity, the policy's value and earnings are tied to the performance of a particular mutual fund or other investment.

Some variable life policies let you switch from one investment to another as you see fit. Even when you switch out of an investment that has earned a big profit, no tax is due.

The pool of investments tied to a company's variable life policies is segregated from the company's other assets. If the insurance company were to go bankrupt, those segregated assets would be used solely to cover the claims of variable life policyholders.

Selecting

In comparing variable life policies, add up the same elements of recurring expense that apply to a variable annuity—policy fees, investment expenses and mortality charges. These expenses vary widely from company to company. Some companies charge considerably more than the least expensive companies, so shop carefully.

HELP

You are more likely to need help finding the right life insurance policy than you are in choosing any other type of investment. The information on discount life insurance brokers and life insurance shopping services given in Chapter 35, "Where to Get Help," should make things a little easier.

INSURANCE CHOICES

The insurance industry offers three types of policies especially well suited for tax-advantaged investing: single-premium life, seven-pay life, and the deferred annuities discussed in the preceding chapter.

Single-Premium Life. As the name suggests, a single-premium life insurance policy is paid for all at once, with just one premium.

For money you are confident you won't need during your own lifetime (so that the potential taxability of loans wouldn't matter), a single-premium policy is the best choice. Single-premium life lets you move as much money as you want into the life insurance tax-shelter tent immediately. Eventually, when your beneficiaries receive the proceeds, it will all be tax-exempt income.

Seven-Pay Life. A seven-pay life insurance policy is paid for with seven equal annual premiums.

If you expect to spend the policy's value yourself (so that tax-free borrowing would be important), and if mortality coverage is desirable (so that its cost would not be a waste), then a seven-pay policy probably is the best choice. The disadvantage, as compared with single-premium life, is that it will take longer (six years and one day) to complete your investment.

But don't purchase a seven-pay (or any other) policy as an investment for yourself if you are in poor health or otherwise are rated a poor risk by the insurance company. The mortality charges (for the one-year risk contracts) would outweigh the tax advantages.

You shouldn't consider any seven-pay policy with a net borrowing cost greater than 1%. A rate of zero would be better.

Deferred Annuity.   If you are in poor health, expect to spend most of the money yourself, and have no need for mortality coverage (because no one is depending on you to earn a living), a deferred annuity is probably the best choice, since life insurance of any kind would entail high charges for the risk that you will die prematurely. A deferred annuity also is a good choice if you find life insurance too complicated to use as an investment or if you have no potential heirs to provide for. ⌐╼

13

PENSION PLANS

Qualified pension plans are investment programs that satisfy certain IRS requirements. They have some strong advantages and some troubling disadvantages. On balance, the good outweighs the bad—and by a big margin. So, if you have the opportunity, you probably should use a qualified pension plan to hold some of your investments.

A pension plan's tax advantages are simple and big. You or your employer receives a tax deduction for money put into the plan. And everything the plan earns—interest, dividends and gains—is tax deferred. Thus pension plan earnings compound faster, and the plan can switch investments without tax.

The primary disadvantages are:

- Penalties on withdrawals you make too early or too late
- A special excise tax if a plan gets too big
- Limited possibilities for tapping a plan's value without paying tax
- A plan's comparative vulnerability to direct or indirect government confiscation

The last is the greatest disadvantage, but all four argue against putting too large a portion of your assets into pension plans.

Welcome to the Zoo

There is a whole zoo of qualified pension plans. Each of the animals in the zoo was created by Congress at a different time, and each has undergone numerous mutations, amputations and organ transplants. The assortment is complicated—and it keeps changing, generally toward greater complexity.

The topic is important, however—even if you have no interest in building a retirement fund. While your pension plan should be limited to a minority share of your overall portfolio, it can defer a majority of the portfolio's tax bill.

In this chapter we'll examine the principal types of qualified pension plans. If you already have a qualified plan, the information may help you use it more effectively. If you don't have one, this chapter may inspire you to get one.

COMMON FEATURES

Among the ever-changing jumble of qualified pension plans, there are some recurring features.

Sponsorship. Except for IRAs (explained later in this chapter), all qualified plans are set up by employers for the benefit of their employees. Any employer—corporation, partnership or sole proprietorship—may establish one. If you are self-employed and are your only employee, you (as employer) may set up a plan for yourself (as employee).

Deductible Contributions. Contributions to a qualified plan are tax deductible when made, but only up to a certain amount. Some plans permit additional, nondeductible contributions, but only up to a certain amount. Participants in the plan (the employees on whose behalf contributions are being made) are not taxed on contributions.

Tax Deferral. A qualified plan's investment income and profits accumulate and compound free of tax until you withdraw the money.

Tax on Withdrawals. Money withdrawn from a qualified plan (and not reinvested in another qualified plan) generally is taxable as ordinary income—even if it represents investment gains. But you don't pay tax on a withdrawal of money that wasn't tax deductible when it went in.

Investment Freedom. A qualified plan can invest in almost anything you want—including stocks, bonds, real estate, mortgages, foreign currencies, and options on such investments. However, precious metals and collectibles are not permitted in a *self-directed* plan (one that lets you select your own investments). And a plan cannot buy investments from the plan's sponsor or participants or sell investments to them.[1]

Lock In. The taxable portion of money you withdraw from a qualified plan before the year you reach age 59½ is subject to a 10% penalty. However, the penalty doesn't apply if you are leaving your job—that is, if you die, are permanently disabled, quit, or are fired.

Lock Out. You must begin withdrawing money in the year you reach age 70½. The minimum yearly withdrawal is the value of your interest in the plan divided by the number of years of your life expectancy (as shown in a standard mortality table). Severe penalties apply to tardy withdrawals.

Portability. If you leave your job, you can take the entire value of your plan (a lump-sum withdrawal) and reinvest it (a *rollover*) into a qualified plan sponsored by your new employer—if the new plan accepts rollovers. Or you can roll the money into your own IRA.

Borrowing. There is a broad ban on transactions between a pension plan and anyone related to it. However, participants in some plans sponsored by a corporation may, within certain limits, borrow from the plan to buy a home or for any purpose if the loan is repayable within five years.

Excise Tax on "Excess." If the plan gets too large, a 15% excise tax is levied on the overage. The tax is complicated, but as a rule of thumb, you should assume that any amounts in a qualified plan exceeding $750,000 when you reach age 65 will be subject to the tax.

VARIETIES OF QUALIFIED PLANS

Most qualified plans fall into one of four categories.

1. Defined-Benefit Plans

A defined-benefit plan promises each employee a pension of a certain amount, based on his anticipated retirement age, years of employment and

---

[1] A qualified plan is taxable on "unrelated business income," including income from an equity interest, other than stock, in an operating business, and income from investments, other than real estate, purchased with borrowed money.

salary history. Each year the employer contributes what it calculates the plan needs to pay for the pensions.

The "defined benefit" may not exceed an annual pension of 100% of a participant's salary.[2] The pension is also subject to a separate dollar limit, which increases with the expected retirement age and is $90,000 per year if the expected retirement age is between 62 and 65.

An employee's pension rights usually aren't affected by a defined-benefit plan's investment results. Those results are important to the employer, however. The better they are, the less the employer needs to contribute.

2. Defined-Contribution Plans

With a defined-contribution plan, the employer makes an annual contribution to an investment account for each employee. The contribution equals a certain percentage of the first $150,000 of the employee's salary. Depending on the type of plan, the percentage may be as high as 25%.

The percentage may be fixed permanently (a money-purchase plan). Or it may be determined each year by the employer, subject to a certain limit (a profit-sharing plan). Or the employee himself may decide each year how much of his salary to put into the plan (a deferred-compensation, or 401 (k), plan).[3]

A defined-contribution plan doesn't promise a pension of any particular amount. Instead, the employee is entitled to receive the contributions made on his behalf and the accumulated investment returns. Thus it matters very much to the employee how a defined-contribution plan handles its investments.

Some defined-contribution plans invest all their money in a single pool. Other, "self-directed," plans let each employee choose the investments for his portion of the plan.

3. Individual Retirement Accounts and Annuities (IRAs)

Any employee, including someone who is self-employed, may contribute up to $2,000 per year to his own Individual Retirement Account or

---

[2] The limitation applies to the participant's "base" salary—his average salary in the three highest-paid of his last five years of employment.

[3] A "401 (k) plan" is so named after Section 401 (k) of the Internal Revenue Code.

Individual Retirement Annuity. If you aren't in an employer-sponsored retirement plan, your IRA contribution is tax deductible.

If you are in an employer-sponsored plan, you still can deduct your IRA contribution if your adjusted gross income is less than $40,000 (filing jointly) or less than $25,000 (filing singly). Above those levels, the tax-deductible amount is reduced by one dollar for every additional five dollars of adjusted gross income.

An IRA may be an Individual Retirement Account or an Individual Retirement Annuity.

An *Individual Retirement Account* is a pool of investments financed by your contributions and held by a custodian bank, stockbroker or other institution in accordance with certain formalities. The account has the same wide freedom as an employer-sponsored plan to hold the investments you want. In addition, it can purchase American Eagle gold or silver coins.[4]

An *Individual Retirement Annuity* is issued by an insurance company and paid for by your contributions. It is similar to the deferred annuities described in Chapter 11. In addition, by its terms, the policy's value cannot be forfeited to the insurance company in any circumstances; the policy cannot be sold or pledged for a loan; and the required premiums, if any, cannot exceed $2,000 per year.

Common Features.   All IRAs are portable. You can transfer an Individual Retirement Account from one custodian to another, an Individual Retirement Annuity from one insurance company to another, an Individual Retirement Annuity to an Individual Retirement Account, and vice versa— all without tax.

In addition, once per year, you can withdraw money from your IRA and deposit it, untaxed, with a new custodian or insurance company within 60 days.

But beware: if you make a lump-sum withdrawal from your IRA, the current custodian must withhold 20%—even if you intend to move the money to a new custodian. If you deposit only the net amount you received (the 80%) with the new custodian, the 20% that was withheld is taxable— with penalties if you won't reach age 59½ before the end of the year! To avoid this withholding trap (which must provide hours of laughter for IRS

---

[4]American Eagle coins are minted by the U.S. Mint, and are sold to the public at prices usually 3% to 5% above the value of the bullion the coins contain.

agents), always direct the current custodian to make the transfer directly to the new custodian.

4. Simplified Employee Pensions (SEPs)

A *Simplified Employee Pension* (SEP) is a kind of jumbo Individual Retirement Account. Generally, SEPs are governed by the rules that apply to regular IRAs, but the employer makes the contributions.

The employer may vary contributions to its SEP from year to year. The maximum in any year for any employee is $30,000 or 25% of his salary, whichever is less.[5]

The employer receives a tax deduction for its SEP contributions. Employees report the contributions in their own tax returns, both as income and as an offsetting deduction, and hence pay no tax until they withdraw the money.

WHAT TO DO WITH IT

To get the greatest benefit from your qualified plan, disregard the words "pension" and "retirement." Congress's decision to call something a "pension plan," doesn't mean you can't exploit it for other purposes—such as minimizing your tax bill and making your portfolio safer.

And your pension plan may not be the best source of income when you retire. It often is better to draw income from some other element of your portfolio and let the pension plan continue to defer taxes for as long as the rules permit.

For example, suppose you're between the ages of 59½ and 70½, so you can leave money in your plan or withdraw it without penalty. A withdrawal generally would be fully taxable as ordinary income. But if you draw your living expenses by selling investments you own directly, the proceeds will be partly a tax-free return of capital and partly a capital gain, resulting in a lower tax bill.

Coordinate All Investment Decisions

If you manage your own pension plan (as you can with an IRA, SEP and many defined-contribution plans), select investments that complement what

---

[5] The $30,000 limitation is subject to annual adjustments for inflation.

you own outside the plan, as explained below. That will give your overall portfolio the balance you want, while allowing the plan to absorb a disproportionately large share of the portfolio's income.

If you don't manage your plan's investments (as with any defined-benefit plan and many defined-contribution plans), you still can increase your overall financial safety by adjusting your other investment holdings to complement those in the plan.

If You Have Control

If you control your plan's investment policy, first decide what investments you want to have in your overall portfolio. From that list, earmark for the pension plan the investments with the greatest propensity to generate taxable income. The usual candidates would be:

- Fixed-dollar assets (bonds and money market investments), since all or most of their return is subject to current tax

- Short-term speculative assets, since you may want to sell them soon if they are profitable

- Small amounts of everything else you want to have in your portfolio, which allows you to keep your portfolio in balance by trimming back your most successful investments without concern for capital gain tax.

In Chapter 29 we'll discuss just how much, if any, of each investment to include in your plan.

If You Do Not Have Control

If you can't choose the investments for your plan, you should find out exactly how the plan works, so you can make the right decisions for the rest of your portfolio.

Defined-Contribution Plan. Assets in a defined-contribution plan affect your wealth in the same way as investments you own directly. You benefit if they are profitable, and you suffer if they are not. So allow for what your employer has put in the plan when you decide what to own outside of the plan. For example, if your pension plan holds $200,000 worth of stocks, you already have a $200,000 position in the stock market. So you should purchase stocks on your own only if you want to have more than $200,000 worth.

Defined-Benefit Plan. A defined-benefit plan promises you a pension of a certain amount. What the plan owns doesn't affect what you are entitled to receive, so you should disregard its investments.

Instead, unless the plan has a cost-of-living clause (inflation protection), think of the plan as a fixed-dollar asset. Until you retire, it's like a deferred annuity or other floating-rate investment. After you retire, it's like a lifetime annuity. So if your interest in a defined-benefit plan is worth, say $250,000, you should buy fixed-dollar assets on your own only if you want your overall portfolio to hold more than $250,000 of such investments.

If the plan does have a cost-of-living clause, it is not a fixed-dollar asset. It is a promise to pay you a certain amount of purchasing power.

THE BAD NEWS

Qualified pension plans combine generous tax benefits with a high degree of investment flexibility. Almost any taxpayer with employment income would be better off having one.

Caution

But don't overdo it. There are four reasons you shouldn't let your pension plan become too large a part of your overall portfolio.

1. Credit Risk. A defined-benefit plan always involves some degree of credit risk. Your interest in the plan is simply a promise made by your employer—an IOU. In principle, the plan's investments should be security enough for the promise, since the employer's annual contributions reflect the estimated cost of delivering the defined benefits. But the estimates might turn out to be too low, if investment returns are disappointing or retirees live longer than expected.

If a defined-benefit plan needs more money, the employer is legally obligated to provide it. If the employer can't, the Pension Benefit Guarantee Corporation (PBGC, a U.S. government agency similar to the Federal Deposit Insurance Corporation) is supposed to come to the rescue.

As with all government insurance plans, the PBGC is able to handle isolated problems—but not epidemics. If your defined-benefit plan and only a few others need help, they will receive it. But in a serious economic downturn, when many companies and their plans might be in distress, the PBGC could be swamped. It would not have enough money to bail out all the pensions it pretends to guarantee. Your pension might not get paid in full.

While it is real, the credit risk is small. I think it is prudent to disregard it if your interest in a defined-benefit plan is no more than 20% of your overall portfolio. But if the percentage is much more than that, the plan's unavoidable credit risk makes your financial program too vulnerable.

2. *Risk of Seizure.* Your pension plan is an easy target for government seizure.

Any tax-deferred plan must file reports and handle its investments in certain ways. So if the U.S. government wants to collect a fine, penalty or tax from you, your pension plan is roast pigeon.

An IRS pamphlet on collection procedures sheds big crocodile tears when it discusses the seizure of pension plans. But the crocodile will dine one way or another.

However, many qualified plans are protected against private lawsuits. Under federal law, your interest in a defined-benefit or defined-contribution plan covering at least one non-owner employee cannot be attached by any creditor except the IRS—even if you file for bankruptcy. IRAs, SEPs and plans covering only self-employed persons don't have this blanket protection, but they often are protected from creditors by state law. Even so, depending on your state, any money you withdrew from a qualified plan might be seized by your creditors as soon as you take it out.

3. *Political Vulnerability.* Pension plans are politically vulnerable. They represent an enormous amount of loosely guarded money—a Big Piñata waiting to finance the happy dreams of government spenders.

Trillions of dollars are sitting in qualified pension plans. Much of it is being accumulated on behalf of employees who are barely aware of its existence or who place only a small value on benefits they've been told will be theirs in the far, far future. The squawk ratio—the amount of squawking per billion dollars raised—would be fairly low if the government decided that some "urgent public purpose" compelled it to tap pension money.

Of course, the government wouldn't simply say, "All pension plans now belong to us." It would devise a more politic way to whack the Big Piñata. It might levy a surtax on withdrawals by taxpayers whose income exceeds a certain minimum. It might impose a "one-time, deficit-reduction" levy on all plans, to recover some of the money that escaped taxes during a past "decade of greed." Or it might compel pension plans to invest in special, low-yielding government bonds or in projects the government designates as "socially useful."

The government has already changed the pension plan rules to boost tax receipts several times. The current prohibition on most borrowing is one example. The excise tax on "excess" accumulations is another. It won't be easy for your pension plan to slip away when the government changes the rules again.

4. No Free Exit.   Some devices for tax-deferral let you withdraw spendable cash without immediately paying tax. A pension plan doesn't. However, see "Roll Away," below.

WHAT TO DO ABOUT IT

Everything you do has risks, and the risks associated with pension plans are not so high that you should forgo the advantages. I don't believe ruinous rule changes are imminent or even likely. I've covered the potential problems only because so many investors overlook them—including investors who have most of their wealth tied up in pension plans.

There are a few steps you can take to control the disadvantages and risks.

Limit Size.   Don't let your interests in pension plans exceed 50% of your net worth. If you are past that limit, make no more optional contributions.

And even if your pension plan is only a small percentage of your net worth, look ahead to assure that its value won't exceed $750,000 when you reach age 65. Any excess would be subject to a 15 percent excise tax.

Roll Over.   If you change jobs or retire, withdraw your interest in your employer's qualified plan and roll the money over into an IRA. This will eliminate credit risk, if you are leaving a defined-benefit plan, and it will let you control how your pension money is invested.

Roll Away.   It is possible to place one foot of your pension plan in a tax haven country. This provides some protection from seizure, and it could rescue from taxation the money you don't spend during your own lifetime. See Chapter 29, "A Plan for Asset Protection and Tax Savings." ⌐╼

14

DEFERRED-PAYMENT SALES

Deferred-payment sales are powerful medicine. In some cases they are the *only* solution to an investor's problem. In the right circumstances they can:

- Defer capital gain tax on real estate, collectibles or privately issued securities into the far, far future.

- Defer tax on interest income for many, many years.

- Protect wealth from lawsuits when it is too late to use a trust or family partnership.

- Export wealth to another country.

Basic Elements

To make a deferred-payment sale, you transfer property to the buyer now and allow him to pay you later. You charge interest—which itself may be deferred—on what the buyer owes you. For your protection, the buyer pledges collateral you can sell if he fails to make a promised payment.

Grape, Cherry and Plain

Deferred-payment sales comes in two "tax flavors"—*installment sales*, which defer tax on capital gain, and *cash method instruments*, which defer tax on interest. Some deferred-payment sales defer both kinds of tax, by satisfying the requirements for an installment sale *and* for a cash method instrument. But a deferred-payment sale can export wealth and protect it from lawsuits even if it doesn't qualify for either kind of tax benefit.

INSTALLMENT SALES

Ordinarily, when you sell a successful investment, you include the entire profit on your next tax return. However, if the transaction qualifies as an *installment sale,* your profit becomes taxable only as the buyer pays you. When the buyer has paid, say, 10% of the selling price, 10% of your profit is taxable. When the buyer has paid 50% of the selling price, 50% of your profit is taxable.

You can defer capital gain tax in this way for as many years—10, 20, 30 years or longer—as you and the buyer agree to defer payments. Meanwhile, you earn interest (from the buyer) on the unpaid portion of the selling price—which includes money you would have lost to capital gain tax if you had sold the investment for cash.

Suppose, for example, that you are selling a plot of land for $400,000, which you bought six years ago for $100,000. If you sell for cash, you must include the $300,000 capital gain in your return for the current year. You'll pay $84,000 in tax, assuming a 28% rate on capital gains.

Or you could sell the land for deferred payments, such as:

- $100,000 down (one quarter of the total price), plus
- $300,000 to be paid at the end of 10 years, plus
- interest at 6% per year on the $300,000.

In that case, you would include a capital gain of $75,000 (one quarter of the total gain) in your tax return for the year of the sale—thereby reducing your immediate tax bill from $84,000 to $21,000, for a savings of $63,000. Not until ten years later would you report the remaining $225,000 of capital gain and pay the remaining $63,000 in tax.

The installment sale lets you earn interest for ten years on $63,000 you otherwise would have lost to taxes. At a rate of 6%, the extra interest is $3,780 per year, or a total of $37,800 over ten years.

And the advantage may be even greater than $37,800. The next ten years might bring some losing investments, even if your overall investment program is highly successful. In year 10 you could use those capital losses to reduce or eliminate the remaining capital gain tax on the installment sale.

Requirements

For a deferred-payment sale to qualify as an installment sale and thereby defer tax on capital gain:

- The property you are selling must be of a kind not traded in an "established market." This rules out stocks, bonds, commodities and foreign currencies traded on an exchange or in an over-the-counter market. But a sale of real estate, collectibles or stock in a private company can qualify as an installment sale.

- You must not be a dealer in the kind of property you are selling. For example, you as an investor can defer tax on the sale of your rare coin collection. A coin dealer cannot.

- The deferred-payment contract must not be payable on demand or be represented by a note or bond that is readily tradable.

- The deferred-payment contract can be secured, but the collateral must not consist of cash, bank deposits or U.S. Treasury bills. And the collateral must not be available to you unless the buyer actually fails to make a required payment.

Limitations

You can defer capital gain tax with an installment sale indefinitely—for as long as you and the buyer are willing to defer the payments. But "payment" is construed broadly. It includes almost any benefit you receive from the buyer. For example, if you sell a building and the buyer pays or assumes your mortgage, the mortgage balance is a "payment" to you.[1]

Losing Deferral

Some events bring an installment sale's deferral of capital gain tax to an abrupt end.

Borrowing. If you pledge the contract as security for a loan, the money is taxed as though it were a payment from the installment buyer.

---

[1] There is a $5-million yearly limit on sales (excluding sales of farms or property held for personal use and sales for $150,000 or less) that can qualify for installment treatment without an "interest" charge on the deferred tax.

Sale or Other Transfer.   If you trade or sell an installment contract or give it away, the deferral of capital gain tax ends.[2]

Subsequent Sales by Related Parties.   If you make an installment sale to a family member who resells or otherwise disposes of the property within two years, your deferral of capital gain tax ends—unless the family member has made an installment sale.

CASH METHOD INSTRUMENT

If a deferred-payment contract qualifies as a "cash method instrument," interest on the unpaid balance isn't taxable until you collect it. It can compound without current tax.

The requirements for a cash method instrument are:

- The property you are selling must not be traded in an established market.

- You must not be a dealer in the kind of property you are selling.

- The deferred-payment obligation must not be payable on demand or be a note or bond that is readily tradable.

- Collateral pledged by the buyer must not be available to you unless the buyer actually fails to make a payment when due.

- The stated price of the sale must not exceed $2.5 million.[3]

- You *and the buyer* must elect to report the interest (as income for the seller and expense for the buyer) as it is actually paid.[4]

As with an installment contract, borrowing against a cash method instrument or selling it brings the tax deferral to an end.

---

[2] Transferring an installment contract to a nongrantor trust (explained in Chapter 16) or to a foreign corporation also would terminate the tax deferral. However, you can contribute an installment contract to a grantor trust or domestic partnership without tax.

[3] The precise limit, as of 1995, is $2,516,900. The limit is adjusted each year for inflation.

[4] There are four other, narrow opportunities for a deferred-payment sale to defer tax on interest—if you: sell your principal residence, sell a farm for $1 million or less, sell land to a family member for $1 million or less, or sell anything if the total payments (interest and principal) do not exceed $250,000.

FINDING A BUYER

Deferred-payment sales, with at least the current interest paid each year, are common in real estate. They are less common for most other types of property, but generally are not difficult to arrange, since they don't cost the buyer any money or great inconvenience.

So, if you only want to defer capital gain tax, a deferred-payment buyer should be nearly as easy to find as a cash buyer. But finding a buyer who will postpone interest payments is more difficult, since you would be asking him to postpone his interest deductions as well.

Of course, there are places where such buyers abound—in tax havens. A buyer there doesn't need tax deductions, so it's easy for him to accommodate your tax planning. Tax havens and how you would find a deferred-payment buyer are discussed in Part 6. For now, simply note that a deferred-payment sale can be thoroughly collateralized and secured, as explained below, which would make it safe for you to deal with a stranger in a strange land.

Triangular Sales

You might identify someone, in the United States or in a tax haven, who can easily accommodate you by deferring payments, but who doesn't want to own what you're selling. In that case, invite him to be an *accommodation buyer* in a three-party, or triangular, sale.

First, negotiate a cash sale with the ultimate buyer—the person who wants the property. (If he needs financing, he must get it from an outside lender, so that he can pay cash when the sale closes.)

Next, negotiate the terms and collateral for a deferred-payment sale with the accommodation buyer, who will buy from you and resell to the ultimate buyer.[5]

Finally, you sell the property to the accommodation buyer for deferred payments, and he sells the property to the ultimate buyer for cash.

The accommodation buyer must provide suitable collateral, such as marketable bonds or money market instruments, which he can purchase with the cash paid by the ultimate buyer. To attract the accommodation

---

[5] If the terms include a deferral of interest payments, the balance owed to you will grow year by year—so the accommodation buyer should be required to pledge additional collateral.

buyer and motivate him to defer payments, you'll need to accept an interest rate just below what he could earn on the collateral. The difference between the two rates would be his profit.

PROTECTING ASSETS

You can "export" a deferred-payment contract to a haven country—provided the collateral consists of liquid assets—even if your buyer is in the United States. This would make it more difficult for a judgment creditor in the United States to seize the value the contract represents.

To export a deferred-payment contract, include the following provisions in the contract and/or its related agreements:

- *Law and disputes.* The contract shall be governed by the laws of the haven country, and any disputes shall be settled in the courts of the same country.

- *Location of collateral.* The collateral shall be held by a financial institution located in the haven country.

- *Place of payment.* The buyer shall make payments to you only by transferring money to a specified bank account located in the haven country.

- *Nonassignability.* You may not assign your rights under the contract to anyone without the consent of a particular third party named in the contract—such as your friend or trusted associate.

The critical provision is the first. It means that any hostile party who hopes to reach the installment contract directly must fight his battle in the courts of the foreign country and by their rules. The other provisions assure that the first will in fact apply, by preventing courts outside the haven from seizing the collateral or the payments.

Not-So-Pretty Wealth

Exporting a deferred-payment contract to a haven country turns it into not-so-pretty wealth. Anyone contemplating a suit against you would know that even if he obtains a court judgment in the United States, he will have to fight a second legal battle, in a foreign country, to reach the contract and turn it into cash.

He could not simply seize the contract and sell it. Seizure would mean going to court in the foreign country to force the buyer to make his payments to the judgment creditor. At a minimum, this would involve delay and extra expense.

A judgment creditor could ask a U.S. court to order you to assign your contract rights to him. You probably would be forced to comply. But the contract's nonassignability clause would raise serious doubts about the effectiveness of any such attempted assignment.

For a potential judgment creditor, a deferred-payment contract is not valueless or absolutely unreachable. It certainly would be easier to reach than assets shielded by a properly structured family partnership or trust. Nonetheless, for reasons explained in Chapter 18, "Dealing with Trusts and Partnerships," a deferred-payment sale may provide a substantial measure of asset protection when you are most desperate for it—when the litigation game has progressed so far that it is too late to try anything else.

PRACTICALITY

Deferred-payment sales can be a cornucopia of financial-planning benefits, and yet few investors ever use them for anything beyond deferring capital gain on real estate. The worries that hold investors back are credit risk and illiquidity. Both can be softened.

Credit Risk

Whenever you extend credit you take a risk. In the case of a deferred-payment sale, you can virtually eliminate credit risk by requiring the buyer to pledge marketable securities as collateral.

Unless the collateral is worth much more than you are owed, it should consist of fixed-dollar assets that themselves are free of substantial credit risk, such as high-grade bonds and money market instruments. The collateral should match the contract itself. If the deferred-payment contract carries a floating, or adjustable, interest rate, the collateral should be restricted to fixed-dollar assets that are short-term or that themselves carry a floating interest rate. If the contract calls for a fixed interest rate, the collateral should be restricted to long-term, fixed-rate investments, such as conventional bonds.

The collateral should be held by a large bank or trust company acting as escrow agent. The escrow instruments should forbid the bank to release the collateral to the buyer without your consent, until the distant day when all the deferred payments have been made.

Illiquidity

Illiquidity is a more difficult problem.

An installment contract is an illiquid asset. You can't just call your broker and say, "Sell." You would have to search for a buyer. And to attract one, you probably would have to offer a discount from the contract's face value. What's more, selling would bring the tax deferral to an end.

But illiquidity is a matter of degree.

You can't defer tax on capital gain or interest with a contract that lets you simply change your mind and demand early payment. But you can have both tax deferral and a measure of liquidity if the contract gives you a stick with which to poke the buyer. For example, the contract could give you the right to audit the buyer's books and records at any time the deferred balance exceeds a certain amount. If you ever called for an audit, the buyer might prefer to pay off the contract early to avoid the trouble.

Liquidity is served as well by minimizing credit risk, since that makes the contract itself into good collateral on which to borrow money. The bank that is acting as escrow agent would be the first place to go for a loan.

And an installment contract's illiquidity, whatever the degree, may not be important if the contract takes up only a modest share (say, no more than 20%) of your portfolio. As explained in Chapter 6, "Portfolio Planning," keeping just a *portion* of your assets readily marketable allows you to make portfolio changes and lay your hands on spendable cash. There is no need for all your investments to be liquid.

ESTATE-PLANNING IMPLICATIONS

If a deferred-payment contract outlives you, so that you do not collect on it in full during your lifetime, it will pass to your estate and your heirs. The payments they eventually receive will have the same character as though you had received them. Thus each payment will be split among (1) tax-free return of capital (in most cases, what the property cost you, minus past deductions for depreciation), (2) capital gain and (3) income. You can't eliminate the deferred tax merely by dying.

EFFECT ON PORTFOLIO

A deferred-payment sale alters your portfolio, usually making it safer. It removes the property being sold and leaves a deferred-payment contract in its place. The contract gives you the right to receive future payments of principal and interest, and thus is a fixed-dollar asset, like a bond or a money market investment.

The contract's function in your portfolio will depend on whether the interest rate you have agreed upon is fixed or floating (adjustable). If it is fixed, the contract resembles a long-term bond. Its earning power won't change, no matter what happens to interest rates. If it is floating, the contract resembles a money market instrument or short-term bond. Its earning power will fluctuate with changes in open-market interest rates, but its potential resale value will be steady.

A deferred-payment contract with tax-deferred interest helps to protect your portfolio from inflation, since the principal's loss of purchasing power is offset by 100% of the interest earnings. ⚷

15

MANAGING CAPITAL GAINS

Capital gain tax is a self-inflicted wound. You do it to yourself by selling a successful investment—perhaps because you believe it is time to take a profit or perhaps because you need the money.

The general strategy for avoiding capital gain tax is to recognize losses promptly but drag your feet about recognizing gains. (You must "recognize" a gain or loss on your current tax return if you sell an investment for cash or transfer it in certain other ways.) If your successful investments outperform the losers by a ratio of three to one, for example, you should wait three times longer to announce the successes to the tax collector. This way, you will always report enough losses to offset your gains, so that no tax is due.

It's easy to hurry up the recognition of losses. You just sell. The only obstacles are the pain you may feel in facing up to a loss, and the (often related) hope that a fallen investment will recover.

Slowing the recognition of gains is more difficult. Caution may prompt you to sell at least part of any investment with a big profit. Or you may need to raise cash—to purchase another investment or simply to spend.

Bigger Payoff

Deferring a capital gain can be even more beneficial than deferring ordinary income. You get to invest money that otherwise would be lost to the tax collector, as you do by deferring interest or dividends.

In addition, every year you defer a capital gain might bring an offsetting capital loss—which would turn the gain into tax-free cash. And, as explained in Chapter 19, "Gift and Estate Tax Rules," the potential liability for capital gain tax is erased for most investments you leave to your heirs. In this respect you are guaranteed that, sooner or later, the horse will speak.

THE LONG AND THE SHORT OF GAINS AND LOSSES, RECOGNIZED AND NET

You *recognize* a capital gain when you sell an investment at a profit and collect the cash proceeds. Recognizing the gain means you must include it in your tax return for the year.

You recognize a capital loss when you sell an investment that has gone down in price.

A capital gain or a capital loss generally is *long term* if you sell the investment at least one year and one day after buying it. Otherwise, the capital gain or capital loss is *short term.*

You are subject to tax on your *net* long-term capital gain and *net* short-term capital gain. Net long-term capital gain is taxed at a maximum rate of 28%. Net short-term capital gain is taxed at the same rate as interest or dividends.

You can deduct up to $3,000 per year of net capital loss (capital losses that exceed your capital gains) from your ordinary income. Any net capital loss not deducted in one year can be used in later years, to offset capital gains and up to $3,000 per year of ordinary income.

RECOGNIZING LOSSES

A sure though bitter tonic for tax on capital gains is capital losses. You should not, of course, seek out losing investments. But when they seek and find you, use them to avoid tax on your winning investments. Whenever you plan to take a profit, first examine your holdings for investments that have fallen in value and can be sold to generate offsetting capital losses.

For many investors, selling a failed investment is unpleasant no matter what the tax benefits. A loss is an insult to the investor's pride, and no mere tax savings will make it tolerable. Selling is too much like putting on a dunce cap.

This attitude is difficult to escape. I can only point out that, if your investment is worth less than you paid for it, the loss has already occurred. So you should feel bad even if you don't sell. Selling is simply a way of getting the tax collector to share your grief.[1]

What to Sell

In selecting depreciated assets to sell, first look for investments you would want to get rid of regardless of taxes.

If that doesn't turn up enough capital losses, look for depreciated assets you can sell and replace with something similar. For example, if you paid $.85 for Swiss francs that now are worth only $.70, you could sell them to recognize the loss and then purchase more francs the next day or even the next minute.

The feasibility of selling and replacing depends on the nature of the investment and on your reason for wanting to keep it. You generally can recognize a loss even if you promptly repurchase the same investment. But if you are selling stocks, bonds or other securities, the "wash sale rule" disallows a capital loss if you buy duplicate securities within 60 days before or after the sale.

The wash sale rule is fairly narrow, however. You can recognize a loss on stock in one company even if you promptly buy stock in a very similar company. Suppose, for example, that you are reluctant to let go of your fallen shares in Tall Stores, Inc., because you see good times ahead for retailers. Despite the wash sale rule, you could sell those shares and recognize the capital loss even if you simultaneously buy shares in Wide Stores, Inc.

When looking for capital losses, you generally should sell assets with the greatest percentage loss, to minimize commissions and other expenses.

How Mutual Funds Help

No-load mutual funds (that impose no commissions) make it practical to recognize even small losses, since the cost of trading no-load funds is negligible.

---

[1] Having sold a losing investment, you are likely to forget it. But if you hold on, it will rebuke you every day.

Rather than buy individual stocks and bonds, buy shares in a mutual fund that invests in the kind of securities you favor. If the market goes against you, but you want to hold on, redeem the shares and immediately invest the proceeds in another fund with the same investment policy. You will recognize a capital loss without abandoning your investment position. The wash sale rule won't apply, since you aren't repurchasing the same security.

CAPITAL LOSS INVESTORS

Someday you might find yourself awash in capital losses. You won't need to defer capital gains—since your losses make them effectively tax free. For you, capital gains will be far more desirable than interest or dividends.

One easy way to earn capital gains instead of interest and dividends is with no-load mutual funds. For example, you can buy shares in a stock market mutual fund and redeem them shortly before each dividend payment. Your share of the fund's dividend earnings will be wrapped up in the price you receive; nonetheless, all your return will be capital gain.

As soon as the dividend is paid, the fund's share price will drop by an equal amount. Reinvest at the lower price and hold the shares until just before the next dividend.

The same technique will work with funds that invest in bonds—turning interest into capital gain. For greater convenience, use a fund that pays dividends annually. Such funds are discussed in Chapter 10, "Easy Tax Planning with Mutual Funds," and more specific information appears in Chapter 35, "Where to Get Help."

TAX-FREE SWITCHING ZONES

Your need for capital losses will be much smaller if most of your profitable investment sales take place within "tax-free switching zones." A qualified pension plan, variable annuity or variable life insurance policy can be such a zone—your own private tax haven. There you can swap one investment for another with no concern for tax consequences.

You probably wouldn't want to hold all your investments in such tax-free switching zones, because of the costs or limitations. But, as we'll see, keeping even modest amounts there can help you defer capital gain tax on a comparatively large share of your portfolio, possibly all of it.

Variable Annuities

The freedom to switch investments within a variable annuity provides a large degree of tax-free control over the composition of your *overall portfolio,* not just over the investments in the annuity. When you purchase the annuity, select investments for it that mimic your direct holdings. Then, when you want to adjust your portfolio, make all of the adjustment inside the annuity.

To give a simple example, if your direct holdings are divided evenly between stocks and bonds, include those same two categories in the annuity's holdings. Later, when you want to reduce your position in, say, stocks (perhaps because they have performed well and you want to lock in some of your profit), do so by switching the stock portion of the annuity into bonds. But don't sell any of the stocks you own directly.

A variable life insurance policy gives you similar tax-free control over the makeup of your overall portfolio.

Pension Plans

You can control the composition of your overall portfolio in the same way through your IRA or other self-directed pension plan. A pension plan is even more powerful for this purpose, because it can own a wider range of investments than most variable annuities.

To continue the example, after you have eliminated all the stocks from your variable annuity and your pension plan, the value of your direct stock holdings may again become uncomfortably large, perhaps because the stock market continues to rise. You can offset the excess stock holdings by having your pension plan buy put options on individual stocks or on a stock market index.[2]

---

[2] A *put option* is the mirror image of a call option. A put gives the holder the right to sell an investment at a stated striking price, up until a stated expiration date.

Put options on 1,100 stocks are issued by the Chicago Board Options Exchange and are traded on all national stock exchanges, alongside call options on the same stocks.

A put option on a stock becomes profitable if the price of the stock declines. So if the stock market weakens, the loss on your excess stock holdings will be offset by a profit on the put options, which would be tax-deferred inside the pension plan.

INSTALLMENT SALES—A LONG-TERM SOLUTION

Installment sales were discussed in Chapter 14, "Deferred-Payment Sales." They can defer capital gain tax indefinitely on sales of real estate, privately issued securities, collectibles, and other investments not traded in a public market.

SLOWING GAINS—TEMPORARY SOLUTIONS

The battle against capital gain tax is won a year at a time. The three devices that follow are easy ways to buy at least a year or two of deferral—perhaps to let offsetting losses emerge.

Short Sale Against the Box

A short sale against the box eliminates the risk of keeping an appreciated investment, without immediately triggering capital gain tax. And it generates spendable cash.

A short sale is the sale of borrowed property. When you sell short, your broker lends you an investment (shares of stock, for example, or a quantity of bonds), sells the investment for you and then credits your account with the cash proceeds. You close the short sale, eventually, by purchasing the borrowed investment and returning it to the broker. You profit if you can buy the investment for less than you sold it for—that is, if its price declines.

While a short sale remains open, the broker requires you to leave cash or investments in your account worth more than the borrowed property, as that property's value changes from day to day. Provided this requirement is satisfied, you can withdraw the cash proceeds of the short sale or use the money to purchase another investment.[3]

---

[3] A simple short sale is a way of speculating that the price of the borrowed investment will decline.

Cloning Around

A short sale "against the box" is a short sale of an investment identical to one you already own. For example, if you own 1,000 shares of Intel stock, a short sale against the box would involve borrowing another 1,000 shares of Intel from your broker and selling it in the open market.

Selling short against the box eliminates all chance of gain or loss in the investment, as though you had sold it outright—since the shares you own are offset by the shares you owe. But you don't recognize gain or loss until you close the short sale by returning the borrowed property (either by buying it in the open market or by delivering the property you already own).

Brokers often impose a heavy rental charge for lending investments to short sellers. So, unless you can negotiate to borrow the investment at nominal cost, a short sale against the box is too expensive for long-term deferral. But if you otherwise would sell a profitable investment late in the year, a short sale against the box is a simple way to push the capital gain into the following year—when you may have capital losses to offset it. Close out the sale on January 2, to halt the rental charge.

Or perhaps your plans will change. If the investment continues to rise, you can, if you wish, close out the short sale by purchasing the investment in the open market. By so doing, you would recognize a capital loss, which you could apply to offset the gain on *part* of your original holdings.

Forward Sales of Precious Metals

If you hold gold or silver at a profit, a forward sale will reduce your holdings without immediately triggering capital gain.

Precious metals (and many other commodities) are traded in both *spot* and *forward* markets. Spot sales are paid for and delivered immediately. Forward sales call for payment and delivery at a specified future date, but at a price agreed upon now. You recognize the gain or loss on a forward sale only when that future date arrives.

Prices in a commodity's spot and forward markets move together. In the case of precious metals, the relationship is especially simple and steady. As a general rule, the price for delivery on any future date stays close to the spot price plus the interest you could earn by investing the same amount in CDs until the delivery date. For example, if the spot price of gold is $400 per ounce and the interest rate on CDs is 10%, the price for gold to be delivered one year from now will be about $440.

A forward sale does not generate any cash until it finally is settled. Instead, the sale converts your precious metals into a fixed-dollar asset, whose value is insulated from changes in the metal's price. The difference between the spot price and the forward price is the "interest" you earn.

When the delivery date arrives, you will recognize a capital gain based on the spot price at the time you made the forward sale. The rest of the profit—the interest element—will be taxable as ordinary income.[4]

You can arrange a forward sale with a dealer in precious metals in the United States or wherever your metals are stored. Most forward contracts are for two years or less, but contracts for longer periods—perhaps much longer—can be negotiated.

Selling Call Options

You can sell a call option to raise cash and reduce the risk of holding on to an appreciated investment, without immediately recognizing a capital gain.

A call option gives its owner the right to purchase an investment at a stated *striking* price on or before a stated *expiration date*. When you write (create and sell) a call option, you agree to deliver the underlying property if the option holder *calls* for it.

You are paid for a call option when you write it, but no taxable event occurs until the option is closed out: when the holder exercises it, you repurchase it, or it expires.

- If the owner exercises the option, you must sell him the underlying investment at the striking price. In calculating your capital gain, you include what you received for the option as part of the proceeds of the sale.

- If you repurchase the option, you will have a capital gain or capital loss—depending on how much you pay and how much you received when you wrote the option.

- If the option expires, the money you received for it becomes a capital gain.

In any case, there's no tax while the option remains outstanding—even though you've collected some money.

---

[4] The rules for separating capital gain from income are more complex than this, but yield a similar result.

A call option with a striking price far below the current price of the underlying investment (a *deep-in-the-money* option) is relatively valuable— at least as valuable as the difference between the investment's current price and the striking price. By writing such an option, you can raise a substantial amount of cash, *without immediately recognizing any capital gain.* Writing the option also removes most of the risk of owning the investment, since you can be hurt only to the extent the market price of the underlying investment falls below the (low) striking price.

More Cash

When you want to liquidate a highly appreciated investment, you may be able to collect more after-tax cash by selling a deep-in-the-money call option than by selling the investment itself.

For example, suppose you own 1,000 shares of ZIZZ Technology purchased fifteen years ago at $5 per share. Now it is worth $100 per share. An outright sale would trigger a capital gain of $95,000 and a tax bill (at 28%) of $26,600, leaving only $73,400. But an eight-year call option with a striking price of $30 per share might be worth approximately $75,000—which you would collect free of current tax.

If the option eventually is exercised, the striking price will provide more than enough cash to pay the capital gain tax. And there may be no capital gain tax at all if you have suffered capital losses in the meantime or if you no longer are alive.

Or if the stock's market price falls below the striking price (so that the option holder lets the option expire), you will suffer a loss, as compared with an outright sale of the stock—but only to the extent the stock falls below $25 per share.

To get the tax results just described, avoid making the terms of the option too extreme. Allow some uncertainty as to whether the option will be exercised, given the volatility of the underlying investment and the number of months or years the option runs. Thus the striking price may be very low, but not fantastically low. It must be possible for the investment's price to reach the striking price without the occurrence of events taken from a science fiction novel.

Option Markets

Call options on more than 1,100 stocks ("CBOE options") are traded on the New York Stock Exchange, the Chicago Board Options Exchange and other exchanges. For most stocks the maximum option period is only nine months, which at best would permit you to defer gain only into the following year. And deep-in-the-money options are not always available in every stock.

Despite their limitations, CBOE options can help. Even one year of deferral is worth having. And postponing tax for one year may eliminate it altogether—because a loss arises from some other investment or because the underlying investment continues to appreciate and you repurchase the option at a loss.

For 69 stocks, call options can be written for up to three years. Obviously, if your stock is one of the few, such long-term options (or "LEAPs") would be more useful.

Short-term call options on precious metals and long-term Treasury bonds can be written on the New York Commodity Exchange and the Chicago Board of Trade, respectively.

If you have a large holding of a particular stock or of precious metals (say, at least $1 million), you may be able to negotiate a private sale of a long-term, deep-in-the-money call option to an institutional investor. The option could run for many years, even past your expected lifetime.[5]

It sometimes is possible to sell a long-term, deep-in-the-money call option to a prospective buyer of unimproved land.

DAMAGE CONTROL

Despite your best efforts, you may eventually have to sell appreciated assets and pay some tax.

But don't pay too much. In deciding what to sell to raise cash, select the investments whose appreciation is smallest in relation to their market value. They will produce the least tax liability for each dollar you collect.

And getting rid of an oversize investment position isn't a matter of all or nothing. Selling just part of it may be enough.

OTHER MATTERS

Devices for deferring capital gain generally have implications for estate planning and for asset protection. These topics are pursued in later chapters. 🔑

---

[5] As explained in Part 6, certain types of foreign trusts can be used to make the sale of long-term options practical for much smaller amounts.

PART FOUR

TRUSTS AND PARTNERSHIPS

All property is owned one way or another by real, flesh-and-blood people—a fact the government often loses sight of.

The world viewed by the government is populated not just by you and me, but also by corporations, trusts, foundations, partnerships and other imaginary people. Such masques neither eat, nor sleep nor breathe, yet the government confers upon them legal rights and powers, including the right to own property.

This part deals with the two most versatile species of imaginary people: trusts and partnerships. By standing between you and your property, they can spare you the disadvantages of ownership.

If you own nothing, nothing can be taken from you. When the government comes to tax your investment income, the investments won't belong to you, they will belong to an imaginary person who is better situated than you to avoid tax. When a litigant tries to enforce a judgment against you, he will find that you own very little (although a figment of the law's imagination may be as rich as you once were). And when the government comes again, to tax your estate, it may find that financial trolls have chewed on much of it and leprechauns have carried off the rest.

16

TRUSTS

A trust lets you "resign" as owner of an asset but still benefit from it. Your resignation protects the asset: since you no longer own it, no one can force you to hand it over. The protection can continue for as long as you like—even past your lifetime. Then, at whatever time you have appointed, the asset can be delivered to whomever you have chosen.

Trusts are versatile. You can design one to fit your purposes exactly—to shift tax burdens from one person to another, shrink your *taxable* estate, protect wealth from lawsuits, and even protect trust beneficiaries from their own inexperience.

This chapter explains a few simple trust strategies. But it is also a prelude—a necessary prelude—to the more complex strategies discussed later. In addition, the information you gain here should make it easier (and perhaps cheaper) to talk about trusts with your lawyer.

BASIC ELEMENTS

You, as *grantor,* establish a trust by transferring property to another person, the *trustee,* who accepts an obligation to safeguard the property and use it for the benefit of certain persons, the *beneficiaries.*

The three essential groups—grantor, trustee, beneficiaries—needn't be distinct. A grantor may be his own trustee, as you might want to be if you set up a trust for your children. And the grantor may be the beneficiary of his own trust, as is the case with a *living trust.*

A fourth party, the *protector,* can be authorized to monitor the trust and advise the trustee. He may even have the power to fire and replace the trustee. Making yourself the protector of your own trust puts the trustee on a short leash.

Trust Declaration

The terms of a trust ordinarily are set out in a written declaration signed by the trustee and, in most cases, by the grantor.[1] The consent, knowledge or other participation of the beneficiaries isn't needed. However, the beneficiaries have a legal right to enforce the declaration—by suing the trustee if necessary.

In preparing a trust declaration, certain "dials" can be adjusted to achieve exactly the kind of arrangement you want.

- *Property*—the assets subject to the trust. The declaration describes the property you are transferring to the trust, and it can permit you to add more later.

- *Term*—how long the trust shall continue. You can fix the term at a definite number of years or you can tie it to the occurrence of a particular event, such as someone's death.

- *Beneficiaries*—the persons for whom the trustee must apply the income and assets of the trust. You can name the beneficiaries individually or you can describe them by class, such as "all the descendants of the grantor." And you can include yourself.

- *Rights of beneficiaries*—who gets what. You can give a beneficiary a share in the trust's income for a fixed number of years, for his lifetime or for some other definable period. And you can give him a share in the trust's principal. Or, with a discretionary or "sprinkle" trust, you can let the trustee determine which beneficiaries receive what and when they get it.

- *Power of appointment*—a right to give or take. You can have the power to direct the trustee to distribute (or *appoint*) the trust's income or principal to a particular beneficiary—or you can give such a power to a beneficiary or some other person. A *Crummey* provision, for example, allows a beneficiary a brief period, such as six weeks, to withdraw a certain amount of money or certain property from the trust.

---

[1] A trust declaration may also be called a *trust agreement* or a *declaration of trust*.

REVOCABLE LIVING TRUSTS

A much-publicized and popular type of trust is the *revocable living trust*. You might establish one to hold some (perhaps most) of your assets during your lifetime. You would be the grantor of the trust. You also would be one of the trustees and one of the beneficiaries.

As trustee, you maintain day-to-day control. The other trustee (which might be a relative or a local bank) is a standby, ready to assume responsibility if you become incapacitated.

As beneficiary, you have full and unhindered use of the trust's assets and income during your lifetime, with the right to withdraw money whenever you wish. Upon your death, the assets are distributed to the other beneficiaries you named (your heirs) without the cost, delay and loss of privacy of probating a will.

A living trust has no tax advantages, and it does nothing to protect your assets against lawsuits. For those purposes, you may want to establish a foreign trust, as discussed in Part 6. Chapter 29 explains how to coordinate a living trust with a foreign trust.

- *Accumulation*—whether the trustee must distribute the trust's income to the beneficiaries each year, and whether the trustee may distribute the principal during the term of the trust.

- *Investment authority*—how the trustee may invest trust assets. You might require the trustee to invest only in, say, high-grade bonds. Or you might allow the trustee to select the investments it judges to be best—or even to borrow money to make investments. Or you might require the trustee to follow investment advice from you or someone else.

- *Revocability*—whether you can revoke the trust and retrieve its assets. You might make the trust revocable from the first day, only after a certain date, only under certain conditions or not at all.

- *Monitoring*—who watches the trustee and who can replace him. You or someone you name as protector can oversee the trustee.

- *Location*—where the trust is administered, and the state or country whose laws govern it. The trust should be located where the law will respect the terms of the trust declaration. To allow for the unforeseeable, the trustee or the protector should have the power to move the trust to another state or country.

Transfer of Property

To create a valid trust, you must actually transfer property to the trustee. The trust declaration, by itself, may not accomplish this. If, for example, you want to put certain shares of stock in the trust, you should endorse the stock certificate and deliver it to the trustee. If you want to put a piece of real estate in the trust, you should execute and record a deed naming the trustee as owner.

EFFECT ON CREDITORS

As a general rule, so long as property is held in trust, a beneficiary's creditors can't reach it directly—since the beneficiary doesn't own it. ("Creditor" includes anyone who wins a lawsuit against the beneficiary.)

But a creditor can attach a beneficiary's right to receive distributions from the trust, if the right is fixed and definable. For example, if a beneficiary is entitled to receive $50,000 per year, a court might order the trustee to make the annual payments to the beneficiary's creditor.

Giving the trustee discretion to determine which beneficiary gets what, and when, protects against such seizures. If a beneficiary of a sprinkle trust becomes embroiled in a lawsuit, the trustee can postpone direct distributions to him until the matter is settled.

Creditors of Grantor

A creditor can take advantage of any rights the grantor retains. For example, suppose you establish a trust but retain the right to order distributions to anyone you choose. A court could compel you to exercise that right, and have the money paid to your judgment creditor. Or if you had made the trust revocable, a court could order you to revoke it—to let your creditor seize the assets as they came out.

Local Law Controls

A trust's power to protect assets from creditors is limited by the laws where the trust is administered, which differ from state to state and from country to country. In the United States, if the grantor is also a beneficiary—even a discretionary beneficiary—the courts *will* invade the trust to satisfy his creditors.

Many foreign countries, on the other hand, will respect a trust even if you are both grantor and a beneficiary. Thus you can establish a foreign trust and include yourself as a beneficiary, without leaving the door open to your potential creditors. This is an important reason for placing a trust outside the United States.

End Run

If the courts respect the terms of your trust, and if you keep no rights that a court could force you to exercise, another line of attack may be open to your creditors. They can argue that your transfers to the trust were legally invalid when you made them and should be set aside.

The rules on this topic (known variously as *fraudulent transfer, fraudulent conveyance,* or *fraudulent disposition*) differ considerably from state to state and from country to country. But almost anywhere, if you establish a trust in order to defeat a particular creditor, and if you owe him something when you transfer property to the trust, a court will set the transfer aside for the benefit of that creditor. And almost anywhere, if the creditor's claim has no link to events or circumstances preceding your transfer, the transfer will be respected.

This important topic is discussed further in Chapter 18, "Dealing with Trusts and Partnerships."

WHO PAYS TAX

The tax bill for a trust's income may go to the grantor, the beneficiaries or the trust itself—depending on the terms of the trust and on what the trust does with the income.[2] The income tax rules distinguish two broad categories of trusts: grantor trusts and taxable trusts.

---

[2] If a trust too closely resembles a corporation, the IRS will treat it as "an association taxable as a corporation." This is likely to occur only if *(a)* beneficiaries may freely trade their interests in the trust (just as stockholders may freely trade their shares); *(b)* the trustee may invest actively, not merely hold investments; and *(c)* the trust is primarily for the benefit of persons other than the trustee.

GRANTOR TRUSTS

If you, the grantor, retain the right to control or benefit from a trust in certain ways, you are treated as the owner of everything in the trust—and must include the trust's income and deductions on your own tax return. The trust may be important for estate planning or for asset protection, but for income tax purposes, it barely exists. Such a trust is called a *grantor trust.*

Generally, a trust you create will be a grantor trust if any of the following is true.

- *Income or principal to grantor.*   You or your spouse may receive distributions from the trust.

- *Control of distributions.*   You can require the trustee to make distributions to someone you specify.

- *Benefit of administration.*   You can require the trustee to administer investments in certain ways that benefit you. For example, you have the right to repurchase trust assets at fair market value.

- *Life insurance.*   The trust may purchase insurance on your life.

In addition, if you establish a foreign trust with one or more U.S. beneficiaries, it is a grantor trust—even if you retain no rights or powers whatsoever.

There are no income tax consequences to *any* transaction between you and your own grantor trust. You can give property of any kind to it, sell appreciated property to it, lend money to it, borrow money from it, rent property to or from it—all with no effect on anyone's taxable income. For income tax purposes you simply are moving assets from one pocket to another.

There is no income tax on any distribution from a grantor trust. It's all after-tax money.

When the grantor dies, the assets of his grantor trust are deemed to have been transferred to a new, taxable trust—since the grantor is no longer available to pay taxes or even file a return.

Two-Edged Sword

The grantor trust rules are supposed to keep you from dodging tax on income that can be used for your benefit. The rules have a wide sweep—in some respects too wide for the tax collector's own good. As we'll see in later chapters, the grantor trust rules let you remove assets from your taxable estate without complicating your income tax planning, make gifts without paying gift tax, and divert tax liability for a trust's income by tagging someone else as the grantor.

Depending on what you want a trust to do, it may unavoidably be a grantor trust. But if it is not, you can *make* it a grantor trust by including any one of the provisions previously listed.

TAXABLE TRUSTS

If a trust is not a grantor trust, then it is a *taxable trust*, and either the trust itself or the beneficiaries pay tax on the income.

Trust Is Taxed

If a taxable trust accumulates income, it pays tax in much the same way as an individual—and even receives a "personal" exemption of $100. But the schedule of tax rates is more steeply graduated for trusts than for individuals. The maximum rate of 39.6% applies to a trust's annual income over $7,500.

A taxable trust receives a deduction for income it distributes to the beneficiaries. Thus it can reduce its tax bill to zero by distributing all its income each year.

Beneficiaries Are Taxed

Income distributed by a taxable trust is taxable to the beneficiary who receives it. If the income was left over from an earlier year, the beneficiary gets a credit for the tax the trust paid on it.[3]

The beneficiary's tax depends on how the trust earned the income. If it was earned as a long-term capital gain, the beneficiary reports it as such on his own tax return; if it was earned through dividends, the beneficiary reports it as dividends; and so on.

A distribution is assumed to be drawn from trust income unless, at the time it is made, the trust has already distributed all its income. A distribu-

---

[3] When a taxable trust distributes income accumulated in previous years, but after the beneficiary has reached age 21, the beneficiary is taxable under special "throwback" rules—which may somewhat increase or decrease his tax bill, but certainly will increase his accounting bill.

tion is assumed to be drawn from income accumulated in earlier years unless the trust has already distributed all past income.

Any other payout (i.e., one made when the trust has already paid out all its income) is a tax-free distribution of principal.

TAXATION OF TRANSFERS

There is no income tax on the grantor's transfer of assets of any kind to his grantor trust—since the grantor continues to be treated as the owner.

There *generally* is no income tax on the grantor's transfer of assets to a taxable trust. You can transfer stocks, bonds, real estate, precious metals and life insurance to a taxable trust without triggering an income tax bill— even if the assets are worth more than you paid for them.

An important exception applies to deferred payment contracts. Transferring such a contract to a taxable trust triggers all the deferred income.

Transferring an asset to a taxable trust doesn't alter its potential for generating capital gain or capital loss. If the trust sells the asset, it recognizes the same capital gain or loss you would have.[4]

TRUST USES

The use of trusts is discussed throughout much of the remainder of the book. The most important uses are as follows.

Protection for Others

A *domestic trust* is one organized under the laws of one of the 50 states.

The simplest use of a domestic trust is to set aside property for your family or others and protect it from your potential creditors. The assets also will be protected from the beneficiaries' creditors if you give the trustee discretion in making distributions, as discussed earlier in the chapter.

---

[4] A special rule applies to income a trust earns by selling assets with *built-in profits*. If the grantor transfers an appreciated asset and the trust sells it within two years, the trust pays tax on the built-in profit at the grantor's tax rate. The trust is liable for the tax, even if it distributes the built-in profit to beneficiaries the same year, but the beneficiaries pay no additional tax on it.

Protection for Yourself

You indirectly can use a domestic trust of which you are *not* a beneficiary to safeguard your own assets. The trust can serve as a kind of hook, to which you attach the assets you want to protect.

For example, suppose you want to put your personal residence beyond the reach of potential creditors. Transfer at least a modest amount of cash, equal to at least 10% of the value of the house to an irrevocable trust for the benefit of your children. Authorize the trust to purchase insurance on your life, or include some other provision that makes the trust a grantor trust.

Sell the house to the trust at fair market value. The trust pays by (1) giving you a cash downpayment, (2) assuming any existing mortgage, and (3) executing a deferred-payment contract for the remainder of the purchase price. Then lease the house back from the trust, paying the trust a fair market rent.

The trust will use the rent to pay the mortgage, property taxes and maintenance costs, and to pay down the remainder of the purchase price or accumulate money for that purpose. Because the trust is a grantor trust, neither the sale nor the lease affects your tax bill. You get a tax deduction for the mortgage interest and property taxes the trust pays, just as though you were paying them.

The net economic result is a deferred-payment sale of the equity in your house. Because the trust may elect not to make payments for many years, the contract is far less attractive to a potential creditor than your house was.

Beat the Clock

There are other ways (discussed in later chapters) a trust of which you are not a beneficiary can help protect your assets—if the trust itself is safe from attack by your creditors. Thus transferring even a small sum to a trust *early*, before any event that might lead to a lawsuit, can help protect much larger amounts later.

Estate Tax Savings

Trusts are essential to many strategies for avoiding gift and estate tax. These strategies are discussed in Chapters 20 and 32.

Foreign Trusts

You can establish a trust outside the United States (a *foreign* trust) to:

- Do the same things as a domestic trust.

- Achieve substantially stronger and more reliable protection from creditors.

- Protect assets even if you are a trust beneficiary.

- Create powerful tax-saving machinery for your heirs.

We'll investigate foreign trusts in Part 6 and in Chapter 35 ("Where to Get Help"), you'll find an easy and inexpensive way to establish one. ☞

17

FAMILY LIMITED PARTNERSHIPS

A family limited partnership can stand as a barrier—almost a threat—to would-be judgment creditors and other financial assailants. Yet it leaves you in direct control of the assets you want to protect.

A family limited partnership also might mean the difference between a sizable bill for estate tax and none at all.

For all its power, a family limited partnership is simple and inexpensive.

Legal Character

A partnership is an unincorporated association that two or more persons form to earn profits. The partners may include natural (flesh-and-blood) persons, corporations, trusts, or other partnerships. In most states and foreign countries, the partners can shape their partnership agreement in nearly any way they want.

There is no limit to how large or small any partner's share, or interest, may be. For example, one partner might own 95% of the partnership, while five other partners each own 1%. And when a partnership is established, one partner might contribute $1 million to its capital, while another partner contributes only $100.

A partnership can be formed through gifts, which is often the case with family limited partnerships. One member of the family contributes all the capital and simultaneously makes gifts of partnership interest to other family members.

Limited Partners

Most countries have laws governing the formation of partnerships, the dealings of the partners with their partnership, and the partnership's dealings with other persons. Generally, every partner has the legal power to make binding commitments on behalf of his partnership and is liable for all partnership debts—unless he is a *limited partner*.

Forty-nine states have laws closely modeled after the Uniform Limited Partnership Act.[1] Under those laws, a person is a limited partner, and hence is protected against liability for the partnership's debts, if *all* the following are true.

- The partnership agreement calls him a limited partner.
- The partnership agreement prohibits him from participating in management.
- He in fact does not participate in management.
- He does not claim authority to make commitments on behalf of the partnership.

In most cases it is easy for a partner to qualify as a limited partner if he is content to let someone else run the partnership.

A limited partner should be careful not to compromise his status. He should participate in partnership activities only at the instruction or with the authorization of the general partner. He never should sign a contract or other agreement on behalf of the partnership.

General Partners

A partnership must have at least one *general partner*, who bears unlimited liability for partnership debts.[2]

The usual arrangement in a family limited partnership is for one person to be the general partner and all the others to be limited partners. But a part-

---

[1] The Uniform Limited Partnership Act is a model statute devised by the National Conference of Commissioners of Uniform State Laws. When a feature of law is found in exactly 49 states, the 50th state usually is Louisiana—as in this case.

[2] For income tax purposes, the presence of a partner with unlimited liability is a key characteristic that distinguishes a partnership from a corporation.

nership can have more than one general partner, each with full power to act on the partnership's behalf.

The agreement governing your family limited partnership should name a specific person to replace the general partner—in case he dies, resigns or becomes bankrupt. Or it can authorize the limited partners to elect a replacement.

TAXATION AND PARTNERSHIPS

Ordinarily a family limited partnership won't affect your income tax bill, although there are a few exceptions you may need to allow for. The general rules are:

Assets Going In. Contributing investments or other property to a partnership, in exchange for an interest in the partnership, ordinarily is tax free. Thus you (or any other partner) can contribute appreciated investments without triggering tax on capital gain.

Partnership Income. As a general rule, each partner is treated as though he individually carries on his share of the partnership's activities. Accordingly each partner includes in his own tax return his share of the partnership's income, expenses, gains, losses and credits. The partnership itself files a tax return but is not taxed.

Items of income and expense retain their character as they flow out to the partners. Thus dividends received by the partnership are dividend income to the partners, a capital gain earned by the partnership is a capital gain to the partners, and investment interest paid by the partnership is investment interest expense for the partners.

Assets Coming Out. Pro rata distributions of money or other property to the partners are tax free.[3] A distribution to just some of the partners may be taxable if it represents certain kinds of tax-deferred income earned by the partnership (such as the untaxed gain wrapped up in a deferred-payment sale).

---

[3] A distribution is *pro rata* if the amount received by each partner is in proportion to his share of partnership capital.

Exceptions

There are exceptions to the tax neutrality of partnerships. They shouldn't be a hindrance, provided you are aware of them.

- If your partnership invests in real estate or operates a business that generates more tax deductions than taxable income, the limited partners may have to wait until later years to apply their share of *net* deductions to reduce their tax bill.

- If your partnership owns a deferred annuity, the earnings will not be tax deferred.

- If more than 80% of your partnership's assets will consist of exchange-traded stock or other marketable equity securities, you must take certain steps to avoid tax on contributions of appreciated assets to the partnership's capital. Either (1) you individually must provide substantially *all* the partnership's capital, or (2) all the partners must contribute the same kinds of assets and in the same proportions.

- If you transfer appreciated assets to a *foreign* partnership, you probably will have to pay tax on the appreciation. (It's the appreciation, not the value of the assets, that is taxed.)

Most likely, none of the exceptions will make it impractical to use a family limited partnership—although you may have to adjust your plans to allow for them.

ASSET PROTECTION

If someone were to sue you and win, he would be very disappointed to discover that most of your assets are tied up in a family limited partnership.

What happens to a partnership, good or bad, affects *all* the partners. Accordingly, courts in the United States and most other countries ordinarily will not touch partnership assets to satisfy the debts of an individual partner.

Similarly, courts are loath to compel a partnership to distribute money to an individual partner—even if the partner "needs" the money to pay a court judgment. Forcing a distribution might divert resources the partnership needs for its own purposes, thereby injuring partners who are not targets of the judgment. Courts also are reluctant to compel a partner to sell his part-

LIMITED-LIABILITY COMPANIES

Forty-seven states and many foreign countries now permit the formation of *limited-liability companies*—a hybrid that seems to offer the
best characteristics of corporations and partnerships.

Like a corporation, but unlike a partnership, a limited-liability
company (or LLC) can exist without any member being personally
responsible for its debts. Thus the member who runs the company
avoids the open-ended liability of a general partner. But an LLC can
be structured so that, for federal income tax purposes, it is treated as a
partnership—and thus does not pay income tax.

Some attorneys now favor using a limited-liability company, rather
than a limited partnership, to carry out the asset protection strategies
discussed in this chapter. Others see LLCs as an untested innovation.

nership interest to an outsider (to raise money to pay a creditor), because
doing so would force an unwanted association on the other partners.

The most a partner's creditor is likely to get from a court is a *charging
order*. This instructs the general partner that, if and when he makes a distribution for the partner, he must pay it to the partner's creditor. But a charging
order only tells the general partner *where* to send distributions. It doesn't
force him to make any. Thus if the partnership agreement lets the general
partner decide when to make distributions, the partnership is a well from
which no unfriendly party can drink.

Poison Pill

Even if someone is willing to wait patiently for a distribution, a charging
order can be dangerous for him. For federal income tax purposes, the holder
of a charging order is treated as though he were a partner. He must pay tax
on "his" share of the partnership's net income—even if he does not receive
any distributions.

This tax rule is powerful shark repellent. Your family limited partnership
can intensify it by investing in tax-managed mutual funds or deferred-
payment contracts. Such investments would threaten a blast of no-cash, taxable income to anyone who might ask a court for a charging order—a blast
the partnership could set off by liquidating its deferred-income investments.

FURTHER PROTECTION

Courts will readily issue a charging order to assist a partner's creditor, since the order would not disturb the partnership or otherwise injure the other partners. In fact a charging order is *almost* the only way a partner's creditor can benefit from partnership assets—but not quite.

Now and then, when it is clear a partnership does nothing the individual partners could not do just as well on their own, a court will take further steps to assist a partner's creditor. It might force the partnership to make a distribution to the partner. Or it might order a foreclosure sale of the partner's interest. Or it might disregard the partnership altogether and treat its assets as belonging directly to the individual partners.

Such actions are rare, but they may become more common as the litigation explosion grows more violent. So it would be unwise to rely solely on the legal formalities of your family limited partnership. Instead, to fortify the partnership, include as many as possible of the following features—in case you find yourself before a judge who believes the wisest legal precedents are the ones he sets.

Activities. Your family limited partnership will be far more robust if it does more than hold passive investments.

Suppose your partnership does nothing but hold 10,000 shares of stock in General Motors. Your creditor could argue that forcing the partnership to make a distribution to you or ordering a foreclosure sale of your partnership interest would not harm the remaining partners, since their income and profits would not be disturbed.

But there is no harmless way to divide the assets of a partnership that operates a business. Forcing a distribution might waste capital the partnership needs for current or future business activities. And forcing the partnership to accept an unwanted partner (such as the winning bidder at a foreclosure sale) might compromise the partnership's relations with customers, suppliers or lenders.

Of course, business activities expose the partnership's investments to business-related claims. So choose a line of business that is not likely to attract litigation of its own. Selling plain cotton socks through the mail might be a safe choice. Dismantling nuclear reactors would not be.

Agreements. Your family limited partnership should obligate itself to continue at its present size and with its present partners. For example, the partnership might obtain a line of credit that automatically lapses if there is a change in partners or if partnership distributions exceed some limit. Or the partnership might retain an investment adviser under an agreement that lapses if there is a change in partnership size or ownership.

Investment Choices. The partnership should own investments that would be hurt by a change in partners. For example, it might purchase life insurance that terminates if any partner's interest is transferred to another person. Or it might purchase securities subject to an agreement prohibiting their indirect transfer—such as through a change in the ownership of the partnership.

Limits on Transferability. The partnership agreement should prohibit any partner from transferring his interest without the consent of the general partner and at least a majority of the limited partners. This would further discourage a court from ordering a foreclosure sale of a partner's interest, since it would so clearly violate the rights of other partners.

Every partner should have a right of first refusal for any partnership interest put up for sale—the right for, say, 120 days, to match any outsider's offer. This would greatly reduce the price a creditor could hope to collect in a foreclosure sale.

Replacement of General Partner. The limited partners should have the power to replace the general partner, so they can choose a new one if a court ever orders a foreclosure sale of your general partner's interest.

This last provision should be designed with great care and should reflect family circumstances. The selection of a new general partner might be placed in the hands of a simple majority of the limited partners or might require a supermajority, such as two thirds or three quarters. The voting can be in proportion to each person's partnership interest, or each partner can have a single vote.

If you personally are going to own most of the limited partnership, voting should be per capita, so you personally don't have the power to replace the general partner. And it usually is best to require a supermajority, so you can be confident the general partner will be replaced only if you want him to be.

Get Real

Your partnership will be a paper tiger if you fail to observe its terms or fail to manage it in a business-like fashion. Your creditor could plausibly argue that the partnership is a sham and that you still own the property you supposedly transferred to it.

Register all partnership property—stocks, bonds, real estate, bank accounts and everything else—in the partnership's name. Manage all partnership assets for profit. If you personally use any partnership property, pay for the privilege. If a partner receives fees for his services to the partnership, make the fees reasonable. Do not enter into what is undeniably a sweetheart transaction with any partner. Keep proper accounts. Give every partner a financial statement every year. It needn't be audited, but it should be accurate. If any partner is a minor, deliver the financial statement to his parents.

Do not violate the partnership agreement, even if you are confident none of your partners will object. Their acquiescence would be silent testimony that the partnership is a sham.

If practical, include an unrelated but trusted friend as a limited partner. His presence would rebut a creditor's argument that the partnership is governed by an unwritten agreement among family members. Were that argument to prevail, the creditor then could argue that the unwritten agreement allows each partner to withdraw his capital at any time—which the creditor would ask the court to force you to do, to pay his claim.

Greatest Safety Offshore

To protect liquid assets, which are easy to hold outside the United States (as distinct from real estate or a U.S. business), it's best to establish your partnership in a foreign country. The laws in certain countries are especially scrupulous in respecting the integrity of partnerships, and assets in a foreign partnership are more costly and difficult for a creditor to pursue. Recall, however, that there may be a tax cost to transferring *appreciated* assets to a foreign partnership—the amount of tax depending on the amount of appreciation.

DRIVER'S SEAT

Placing your assets in a family limited partnership can put you in a strong position to deal with potential litigants. A hostile party must either leave you alone or bear the costs and risks of litigation for the chance to wait 20 years, 30 years, or longer (perhaps until the partnership terminates) in hope of collecting a judgment through a charging order. He is likely to find even a small settlement attractive, and he might simply go away.

A foreign limited partnership makes your position even stronger, because it undermines a potential litigant's hope of persuading a court to overturn established legal principles and because it adds to his expense in trying.

RISKY BUSINESSES

A partnership protects against creditors of the *partners*, but a partnership might have creditors of its own. And a successful suit against a partnership—based on its alleged wrongdoing—could lead to claims against the general partner.

A partnership that holds only passive investments (stocks, bonds, life insurance, etc.) faces little risk of litigation. But a partnership that holds real estate (on the premises of which a tenant, delivery man, guest or burglar might slip and fall) or that operates a business (which someday may have a disgruntled employee, customer or supplier, or which might inspire the zeal of a government regulator) is a potential target for a lawsuit.

If you have property that might attract litigation, put it in a separate partnership. Then, if a problem arises, only that particular property will be at risk. Assets in other partnerships would be safe. Don't expose passive investments by mixing them in a partnership with property that is legally accident prone.

Corporate General Partner

A general partner has unlimited liability for all partnership debts. If your family limited partnership is going to borrow heavily (in relation to its assets) or if it is going to conduct a business that might attract litigation, consider forming a corporation to act as general partner. A corporation isn't an impenetrable shield. But if the partnership loses a lawsuit, the corporation's presence (rather than yours) as the sole general partner makes it harder for the winner to hold you personally responsible.

Spread the stock among family members or transfer it to a trust for their benefit. Don't hold more than a small amount directly, since what you own might fall into the hands of your creditors—who could use it to control the partnership.

TIME MACHINE

Even if asset protection is important to you, you may not be ready to transfer substantial capital to a partnership. But rather than wait, consider forming a partnership now, with small capital. Then, if a need for asset protection ever arises, the partnership will be available to buy your assets through deferred-payment sales.

To go a step further, the partnership agreement could authorize the general partner (you) to require one or more partners (including yourself) to contribute additional capital at any time.[4] Organizing a partnership with such a provision *early* will enable it to snatch up money or other property later, if you ever suspect that a lawsuit is lurking over the horizon.

If you don't form a partnership now, it someday may be too late to use one for asset protection, for reasons explained in the next chapter.

ESTATE PLANNING

A family limited partnership lets you make tax-exempt gifts without losing control of the wealth you give away. It also cuts the taxable value of those gifts.

Control

You might hesitate to make tax-saving gifts now because you want to continue managing your property or because you believe that the recipients are not yet ready to handle the property wisely. A family limited partnership, with you as general partner, resolves the dilemma.

Organize the partnership by contributing a small amount of property (stocks, bonds, cash, real estate, etc.) in exchange for your general partnership interest. Contribute additional, larger amounts in exchange for a limited partnership interest. Then give all or part of your limited partnership interest to your children or other family members.

The family members eventually will have the benefit of the property, but, as general partner, you will continue to manage it. And you can decide when family members shall receive spendable cash, by deciding when to make partnership distributions.

When you organize the partnership, make the interests transferable only with the consent of the general partner (you). Then no one can upset your plan by selling his interest to a third party.

---

[4] The partnership agreement should provide a penalty, such as an automatic dilution in a partner's interest, for failing to pay the required additional capital.

Less *Taxable* Value

Gift and estate tax is assessed on an asset's *fair market value*—the price an unrelated buyer would willingly pay for it. Because interests in a family limited partnership are illiquid (no matter how liquid the partnership's assets), and because the limited partners have no voice in management, the fair market value of such interests is less than the value of the partnership's assets.

The difference can be considerable—as much as 30% or more. This stretches the exemptions from gift and estate tax, letting you transfer more of your estate tax free. And it reduces tax on the rest of the estate. This is discussed more fully in Chapter 20, "Estate-Planning Strategies."

18

DEALING WITH TRUSTS AND PARTNERSHIPS

To thwart the dreams of litigants, your transfers of property to a trust or partnership must be free of legal defects. If someone wins a judgment against you and then demonstrates a flaw in your transfers, the court will set them aside—thereby making the property available to your judgment creditor.

In most cases, it is fairly simple to make your transfers unassailable—primarily by making them early, before any event that would inspire a claim against you. *Early* is important. When it is too late to do the job well, it may be too late to do it at all.

FRAUDULENT THIS, FRAUDULENT THAT

So powerful are trusts and partnerships that you may wonder how anyone ever collects on a court judgment. What prevents you from dumping your stocks, bonds and everything else into a family limited partnership if someone waves an IOU in your face or if you see you are about to lose a lawsuit? Or could you transfer your 1,000-acre farm to a trust for your grandchildren, reserving for yourself only "the first rose of summer," if you see the sheriff coming up the road to auction the place off? Such maneuvers have been tried, but they don't work.

All 50 states and most foreign jurisdictions have laws limiting the use of trusts and partnerships to frustrate creditors, especially judgment creditors.[1]

---

[1] Transfers to corporations in exchange for stock, gifts to individuals, and sales of property at bargain prices are subject to the same laws.

The legal doctrines, which go under such names as *fraudulent conveyance, fraudulent transfer;* or *fraudulent disposition,* share a common theme: a court may set aside a transfer made to frustrate creditors that existed or were reasonably foreseeable at the time of the transfer. But the rules differ considerably from state to state and from country to country—primarily in what is meant by "foreseeable."

To give an extreme example, suppose that, having been ordered to pay a $1-million judgment, you transfer all your property to a trust for the benefit of your children. In nearly any jurisdiction, including those where shoes are worn only on ceremonial occasions, the courts would call the transfer a fraudulent conveyance and would make the property available to your judgment creditor.

NOT CRIMINAL

Despite the name, in most jurisdictions *fraudulent conveyance* refers only to remedies that creditors may obtain through civil litigation—not to a crime. If you lose an argument about fraudulent conveyance, your creditors may take you to the cleaners, but they can't send you to jail.

However, there are exceptions. In some states a fraudulent conveyance may be a misdemeanor. You should ask your attorney about the rules in your state.

Elements of Fraudulent Conveyance

To attack your transfer to a trust or partnership, a creditor generally must persuade a court to answer "yes" to three questions.

■ When you made the transfer, did you owe the debt the creditor is pressing, or did you have reason to anticipate you would owe it, or had you promised to pay it if someone else failed to?

■ Did the transfer leave you unable to pay the debt when due?

- Did you make the transfer with the intention of hindering or defeating your creditor?[2]

Existing or Foreseeable Debt.   Whether you had a debt at the time of the transfer may be easy to answer, as in the extreme example given above. But other situations aren't nearly so clear.

Suppose that in year 1 you perform an apparently successful medical operation. In year 2 you transfer a substantial portion of your property to a trust. And in year 3 the patient begins to complain of chronic pain, wins a malpractice suit against you and is awarded damages. Should you have anticipated the debt? The answer may depend on which court you ask. In many jurisdictions it will depend on what the court believes you knew about the patient's condition when you established the trust.

Inability to Pay.   Immediately after the transfer, did your liabilities, including the debt in question, exceed your assets? It is easier than you might suspect to get an answer of "Yes," especially in the United States. In many jurisdictions, only assets that creditors can legally seize are taken into account. Property you had earlier placed in a trust or partnership and property that is exempt from creditors under local law (such as, in some states, your primary residence) might not count. And your debts may include liabilities that are only contingent, such as a loan guarantee you had signed.

Intention.   Whether you intended to hinder a creditor may be the trickiest question. Two factors that argue "yes" are (1) you had no other purpose for making the transfer, and (2) you received something of lesser value, or nothing at all, in exchange.

Which Creditors?

Fraudulent conveyance law protects two classes of creditors. Courts will set aside fraudulent transfers to allow those creditors to collect their due. A third class of creditors is not protected.

Present creditors are protected. A present creditor is anyone to whom you owe a debt at the time of a transfer, including:

---

[2] In many jurisdictions mere intent to frustrate a creditor is sufficient to make a transfer fraudulent. But as a practical matter it is difficult to prove such intent without also proving the debtor's insolvency and the existence or foreseeability of his debt at the time of the transfer.

- The holder of an IOU or guarantee you signed before the transfer.

- Someone who wins a court judgment for something you did before the transfer, even if the judgment isn't rendered until after the transfer.

Foreseeable creditors also are protected. A foreseeable creditor is anyone to whom you become indebted through circumstances foreseeable at the time of the transfer, including:

- A person whom you injure after the transfer, if, at the time of the transfer, you intended to begin acting recklessly. For example, suppose you hate your neighbor. If you transfer your assets to a trust and then burn down his house, your besooted victim will be a foreseeable creditor.

- Someone who cannot collect a debt you incurred after the transfer because the transfer made your assets unreasonably small, in light of the kind of business you were in (or intended to enter) at the time of the transfer. For example, suppose you transfer most of your assets to a trust shortly before entering the toxic waste disposal business. If someone gets sick because you left a microgram too much of PCB in his backyard, he may be a foreseeable creditor.

States and countries vary widely in whom they regard as a foreseeable creditor.

Courts in the United States, particularly in the more litigation-happy states, interpret "recklessness" and "unreasonably small assets" broadly—thereby increasing the ranks of foreseeable creditors. Many foreign countries, on the other hand, interpret these concepts narrowly, making it harder for a litigant to qualify as a foreseeable creditor.

A *potential creditor* is everyone else who eventually becomes your creditor. Assuming you are not carrying out a plan of reckless behavior, potential creditors include all the people you have not yet met or affected in any way but who one day may want to sue you. Potential creditors are not protected by fraudulent conveyance laws.

Because potential creditors are not protected, the transfer to a trust or partnership you make today cannot be undone because of something that happens tomorrow and is not related in any way to the transfer or to events prior to it.

Time Limit

Many states and countries observe a statute of limitations on claims of fraudulent conveyance. A creditor has a certain number of years after a transfer to begin a legal action to set it aside. If he misses the deadline, it's too late—no matter what.

PROTECTING TRANSFERS IN TRUST

Transfers to a trust require the most care, since you ordinarily don't receive full value in return for what you give the trust.[3]

- *Timing.*   The first rule is: *hurry up.* The sooner you establish a trust, the stronger it will be. A judgment creditor will find it far more difficult to attack a transfer you made ten years ago than a transfer you made last year.

- *Solvency.*   Don't transfer so much that you become insolvent. Retain enough property to cover all existing debts and any obligations you reasonably can foresee, and then add a margin for error.

- *Purpose.*   Find one or more purposes, aside from asset protection, for establishing the trust—such as obtaining professional investment management, assuring an orderly transfer of assets to your eventual heirs, facilitating international investing or cutting taxes.

- *Smile.*   Do nothing that suggests a plan to frustrate creditors. Don't simply drop your malpractice or other liability insurance after setting up a trust. Wait at least three years. Then reduce your coverage, if you wish, but don't eliminate it. And find some reason for the reduction other than the comfort the trust gives you. Perhaps you've been advised that you don't need so much coverage. Perhaps you like some feature of a different, smaller policy. Perhaps you are worried about your insurer's financial condition. Or perhaps you intend to cut back your business or professional practice.

- *Location.*   Choose the right state or country for your trust. A transfer invulnerable to attack in one place may be a sitting duck in another.

---

[3] The suggestions for protecting transfers to a trust from attack as a fraud upon creditors apply also to outright gifts.

The choice of jurisdiction is a matter on which you need expert legal advice. The advice should consider both your individual circumstances and the laws of various states and countries. If your attorney merely assumes your home state is the right jurisdiction, go to someone else for guidance on this critical question.

PROTECTING TRANSFERS TO PARTNERSHIPS

In many jurisdictions, courts are inclined to respect a transfer, despite the squeals of creditors, if you received "full and adequate consideration" in exchange for the property you gave up. Thus, compared to a transfer to a trust, a transfer to a partnership in exchange for a partnership interest of equivalent value is harder to attack.

Nonetheless, to achieve maximum safety, follow the same rules in making transfers to a partnership as you would in making transfers to a trust. The sooner a transfer is made, the better. Do not transfer so much that you are unable to satisfy existing debts or that you appear to be planning to frustrate likely future creditors. Organize your partnership to do something in addition to protecting assets. And organize it in a jurisdiction that respects transfers made by someone in your circumstances.

Extra Care

Even if you want to give partnership interests to family members, ask at least one person to make a founding contribution to the partnership's capital. This allows the partnership to survive even if your *gifts* of partnership interest later are set aside as fraudulent transfers. With the partnership intact and in possession of your assets, a creditor's only easy recourse would be to seek a charging order (as explained in Chapter 17, "Family Limited Partnerships").

EMPTYING THE CUPBOARD

A court is likely to respect your transfer to a trust or partnership if you retain enough assets to meet your existing and foreseeable debts. But this seems to conflict with the desire to minimize the wealth left exposed to possible lawsuits. The conflict is real, but it can be resolved.

Suppose you have liquid assets of $2 million, you have no substantial debts, and you want to protect all your wealth. You might transfer the entire $2 million to a trust for the benefit of yourself and your family. But if you later were involved in a car accident and lost a lawsuit, your judgment creditor would use your lack of assets to attack the trust. He would argue that your transfer to the trust was fraudulent because: (1) your driving is not merely bad, it is habitually reckless, (2) the transfer left you unable to meet obligations you should have known might arise from your reckless driving, and (3) transferring all your assets to a trust demonstrates an intention to frustrate creditors.

Step by Step

Your trust will be far safer if you give it only, say, $1 million. But that leaves the other $1 million exposed. So drive carefully for a few months, and then put $500,000 into a limited partnership consisting of yourself, the trust, other family members, and perhaps a trusted friend. That transfer is protected from attack by creditors because you receive full consideration in the form of a partnership interest and because it still leaves a substantial amount—$500,000—available to creditors.

Wait another year. Come to a complete stop at every STOP sign. Do not change lanes unnecessarily. Then make a long-term, deferred-payment sale of property worth $400,000 to an unrelated party—preferably a foreigner. The transaction is protected because it is a sale for full and adequate consideration and because it still leaves you solvent. But it turns your liquid assets into a deferred-payment contract—an unattractive prize for a litigant.

If the deferred-payment sale is to a foreign buyer, transfer the contract to a foreign trust in a country selected for the narrowness of its doctrine of fraudulent conveyance.

The three or four transactions spread out over three or four years will tie up all but $100,000 of your liquid assets. A potential litigant would expect you to spend that much on legal defense and on normal living expenses, leaving nothing to pay a judgment—and so would see little chance to profit by suing you.

You still should drive carefully.

LATE PLANNING

Timeliness is the strongest factor working to protect a transfer to a trust or partnership. What can you do if you regret having waited so long to devise a program of asset protection?

Ask a family member who does not face any threat of litigation to establish a trust that includes you both as a discretionary beneficiary and as the protector. Then enter into a partnership agreement with a corporation controlled by the trust. The corporation would be the general partner, and you would contribute much of your assets in exchange for a limited partnership interest. Invite other family members and an unrelated friend to contribute small amounts of capital as limited partners.

This structure should present a serious barrier to anyone contemplating a lawsuit against you. He can't attack your relative's transfer to the trust, because your relative doesn't owe him anything. The integrity of the partnership is protected by the involvement of the other limited partners. And your transfer to the limited partnership is protected by your receipt of a limited partnership interest in exchange.

However, this late-planning strategy is not so much a solution as it is a battle plan. It gives you a fighting chance and strengthens your position to negotiate a settlement—so it is far better than nothing. But in the end it may fail, depending on your particular situation and on your creditor's skill and fervor.

The only true security is to act early, before there is a specific threat. Treat asset protection as you would fire insurance. Get it before you smell even a whiff of smoke. ⚿

PART FIVE

ESTATE PLANNING

There is more to life than avoiding estate tax. On the other hand, you probably wouldn't enjoy an out-of-body experience if it involved watching your children pay huge sums of money to the government.

To the extent your estate exceeds $600,000, it will be subject to tax at rates from 37% to 55%. For a married couple planning their estates together, the threshold of taxation is $1.2 million.

This part explains the basic rules of gift and estate tax and explores a short list of strategies for protecting your family from grave robbers. Additional strategies, needed only for large estates, are covered in Part 8.

19

GIFT AND ESTATE TAX RULES

When you die, your soul leaves your body and turns into your taxable estate. Everything you have accumulated after a lifetime of paying income tax is subject to estate tax at rates up to 55%. And with the generation-skipping tax, property you leave to your grandchildren may be taxed at rates up to 80%.

The next chapter explores specific strategies for preventing such a financial catastrophe. But first we need to examine the estate tax rules themselves, since they tell you how to save your estate from being taxed.

Learning the bare rules is necessary, but it's not too exciting. So if you like to drink coffee, I suggest you treat yourself right now.

But only one cup. To save you from getting bogged down, this chapter skips material you'll need only if your net worth exceeds $1 million ($2 million for a married couple). You can find that material, if you do need it, in Part 8.

TOPIC 1: GIFT TAX

Making gifts during your lifetime can reduce estate tax. So we'll start by looking at the gift tax rules.

Your gifts of money or anything else are subject to tax. You are the one responsible for paying the tax, not the person who receives the gift.

The tax rates on gifts are graduated: the more you give, the higher the rate. But the rate schedule doesn't apply to each gift separately. It applies to the total gifts you make during your lifetime. Thus the tax on what you give away this year depends on how much you gave away in all past years.

The government allows you a lifetime credit ($192,800) against gift tax. The credit "pays" all the tax that, according to the IRS rate schedule, would be due on your first $600,000 of *taxable* gifts—an important figure to remember. The effective gift tax rates, after allowing for your lifetime credit, are shown in the following table.

Effective Gift Tax Rates (After Allowing for Lifetime Credit)

Total of Lifetime Gifts, Not Counting Exempt Gifts	Tax Rate
First $600,000	No tax
Additional amounts, up to $750,000	37%
Additional amounts, up to $1,000,000	39%
Additional amounts, up to $1,250,000	41%
Additional amounts, up to $1,500,000	43%
Additional amounts, up to $2,000,000	45%
Additional amounts, up to $2,500,000	49%
Additional amounts, up to $3,000,000	53%
Amounts above $3,000,000	55%

Notice the first two lines and the last line. Until your "taxable" gifts exceed $600,000, there is no actual tax. Beyond that amount, gifts are taxed at 37% or higher. Gifts above $3 million are taxed at the maximum rate of 55%. But exempt gifts, explained below, aren't counted.

Payment of Gift Tax

Gift tax is payable yearly. You must file a gift tax return for any year in which you make a gift that does not qualify for an exemption, even if no tax is due. The return must be filed by April 15 of the following year.

EXEMPT GIFTS

Some gifts are exempt from tax. There is no absolute limit to the amount of exempt gifts you can make, and *they do not count against the $600,000* you can give away tax free with your lifetime credit.

$10,000 Annual Exemptions

The most important exemption is the *annual exemption,* which allows you to make tax-free gifts of up to $10,000 per year to as many people as you wish. If you have three children, for example, you can give $10,000 per year to each of them, or a total of $30,000 per year, all tax free. And your spouse can give each of them another $10,000, for a joint total of $60,000 per year.

With your consent, your spouse can use any portion of your annual exemptions that you don't. To continue the example, if you give a total of $20,000 to your three children, your spouse can give them $40,000—for the same $60,000 joint total.

A gift needn't be to your children to be exempt. The annual exemption is available for gifts to any individual—including parents, grandchildren, godchildren, friends, neighbors, bimbos and complete strangers. But the gift must be to a specific, natural (flesh-and-blood) person. Gifts to partnerships or corporations don't qualify.[1]

Can your gift to a trust for a particular individual qualify for an annual exemption? It can, if the beneficiary has the right, at the time the gift is made, to withdraw it from the trust (called a "Crummey" provision, named after taxpayer D. Clifford Crummey). A gift in trust for a minor can qualify for the annual exemption if he is permitted to withdraw the property and any accumulations of income on his twenty-first birthday.[2]

It is the annual exemption that lets you give Christmas presents without filing a gift tax return.

Other Exemptions

Also exempt from gift tax and not counted toward the $600,000 you can give away tax free are:

- Gifts you make to your spouse
- Gifts you make to charitable organizations
- Tuition you pay directly to a student's school
- Medical expenses you pay directly to a patient's doctor or hospital.

---

[1] To qualify for an annual exemption, the thing given must be a *present interest,* which is the right to possess or enjoy property *now,* such as outright ownership of property or an income interest beginning now.

[2] A gift in trust is a present interest (see preceding footnote) only if the beneficiary has the right to withdraw the gift from the trust.

INCOMPLETE GIFTS

Only *completed* gifts are subject to tax.

A gift is *incomplete* if you can undo it or change the recipient. No tax is due. Features that make a gift incomplete include:

- Retaining the right to have the property returned to you eventually
- Retaining the right to name additional people to share in the gift
- In the case of stock in a closely held corporation, retaining the right to exercise the stock's voting power
- In the case of life insurance, retaining the right to borrow on the policy, withdraw its cash value, or change the beneficiaries

A special rule applies to gifts of life insurance. Even if you give away a life insurance policy entirely, retaining no rights or powers whatsoever, the gift will be incomplete if you die within three years.

Income a beneficiary receives from an incomplete gift—such as dividends from shares of stock you can take back—represents a completed gift, which could be subject to gift tax.

TOPIC 2: ESTATE TAX

Estate tax is based on the value of your estate's assets as of the date of your death. Alternatively, the executor can choose to value the assets (all of them) as of a date exactly six months later, if that yields a lower estate tax.

Your taxable estate includes the gross value of everything you own at the time of death—such as your house, your investments, your interests in a business, your share of a pension plan and your 50% share of any community property.

Deductions

Certain items are deducted in calculating your net taxable estate. They include:

- Debts payable by the estate, including your personal debts
- Income taxes paid by the estate on its own income

- Expenses of settling the estate
- Bequests to your spouse
- Bequests to charities

There is no limit on the deduction for bequests to your spouse (called the *marital deduction*). Thus if you leave everything to your spouse, there generally will be no tax on your estate.[3]

ESTATE TAX CALCULATION

Your taxable estate is the *total* of:

- the net value of the estate (the assets described above, minus the deductions described above),
- the completed gifts you made during your lifetime, but excluding exempt gifts (such as gifts to your spouse and gifts subject to the annual exemption), and
- any gift tax you paid.

Your estate is taxed on this total at the rates shown in the table on page 000—the same tax rates that apply to gifts. But the estate receives a credit for all the gift tax you paid during your lifetime.

Payment of Estate Tax

Your executor has primary responsibility for paying the estate tax.

An executor is the person legally empowered by a state probate court to pay the estate's debts and distribute the rest to the heirs. He may be the individual (or institution) requested in your will, a person requested by a member of your family, or a person selected at the initiative of the court—such as a county political hack.

The executor is responsible to the probate court for distributing your assets properly, and he must deal with complaints from anyone who feels

---

[3]If you bequeath an income interest to your spouse but provide that someone else eventually will receive the property generating the income (for your spouse, a *terminable interest*), the bequest won't qualify for the marital deduction, unless it is *qualified terminable interest property* (QTIP). Property held in trust is QTIP if *(a)* your spouse has the right to receive all the income or a fixed portion of the value of the trust property each year, and *(b)* no one else can receive distributions from the trust during your spouse's lifetime.

YOUR RESPONSIBILITY

As a prospective dead person, you have no obligation to maintain records that would assist your executor in identifying and valuing the property you have left.

slighted by your will. In addition, he is responsible to the U.S. government for filing an estate tax return and paying the correct tax.

If the executor distributes assets to the heirs without reserving enough to pay the tax, the government can require any heir to use everything he received from the estate to pay the *entire* amount of the tax deficiency and any interest due on it.[4]

Apart from the possibility of an estate being settled improperly, an heir does not personally pay federal estate tax.

TOPIC 3: FREEDOM DAY FOR CAPITAL GAINS

With a maximum estate tax rate of 55%, dying can be the most expensive trip you ever take. But in some circumstances it results in an overall tax savings.

When you sell an asset, the taxable gain is the difference between the selling price and the asset's *basis*. For most assets, *your* basis is the same as your original cost. (In the case of a depreciable asset, such as a building, your basis is reduced by all depreciation deductions you have taken.)

Your *estate's* basis for an asset generally is its fair market value on the date of your death (as declared on the estate tax return). The basis will be the value as of six months later, if the estate elects the alternative valuation date. Thus when assets that appreciated during your lifetime pass to your estate, the potential liability for capital gain tax is, in effect, forgiven.

For example, if you buy IBM stock at $50 per share and die when the price is $75, the basis of the stock is reset to $75. The estate could sell the

---

[4] If one heir is forced to pay more than his share of the tax, he can sue the other heirs to recover, out of their inheritance, their share of the tax not paid by the executor. But he still won't like what has happened to him.

stock for $75 without paying capital gain tax. Or if the estate distributes the stock to your heirs, they receive it with a basis of $75—and so could sell it without capital gain tax.

The resetting of basis applies to *both halves* of any community property you own. Thus, in a community property state, the basis of the 50% of community property that already belonged to the surviving spouse also is reset.

The rule on resetting of basis is rich with opportunity and significance.[5]

- Investing in appreciating assets rather than income-earning assets doesn't just defer income tax. It can eliminate the tax— since the potential liability for capital gain tax evaporates at the end of your lifetime.

- Highly appreciated assets are the last choice to give to your prospective heirs late in your life, since you would be removing the assets from the operation of the resetting-of-basis rule.

- Highly appreciated assets are the last choice to sell late in life. Instead, look first to assets with little or no appreciation if you need to raise cash.

- If you expect your taxable estate to be less than $600,000, hold on to highly appreciated assets even if you could remove them from your estate with exempt gifts—so your heirs won't have to pay capital gain tax.

Deferred Income

The resetting of basis generally does not apply to assets that represent ordinary income you earned but didn't collect during your lifetime. Such assets include pension rights, deferred annuities, amounts due from deferred-payment sales, and stock in certain types of foreign corporations (explained in Appendix B). However, the person who eventually collects the income (the estate or an heir) receives an income tax deduction for the estate tax attributable to it.

---

[5] The resetting of basis is often referred to as a *step-up*—although it also can result in a decrease in basis.

TOPIC 4: VALUATION

In principle, an asset's value for gift, estate, and generation-skipping tax is its fair market value—the price a willing buyer and a willing seller would agree upon, "neither being under any compulsion to buy or sell and both having a reasonable knowledge of all relevant facts." The asset's actual value to your estate or heirs doesn't matter.

As you might imagine, estate executors and IRS agents sometimes disagree about an asset's fair market value. If the dispute can't be settled by argument and negotiation, it is settled in Tax Court—often with testimony from contending appraisers recruited by the estate and the IRS. The IRS's valuation is presumed to be correct. It is up to the estate to prove otherwise.

Devaluation

Much estate planning consists of reducing the "fair market value" of your assets with packaging that makes them temporarily unattractive to most potential buyers—but without altering their actual value to you, your heirs or other beneficiaries. A family limited partnership, discussed in Chapter 17, is one example. Other devices, likely to be useful only if your net worth exceeds $1 million ($2 million for a married couple), are discussed in Part 8.

TOPIC 5: DRASTIC MEASURES

Since gifts to a spouse are exempt, could someone avoid estate tax by marrying his own child or grandchild? No one knows. But if the top estate tax rate stays at 55%, I suspect we are going to find out. The day may come that you read about the proceedings of the Tax Court in the *National Enquirer*.

While we're waiting for the news, you should consider using some of the less lurid strategies explained in Chapters 20 and 32. ⌐

20

ESTATE-PLANNING STRATEGIES

Estate planning lets *you* determine who benefits from your property. If you don't plan, the government will help itself to as much as it wants.

And you can do more for your heirs than just trim your estate's tax bill—although that's a great kindness in itself. A thorough plan also helps your heirs protect and nurture what you leave them. It gives *them* opportunities to avoid tax on the income you've deferred, to shelter their own income, and to protect themselves from lawsuits. Thus a thorough plan leaves assets *plus* the means to safeguard them.

Attitudes toward estate planning vary widely. Some people want "to be buried by the county," meaning they want to spend everything themselves, leaving no estate at all. Others hope to leave a large estate for their children or other heirs. Most fall somewhere in between. They would like their remaining assets to reach their heirs intact, but they don't want estate planning to get in the way of their own enjoyment of what they've accumulated.

I'll assume you share this middle attitude. We'll look only at strategies that entail little cost or inconvenience. In other words, we'll look for advantages you can give your heirs almost "for free." Fortunately the strategies that do so may be sufficient even if you place great importance on leaving a large estate.

COMPETING GOALS

Estate planning would be easy if nothing else mattered. But, of course, other things are important—some of them much more important—and your estate plan mustn't get in their way. So before we examine specific estate-planning techniques, let's look at the constraints—the goals that won't yield to the goal of reducing estate tax.

Budget Constraint

You obviously do not wish to give away so much that you create financial problems for yourself. It's one thing to plan to die broke. It's something else to be broke years too soon.

Even if you are cautious, there are ways this unwelcome result might creep up on you.

Investment Failure. If the investments you plan to live on lose value, produce less income than expected or fail to keep up with inflation, you will regret having given so much away.

Higher Expenses. Unforeseen problems may add to your expenses. If today you live comfortably on $100,000 per year, tomorrow you might need much more—if, for example, you become severely or chronically ill. You don't want to give away capital you might later need to dip into.

Longevity. Another hazard is being too healthy, so that you live much longer than expected. You can, for many years, spend a little more than your investments are earning—but not forever. Unless you hold on to enough of your assets, long life will be a hard blessing.

The need to provide adequately and certainly for your own welfare is the "budget constraint." No estate plan will be acceptable if it puts your own security at risk.

Management Constraint

Even if you can give generously without endangering your own comfort and security, there still may be reasons to hold back. You might suspect that a recipient would waste the money you give him or lose it to creditors or a wily spouse. Or you might be concerned that a gift could subvert the recipient's ambition or sense of responsibility. It is a rare grandparent who wants to pay for his eighteen-year-old grandson to tour America on a $40,000 motorcycle.

Or you might worry that some prospective heir someday will be especially needy. By holding back on gifts now, you conserve your ability to rescue whoever turns out to need rescuing. Or you might simply enjoy running your own affairs—and believe the entire family will be better off if you continue to do so.

The desire to control the wealth destined for others is the "management constraint." No estate plan will be acceptable if it deprives you of the management power you want.

Satisfying the Constraints

Exactly how you satisfy the two constraints—making sure you don't give away too much too soon and retaining sufficient control over your wealth—must wait until Chapter 29, "A Plan for Asset Protection and Tax Savings." But it's important to notice the constraints now, so you can evaluate each estate-planning device for its practicality. The devices covered in this and later chapters are not just for people with money to burn. They are for investors who watch every nickel.

INSTRUMENTS

What follows is a description of eight instruments for disinheriting the estate tax collector. Five additional instruments, useful only for large estates, can be found in Chapter 32. But with just the devices in this chapter, most investors can do most of the job.

EXEMPT GIFTS

The simplest, most straightforward way to reduce estate tax is to make exempt gifts of cash or other property. If you have, say, three children and six grandchildren, the $10,000 annual exemption allows you and your spouse to give them a total of $180,000 per year without gift tax—thereby reducing your taxable estate by at least the same $180,000.

If no planning constraint is holding you back, start giving. You can't save up exemptions—each year's opportunity is lost if you don't use it by December 31. The exemptions for tuition and medical expenses also go to waste if you don't use them when you have the chance.

NONEXEMPT (TAXABLE) GIFTS

There seems to be no hurry about using the lifetime credit (which covers the tax on your first $600,000 of nonexempt gifts and bequests), since your estate can use any portion you don't.

But there are reasons not to dawdle. The value of what you don't give away today may double or triple by the time the estate tax collector notices it. So by giving now, you keep the gift's future earnings and appreciation out of your taxable estate.

And the lifetime credit is no more permanent than any other feature of the law. Congress could reduce it at any time, or eliminate it. What now seems like an opportunity you can exploit at your convenience would disappear.

FAMILY LIMITED PARTNERSHIP

With little effort or inconvenience, a properly structured partnership shrinks the fair market value of the assets you put into it—thereby reducing their gift tax value, if you give them away, or their taxable value for your estate, if you keep them. (Family limited partnerships were discussed in Chapter 17.)

To start, simply form the partnership and transfer property to it. You needn't make any substantial gifts of limited partnership interest until you are ready.

But when you decide to make a gift, a limited partnership interest can be the perfect thing to give. As general partner, you control the partnership's assets and determine when the recipient actually receives spendable cash. And giving a partnership interest lets you pack more real wealth into a $10,000 annual exemption—since, as explained below, the gift tax value of a partnership's interest may be much less than its real value.

You can slice limited partnership interests as thick or as thin as you like. You can give a limited partnership interest in a single, large gift or in a series of small gifts. And you can make the gift in trust, if you wish.

Credible Shrinking Value

To depress the fair market value of interests in a family limited partnership—and thereby reduce their value for gift and estate tax purposes—the partnership agreement should provide that:

- The general partner decides when distributions will be made.

- Partnership interests may not be transferred except with the consent of the general partner and a majority of the limited partners.

- Each partner has a right of first refusal to purchase any partnership interest any other partner offers for sale.

These provisions may reduce the value of a limited partnership interest by as much as 30%, compared with the partnership's assets. The discount applies because, for an outsider, owning the limited partnership interest would be far less desirable than directly owning the investments the partnership holds.

Imagine how you would appraise an interest in a limited partnership with such provisions if you were simply a willing buyer, unrelated to the general partner.

- You would have no control over how the partnership is managed.

- Being an outsider, your wishes would be of no importance to the other partners.

- The interest—unlike the investments the partnership may own—is not readily marketable. You can't simply call a broker and sell; you would have to search for a buyer.

- If you attempt to sell to another outsider, each of the existing partners has the right to match any offer you receive—which leaves potential buyers with little incentive to make an offer.

To protect the discount for estate tax purposes, the partnership must be able to continue after your death without the consent of the estate. Accordingly, the partnership agreement should provide for the installation of a new general partner whenever needed. The new general partner can be named in the partnership agreement or, if the estate will own less than a majority of the limited partnership interest, can be a person elected by the limited partners.

GIFTS IN TRUST

Making a gift in trust, rather than directly to the beneficiary, assures that the money or other property will be invested the way you want and will be used for the purposes you have in mind. It also protects the gift from the beneficiaries' creditors and may create a vehicle for the beneficiaries to shelter their other assets through transactions such as those described in Chapter 18, "Dealing with Trusts and Partnerships."

Bonus Gift

Placing a gift into a *grantor* trust allows you to make an additional gift without any additional gift tax. The extra gift is your payment, under the grantor trust rules, of income tax the beneficiaries otherwise would pay. (The grantor trust rules are explained in Chapter 16, "Trusts.")

Include provisions in the trust declaration, such as a power to purchase insurance on your life, that make the trust a grantor trust. Since the trust's income therefore will be taxable to you, distributions will be income tax free to the beneficiaries.

This strategy may remind you of a nasty-tasting vegetable someone once insisted was good for you. But in fact it is sweet. It can leave both you and your beneficiaries wealthier—because it leaves the tax collector poorer.

Putting a gift in a grantor trust does not mean requesting a large income tax bill, since you can continue to manage the trust's investments for tax deferral. It means only that the income tax bill, however much it is, goes to you rather than to your beneficiaries. The size of the bill isn't affected.

If this still seems like more generosity than you care to practice, reduce the amount to place in trust to offset your expected income taxes. The beneficiary will receive the same amount of wealth, after income tax, as he would from a direct gift—but the size of the gift, for gift tax purposes, will be less.

Making gifts by paying the recipient's income tax bill also eases your estate-planning budget constraint, because you can slip away from the income tax liability if you ever need to. Simply retain the right to revoke the provisions of the trust declaration (such as the power to buy insurance on your life) that make the trust a grantor trust. This gives you the ability to convert the trust to a taxable trust at any time by actually revoking those provisions.

Exempt Gifts in Trust

A gift in trust can qualify for a $10,000 annual exemption from gift tax if it is subject to a Crummey provision allowing a particular beneficiary a fixed period, such as 60 days, to remove the gift from the trust. Beneficiaries seldom yield to the temptation to take the money and run, since most understand that doing so might discourage further gifts.

You can't make an exempt gift in trust and also retain the income tax liability for the property. The beneficiary who declines to withdraw the gift—not you—will be treated as the grantor for income tax purposes.

LIFETIME ANNUITIES

A lifetime annuity is a promise to pay you a fixed amount of money each year for the rest of your life.

Buying a lifetime annuity effectively removes the purchase price from your taxable estate, since the annuity ends with your death. The annuity also helps satisfy your budget constraint (increasing the amount you can give away without imperiling your standard of living), because it provides an income you can't outlive.

A lifetime annuity will pay you a higher yearly income than, say, high-grade bonds, because the issuer will have no obligation to return your capital if you are short-lived. An old investor can receive much more from an annuity than from a bond investment.

Commercial Annuities

The simplest way to buy a lifetime annuity is from an insurance company in the United States.

Such an annuity has two potential disadvantages, however. First, a portion of each annuity payment is taxable income. Thus your income tax bill *may* be higher than if you had bought some other fixed-dollar investment. Second, finding the right annuity may require some shopping, as explained in Chapter 11, "Deferred Annuities."

Despite the potential disadvantages, a lifetime annuity from an insurance company may be a good choice if you acquire it by converting a tax-deferred annuity with substantial accumulated earnings—since conversion allows tax deferral on money left in the annuity to continue.

SPOUSAL BEQUESTS

Bequests by one spouse to another are effectively exempt from estate tax. This allows the estate plan of one spouse to piggyback on the estate plan

MORE STRATEGIES

Additional estate-planning strategies, which you may need if your net worth exceeds $1 million (or $2 million for a married couple), are explained in Part 8, "Planning for Large Estates."

of the other. The estate of the first spouse to die escapes tax simply by being left to the second.

Piggybacking can buy time to devise and execute an effective estate plan for the assets left to the second spouse. The surviving spouse has more years to find untaxed avenues for transferring wealth to the next generation—perhaps using some of the devices discussed in this chapter or in Chapter 32.

Spousal bequests are the estate-planning device of last resort. If you can't devise a better plan, or if you don't have time left to execute it, leave your taxable wealth to your spouse. When you are gone, the horse may speak clearly to your spouse, even if it only whinnied at you. ⚏

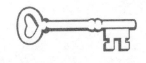

PART SIX

TAX AND
PRIVACY HAVENS

While most modern governments take a predatory attitude toward business, a few consider *themselves* to be businesses. The service they sell is safety—safety from taxes, safety from lawsuits and safety from prying eyes.

A government that operates such a business is called a *tax haven* or a *privacy haven*. Its customers are people from outside the country who can't find enough safety at home. The haven government earns money by charging them fees for establishing companies and trusts—and then leaves them alone.

This part explains how you can become a customer of a tax or privacy haven.

21

INTRODUCTION TO HAVENS

More than a dozen countries have no income tax. The best known to Americans are Bermuda, the Bahamas and the Cayman Islands. Other countries, such as Hong Kong and British Virgin Islands, tax the income of local businesses but not of investors. If you somehow could divert your investment profits to a tax haven and away from your U.S. tax return, the money could accumulate and compound tax free.

It's a nice idea, and it can be made to work. But it's far from simple. As we'll see in this and later chapters, the government has done an energetic—but imperfect—job of blocking the opportunities for you to use tax havens.

As a U.S. citizen or resident, you are taxed on your worldwide income. Just leaving profits in a foreign account won't cut your tax bill. To avoid U.S. tax, some entity, such as a corporation or trust, must stand between you and the income. However, merely putting investments in a foreign corporation or trust isn't sufficient either. The foreign entity will reduce your tax bill only in certain circumstances and only if it operates in certain ways.

Why There Are Tax Havens

Some governments believe they can collect more revenue by attracting foreign investors than by levying high taxes.

Immense wealth is controlled by individuals and corporations that are financially mobile. Tax havens attract that money by offering a better deal than its owners can find elsewhere—a 0% corporate tax rate in the Bahamas, for example, versus a 40% rate in the United States or a 33% rate in the United Kingdom. With low or zero tax rates, haven governments hope to earn a large volume of registration fees and other incidental charges.

OTHER HAVEN BENEFITS

Tax havens offer more than just tax relief. Their governments, being businesses, know that additional services—such as secrecy and asset safety—bring in additional customers and higher revenue.

In the United States your bank and other financial records are no more private than the color of your eyes. The government has ready access to those records, and few of the companies you deal with try to keep the details of your financial life from anyone.

But in many countries, including some that aren't tax havens, financial institutions consider privacy a duty. Some European countries, notably Switzerland and Austria, have laws to reinforce bank secrecy; not even the government can breach it without first persuading a court that it needs bank records to prosecute a crime or uncover loot.

Some havens take financial privacy a step further and use it as a marketing tool. They promise that no one—certainly not your own government—need know you are a customer.

With a numbered account, for example, records available to clerical personnel are identified by number only. Your name is not shown. Only a handful of senior bank officers have access to a directory linking your account number to your name.

If you wish to operate through a corporation, a local attorney can be the *nominal* owner of your stock. His name appears as the owner of record, while you remain the true, but invisible, owner. Or you can own a corporation through bearer shares, which are the property of whoever possesses them.

Of course, havens are not equally adept at fulfilling the promise of financial privacy. Bermuda has no bank secrecy statute, yet it is one of the most reliably silent havens. Panama has the world's strictest secrecy laws—and a reputation for leaks, especially during invasions.

Asset Safety

Territoriality is a legal concept honored in most tax and privacy havens. It means local courts don't accept the official acts and decisions of foreign governments at face value or heed complaints arising from events in other countries. Territoriality is a great comfort if you fear your assets might be seized by your own government—whether through lawsuits, reckless tax collection or otherwise.

No haven observes territoriality absolutely. Generally, if a foreign government demonstrates to the haven government that a serious crime has been committed, and if the foreign government properly follows all local legal procedures, the haven government probably will force a local bank to hand over records and hidden assets. But the matter must be grave—kidnapping, for example, or drug smuggling or embezzlement on a grand scale. The evidence must be compelling. And the culprit's guilt must be too embarrassingly obvious for the haven government to overlook. Bodily injury suits by whiplash victims don't count for much, nor do charges of tax evasion.

TAXERS FIGHT BACK

Most governments look upon tax havens as a costly annoyance and apply antiavoidance laws to prevent their citizens from using havens. The measures differ considerably from country to country, but nearly all impose withholding on income paid to foreign investors. A few countries, including the United States, tax their citizens on income earned by corporations in which they own stock or earned by tax haven trusts to which they have transferred property.

WITHHOLDING

The economies of most tax havens are too small to absorb much capital, so money that reaches a tax haven seldom stays there for long. It moves on to Europe, the United States or another high-tax area—perhaps returning to its country of origin. If you deposit money in a tax haven bank or buy shares in a tax haven mutual fund, the bank or fund may invest your money in London, Zurich, Tokyo or New York.

U.S. Withholding

Understanding the U.S. withholding rules is an important first step in laying out a tax haven strategy. The shape of the withholding system identifies the kinds of income you can route from the United States to a haven without leakage to taxes.

The United States generally withholds 30% of any investment income (interest, dividends, rents, royalties and annuities) paid to a foreigner—

including foreign individuals, foreign corporations, foreign trusts and foreign partnerships.[1]

But there are exceptions—big ones. The government allows them to enable the United States to compete as a world financial center, to permit American companies and the government itself to borrow abroad, and to accommodate industries that are politically influential. Under the exceptions, there is no U.S. withholding on:

- Interest on deposits at banks and savings and loans

- Interest on deposits with insurance companies

- Interest on U.S. Treasury bills

- Interest on corporate and U.S. Treasury bonds issued after July 18, 1984[2]

- Capital gains on stocks, stock options, commodities and futures contracts—and on almost everything else except real estate

- Life insurance death benefits

Dividends and income from pensions and annuities paid to a foreign person *are* subject to 30% withholding.

Withholding by Foreign Countries

Foreign withholding systems generally are more elaborate than the U.S. system. Most apply different rates to different types of income—distinguishing, for example, between interest and royalties or between dividends paid by closely held corporations and dividends paid by public corporations. Here is the usual pattern.

- Dividends are subject to the highest withholding rates, generally 25% to 35%.

- Interest on bank deposits is subject to low or zero rates.

---

[1] Anyone in the United States (whether an individual or an institution) who makes a payment of investment income to someone outside the United States is a *paying agent*. It is the paying agent who is obligated to withhold the 30% and remit it to the U.S. Treasury.

[2] The bonds must be in registered form, and the recipient of the interest must certify that the bonds are not being held on behalf of a U.S. taxpayer.

TAX TREATIES

Tax treaties between the United States and foreign countries reduce or eliminate withholding on certain types of payments. For example, under the treaty with the United Kingdom, there is no withholding on interest paid by a borrower in the United States to a lender in the United Kingdom, or vice versa.

There also are numerous tax treaties between foreign countries, to which the United States is not a party. Most are between high-tax countries. Few reduce withholding on income paid directly to tax haven trusts or corporations.

Treaty Shopping

The web of tax treaties, the variety of withholding systems and the different rates applied to different types of income have led to "treaty shopping."

If a tax haven corporation wants to invest in a business in a high-tax country, it may use a chain of corporations running through countries selected for the particular wrinkles in their tax treaties. As income passes from link to link, its character may change along with its location. Rent turns into royalties, then into dividends and then into interest. At the end of the chain, the well-traveled income builds up tax free in the haven.

Treaty shopping is very clever, but very complicated. None of the strategies explained in this book requires it.

Refunds and Credits

You may benefit from a U.S. tax treaty if you invest in a foreign country. As a U.S. taxpayer, you may be entitled to a reduction in withholding on dividends, interest or other income.

If you invest directly in a foreign country and lose money to withholding at a rate higher than called for by its tax treaty with the United States, you can apply to the foreign government for a refund. And you can claim a tax credit on your U.S. return for any amount not refundable, so that you are not taxed twice.

If you invest in the United States through a foreign bank, broker, or trust and lose money to U.S. withholding, you can claim a tax credit for the full amount on your U.S. return.

- Interest on bonds may be subject to withholding at a rate that may be high or low.

- Capital gains on stocks, stock options, bonds, commodities and futures contracts are exempt.

- Life insurance proceeds are exempt.

- Annuity income might be exempt; if not, the rate probably is the same as for interest on bonds.

No Withholding on Many Investments

Not every investment can easily escape withholding. But the variety of investments that can is very wide—wide enough to let you execute almost any investment strategy from a tax haven without loss to withholding.

What is not free of withholding in one market may be in another—such as New York, London, Zurich, Hong Kong, Singapore or Jersey (Channel Islands). For example, bond interest paid by Swiss companies is subject to 35% withholding. But Swiss franc bonds also are issued in Luxembourg, which doesn't withhold on interest. Annuity income paid to foreign investors by U.S. companies is subject to 30% withholding, but there is no withholding on annuities paid by Swiss insurance companies to non-Swiss investors.

The investment hit hardest by withholding is stocks. All major countries withhold on dividends that public companies pay to foreign shareholders. However, an offshore corporation or trust can avoid the tax by investing in mutual funds and redeeming its shares each year just before dividend day or by buying call options on stocks or futures contracts on stock market indices.

BEYOND WITHHOLDING

Unlike most countries, the United States goes far beyond mere withholding to take the fun out of tax havens. The United States seeks to tax the entire worldwide income—direct and indirect—of its citizens and residents. Among the more astounding features of the U.S. system are:

- If you own stock in a foreign corporation, you may be taxed on your share of the corporation's income, even though you receive no dividends.

- If you place assets in a foreign trust, you may be taxed on the trust's income, even if you have no right *ever* to receive anything from the trust or to determine who does.

- If you invest in a foreign mutual fund, special taxes may consume your entire profit.

- In some cases, you may be required to file *monthly* information returns on tax haven activities.

These and other extraordinary features of U.S. tax law have gone a long way to discourage Americans from using tax havens. But the rules are not the primary deterrent. Far stronger is the anxiety of dealing with the un-familiar.

Escaping Fear

In all things, it is familiarity that puts you at ease. If you're comfortable with your local bank, it's not because you've blocked every possibility for the bank to cheat you, and it's not because you know all the ins and outs of commercial law in your state. You're at ease because you've been doing business with the bank for many years, you understand how it operates, nothing especially bad has happened so far, and you know the bank has a reputation to protect.

The farther you go from home, the less familiar things become, and the more cautious you grow. When you move to a new town, you are a bit more watchful of the local merchants. You have no reason to suspect them of being less honest or less reliable than the merchants you left behind. It's simply that you don't know them. But in time the anxiety subsides. You haven't learned anything remarkable about the stores in your new town, but after buying the sixth pair of socks from the local haberdasher, you stop worrying.

When you move to a new town, familiarity with the local merchants eventually is unavoidable. But nothing in your day-to-day life forces you to deal with banks, brokers or trustees in countries thousands of miles away— so you never do get acquainted.

Even though there are safe, lawful ways for you to benefit from tax havens, worry over the unfamiliar may deter you and keep your money at home, paying taxes. The unmatchable benefits of tax havens will never be more than a pipe dream unless you acquire enough knowledge about the tax rules on foreign investments and acquire sufficient familiarity with at least one tax haven to give yourself the confidence to act. The next six chapters will give you a strong start and show you how to move on from there. ⚷

22

FOREIGN
FINANCIAL
SERVICES

Later chapters explain how a foreign trust can protect your assets and reduce your taxes, and how it now has become *practical* for many investors to establish such a trust. But, even though foreign trusts can be far easier and cheaper than they used to be, they still demand an extra measure of effort and planning. The benefits, while big, come at the price of some complexity.

This chapter shows what you can achieve easily, by using off-the-shelf financial services provided by financial institutions outside the United States. All you need to know is that the services are available and where to get them.

FOREIGN BANK ACCOUNTS

If you could take just one step to protect your assets, it should be to open an account at a foreign bank.

The mere fact the account is foreign will work powerfully to make it private. A foreign bank won't ask for your Social Security number, won't respond to inquiries about you from U.S. credit-rating services, won't make reports on your account to the U.S. government, and won't contribute information about you to any U.S. data bank. Thus, someone sizing you up for a lawsuit could easily overlook your foreign account.

And even if your foreign account were public knowledge, it still would be protected by its foreignness. Enforcing a judgment against you outside the United States would be troublesome, expensive and time consuming—

and in some countries impossible. And the time consumed might permit you to take further steps to protect the assets—if only by moving them to another, more private location.

A foreign account also protects you against a lightning strike by government agencies. A variety of laws enable the IRS and other federal agencies to seize your property, without warning, merely on a suspicion. In principle, you can recover your property (eventually) by suing the government. But you would need money to hire a lawyer, which would be impossible if the government had taken everything. A foreign account lets you escape such a trap.

Opening an account at a foreign bank can be as simple as any other bank-by-mail arrangement, although it may seem exotic at first.

Types of Accounts

Foreign banks generally distinguish between two types of accounts: fiduciary accounts and deposit accounts. The distinction can affect your privacy.

A *fiduciary account* holds stocks, bonds or other investments for which the bank acts as your agent—buying and storing the investments for you. It also may be called a *custodial* or *safekeeping account.*

A *deposit account,* on the other hand, represents something the bank owes you. It is a claim against the bank's assets—a checking or savings account, for example.

Some investments can be handled by either type of account. For example, a metals claim account, which represents the bank's obligation to deliver so many ounces of gold or silver whenever you ask for it, is a deposit account. But if you buy physical gold or silver at a foreign bank and leave it there, you have a fiduciary account.

Assets in a fiduciary account may be held in bulk custody or in segregated storage. If your gold is in bulk custody, the bank maintains just one "pile" of gold for all its customers, noting in its books how much (to a thousandth of an ounce) each customer owns.

With segregated storage, on the other hand, each bar or coin is earmarked as the property of a particular customer. The bank can place into your hands the particular bars or coins you own. Of course, this limits you to discrete quantities—such as one-kilogram (32.15 ounces) bars of gold, one-ounce gold coins, or 1,000-ounce bars of silver.

Credit Cards

Banks all over the world issue VISA and MasterCard credit cards. A foreign-issued card can be a handy tool for financial privacy.

Every bank that issues you a credit card maintains a permanent record of your transactions, but there is no other centralized record. So a credit card from a bank in a privacy haven can be used privately in the United States. Even if someone eavesdrops on a merchant requesting authorization for your purchase, you personally will go unnoticed—since the authorization message refers only to an account number, not to a name.

Some offshore banks will issue a credit card without investigating your credit if you deposit money or establish an investment account and pledge it to assure payment of your credit card bills. The card will look just like a credit card from a U.S. bank.

Privacy with ATM Cards

You can get an ATM (automated teller machine) card on the same terms. A foreign-issued ATM card is a safe, private way to bring money back into the United States. You can use the card to withdraw cash from ATMs anywhere in the United States (or anywhere in the world). This is even more private than using a foreign-issued credit card, since ATMs don't ask for a signature.

Having a foreign-issued credit card or ATM card does not, by itself, obligate you to make reports to the IRS. However, you might have to report the deposit or investment account that secures the card (see below), and you definitely must report any taxable income the account generates.

Other Services

In many countries, particularly in tax or privacy havens, banks provide a wider range of services than banks in the United States. Virtually any type of financial or finance-related service—including securities trading, commodities, insurance and accounting—can be obtained directly from a haven bank or from a source the bank will refer you to.

U.S. REPORTING

How you use a foreign bank depends on whether you want to avoid reporting your account to the U.S. government. If strict privacy is a goal, you will have to limit your use of foreign banks.

Reportable Accounts

You are required to indicate on your U.S. tax return whether you have more than $10,000 in *foreign financial accounts,* which are financial accounts at a foreign bank, securities or commodities broker or depository. This leaves three ways to use a foreign bank lawfully without reporting the existence of an account.

- Keep an account with less than $10,000, simply to open a foreign window—in case you someday want to transfer more in a hurry.

- Use a foreign account to send large amounts of money to purchase nonreportable investments outside the bank, taking care never to let the bank account balance exceed $10,000.

- Keep investments at a foreign bank that are not "financial accounts."

Black and White

Some things clearly constitute a foreign financial account and would be reportable. Other things clearly are not. Still others are in a gray area—light gray.

A checking or savings account at a foreign bank is clearly reportable if the balance goes over $10,000. Similarly, if the bank buys more than $10,000 worth of stocks or bonds for you and holds them in its name (a fiduciary account with bulk custody), your account is reportable.

On the other hand, suppose you visit a Swiss bank and leave your wallet behind. Calling the bank to ask it to take care of the wallet until you return won't create a "financial account," because the bank won't owe you the wallet or the money it holds. The bank will owe you only a duty of safekeeping, as it does for investments held in segregated custody. And what you own will still be a wallet—not an account.

The same argument applies to other types of assets. If a bank purchases something for you, takes delivery of it and holds it in segregated custody— you own the thing itself, not an account representing the thing.

By this line of reasoning, you can own gold, silver, other precious metals and bearer securities in segregated storage at a foreign bank without having to report a foreign financial account. You also can invest in stocks and bonds in registered form without creating a reportable account if the bank takes delivery of actual certificates and endorses them in blank (effectively converting them to bearer instruments) and earmarks them as your property.

GETTING MONEY THERE

The privacy of a foreign investment depends on how you get the money out of the United States. Even if your foreign account is not reportable, you may have to compromise your privacy—unless you transfer money to the foreign bank in a way that is lawfully silent.

Currency Reporting

You are required to report any export of currency or bearer instruments with a value of more than $10,000. (*Bearer instruments* are anything that is effectively the property of whoever holds it—such as checks payable to cash, unsigned travelers checks, bearer bonds and stock and bond certificates endorsed in blank. They don't include personal, company or cashier's checks with a named payee.)

Private Transfers

The simplest way to send money to a foreign bank is to write a personal check. But that isn't very private.

The first place a curious person will look for information about you is at your bank, where copies of your canceled checks are kept. Writing a personal check to Swiss Friendly Bank is only slightly more private than advertising your plans in the local newspaper.

Buying a cashier's check will increase your privacy a little. Even if you pay for the cashier's check with a personal check, a curious person would have to sort through your checking account records, notice you had written a check to your bank or for cash, and then look through the bank's records of cashier's checks to discover you had sent money to a foreign bank. And you can make things more difficult for him by buying the cashier's check at a different bank from where you keep your checking account.

Traveler's checks will give you still more privacy, especially if you buy them from more than one bank. However, when a traveler's check eventually is returned to the issuer, it will show the endorsement of your foreign bank. Thus a determined effort could trace your money.

But the effort would have to be considerable. First, the investigator must look through your personal bank records for checks that could have been used to purchase travelers checks—which would include every check made out to "cash." Then he'd have to track down every traveler's check you bought to determine what, if anything, had gone to a foreign bank. It's a big project, one that might take him to the microfilm readers of banks in half a dozen cities.

If you are suspected of being a nuclear spy, someone will go to this trouble. Otherwise, it's not likely anyone will.

No Trail

To approach an absolute assurance of privacy, you need to break the paper trail between you and the foreign bank by using actual cash at some point. For example, you could withdraw small amounts of cash from your bank account from time to time and buy cashier's checks or traveler's checks at another bank, where you don't have an account.

Whether you'll want to depends on how important secrecy is to you and on how much money you want to send. Moving $50,000 or $100,000 to a very secret foreign account is a chore, but it's not impractical. But if you want to send, say, $1 million, you may decide that handling 200 cashier's checks is too much trouble.

Two-Step

Another way to break the paper trail is to use two foreign banks.

First, send money to Bank #1 by the least conspicuous means you find convenient—even a wire transfer. Then visit Bank #1 and withdraw the money in cash. Carry it to Bank #2 and make a deposit.

Obviously, you'd want to do this only in a good neighborhood, such as Switzerland. But for large amounts it is the most practical, lawful way to break the paper trail.

If you would not be comfortable carrying cash from bank to bank, buy a cashier's check from Bank #1 and take it to Bank #2. This doesn't break the paper trail, but places a section of it in a privacy haven.

Cooperation

In any country where it is safe to do business, a bank will want to know who you are. If you are sending large amounts, it will want to be satisfied that the source of the money is legitimate—especially if you are sending it by means that are hard to trace. The bank may ask you for a letter of reference from your attorney, accountant or local banker (which may be addressed "To

Whom It May Concern"). If you provide this comfort, the bank will cooperate in almost any lawful plan to transmit money.

CASH REPORTS

If you want to use cash to break the paper trail between you and your foreign bank, be aware that your U.S. bank is required to report any cash withdrawal in excess of $10,000 or that is "unusually large."[1] No one knows what "unusually large" means, so you should assume any withdrawal over $5,000 will be reported.

Also, don't abruptly begin making withdrawals of even $5,000. Start with small amounts, taking six months to a year to let the withdrawal size grow to $5,000 or so. Let your local bank tellers wonder whether you are developing an expensive vice.

Structuring

There now is a federal law against *structuring*, which is a crime for which you can be fined or imprisoned.

Structuring consists of breaking a single transaction into pieces small enough to avoid the $10,000 reporting threshold. For example, suppose you owe someone $16,000, due on a certain date. If you buy a cashier's check with $8,000 in cash at one bank and buy another $8,000 cashier's check for cash at a second bank, and then use the two checks to pay your debt, you have illegally "structured" the transaction. You could be prosecuted and sent to jail, even if the transaction is completely innocent—even if you are giving the money to Mother Teresa or paying a tax bill.

Making a series of small cash payments or withdrawals that add up to more than $10,000 is structuring only if some single transaction ties them together. Using money orders or cashier's checks purchased for cash to make a series of unrelated deposits would not be structuring.

LIFE INSURANCE AND ANNUITIES

Life insurance and annuities issued by foreign insurance companies have the same tax advantages as policies issued by U.S. companies: tax-free

---

[1] Certain types of businesses are exempt from the cash reporting rules.

compounding of earnings and, in the case of life insurance, tax-free payments to beneficiaries.

A policy issued by a foreign company has the additional advantage of being private, especially if you buy it in a country where financial privacy is the norm. And, because an insurance policy isn't a "financial account," you can put as much as you like into foreign life insurance and annuities without mentioning the policies in your tax return.

You can pay the premiums in the same way you would send money to a foreign bank account.[2] For maximum privacy use small, nonreportable money orders or cashier's checks bought with cash. But in that case select a policy with a periodic premium below $10,000, to avoid any suggestion of "structuring."

Considering how simple it is to buy a life insurance policy or a deferred annuity, the tax and privacy benefits are remarkable. You should consider this alternative closely if you find the benefits of a foreign trust attractive but you don't like the complications.

You also can use foreign life insurance and annuities to fund a foreign trust for your heirs, without ever having to report the trust. Make a trust the beneficiary of your foreign life insurance or annuity, but don't transfer *any* property to it during your lifetime—so that the trust will not be reportable. Eventually the proceeds of the policy will be paid silently and invisibly to the trust.

You can use a foreign annuity to fund a pension plan. If the annuity is properly structured (see Chapter 29, "A Plan for Asset Protection and Tax Savings"), it can be distributed by the plan directly to you without disturbing the pension plan's tax deferral. And, if you have established a foreign trust for your heirs, you can make the trust the secondary beneficiary of the annuity, so that anything you don't collect during your lifetime will flow to the trust without U.S. income tax.

OFFSHORE MUTUAL FUNDS

Some tax haven mutual funds never pay dividends. Instead, they accumulate all their income and profits, adding them to the redemption value of investors' shares. There's no tax to pay until you redeem or otherwise dispose of your shares.

---

[2] Or you can first let money accumulate in a non-interest-earning foreign bank account (up to $10,000, so as not to be reportable), and then pay the premiums from the account.

However, the tax rules on passive foreign investment companies (PFICs) explained in Appendix B generally make these funds useless for U.S. investors—except for one purpose.

You can put away shares in a foreign mutual fund for the day of some extreme emergency—when tax rules might not be an overriding concern. Until that day (if it ever comes), your investment can build up value without current income tax. You must report the fact that you own stock in a particular PFIC by filing Form 8621 with your income tax return each year. But you don't need to disclose the size of your holdings until you receive a dividend or dispose of the stock.

DEFERRED-PAYMENT SALES

A deferred-payment sale can compound interest income free of current tax. But, as a practical matter, you must find a buyer that itself is not subject to income tax—such as a company in a tax haven. It is not necessary for the tax haven company to want the thing you are selling, provided it has a convenient way to promptly resell the property.

A foreign bank can facilitate a deferred-payment sale in two ways. First, it can hold the collateral you would want the deferred-payment buyer to pledge. Second, it can provide the deferred-payment buyer—probably a corporation managed by the bank for another of its customers.

CHOICE OF HAVEN

Your choice of haven country will depend primarily on what you want—privacy, tax savings, investment flexibility, or other benefits.

But you should disregard some countries entirely, regardless of their apparent advantages. Some would-be havens are riven by deep social conflicts that threaten their political stability. In some countries bank secrecy is only a legal fiction, and in some others, banks will accept money from anyone, including Long John Silver. Sending your money to any of these countries would undermine your safety, not add to it.

The following sections describe five important havens.

SWITZERLAND

Swiss banks combine services comparable to those of a U.S. commercial bank and an internationally minded stockbroker. You can deposit money in U.S. dollars, Swiss francs and a variety of other currencies; invest in stocks, bonds and commodities traded in Switzerland, the United States, or anywhere else; and buy, store and sell gold, silver and other precious metals.

"Swiss bank" is a cliché for privacy and financial conservatism—a cliché that happens to be true.

Swiss Safety

Switzerland is a healthy place for banks. It is politically stable, due to the character of the people and a long-standing attitude of live and let live among the country's cultural groups. And Switzerland's mountainous terrain and policy of well-armed neutrality make it the haven least likely to be attacked by anyone.

A spirit of caution rules the banking system. While Swiss law strictly regulates bank capital and lending policies, there is no government insurance program for bank deposits—nothing similar to FDIC coverage. As a result, Swiss depositors pay much closer attention to their bank's financial condition than do depositors in a U.S. bank.

Banks in Switzerland compete to present a picture of safety by maintaining a higher ratio of capital to deposits than required by law and by favoring secured, short-term loans they can liquidate whenever they need cash to repay depositors. A Swiss bank that operated like an ordinary American savings and loan would quickly lose its depositors—and its officers might go to jail.

Swiss Privacy

Swiss banks are private. As a matter of long tradition and of law, any account at a Swiss bank is a secret account. It is a crime for any employee of a Swiss bank to disclose information about a depositor to anyone outside the bank or even to reveal the existence of someone's account. Not even a Swiss government agency can get information about an account without a court order, which it can obtain only by satisfying the court that a crime has been committed and that there is reason to believe a particular account is involved. A Swiss court won't permit a fishing expedition.

A foreign government seeking information about an account would first need to persuade the Swiss government that it could satisfy those same conditions. Then the Swiss government, if it wished to cooperate, would attempt to get a court order. The Swiss government would cooperate only if the incident under investigation were a crime under Swiss law.

In Switzerland nearly all tax litigation is handled in the *civil* courts. If the Swiss government believes additional tax is due, it sues the taxpayer. Thus most of the tax questions that are criminal matters in the United States have no criminal flavor at all in Switzerland. The only tax crime is actual fraud, such as submitting counterfeit documents to the tax collector—the only kind of tax matter Swiss bank secrecy doesn't protect.

Court orders to breach Swiss secrecy also are issued for nontax crimes, such as robbery or extortion. If you are looting entire countries, buying and selling dope by the boatload or piling up megamillions through insider trading, the Swiss courts will help the U.S. government find and seize the fruits of your enterprise. But if you are using a Swiss bank account simply to protect what you have earned honestly, the Swiss courts will respect your privacy.

Swiss Taxes

Switzerland is a premier haven for investors seeking safety and privacy, but it's not a tax haven. Swiss banks are required to withhold 35% of all interest and dividends paid by Swiss companies and banks.

Tax treaties reduce the effective withholding rate, however. U.S. investors may apply to the Swiss government for a refund of 30 of the 35% withheld on interest and dividends, which reduces the effective withholding rate to 5%. But when you apply for a refund, *you* are revealing information about your bank account, and there is no guarantee the Swiss government won't make the information available to the U.S. government.

The 5% not refundable by the Swiss government can be claimed as a deduction or credit, as you elect, when you prepare your U.S. tax return.

Some types of income avoid Swiss tax. There is no Swiss withholding on payments to foreigners arising from Swiss life insurance or annuities or from non-Swiss investments held through a Swiss bank. And foreign investors pay no tax on capital gains.

With its high tax rates, Switzerland usually is not a suitable place for a corporation or trust. In addition, because the Swiss legal system is not based on English common law, your U.S. attorney couldn't give you much help in using a Swiss corporation or trust.

Names and addresses of Swiss banks that welcome U.S. investors and that will accept accounts by mail can be found in Chapter 35, "Where to Get Help."

AUSTRIA

Austria also is a stable, politically neutral country with a strong tradition of bank secrecy—and a low profile. While it's difficult to say "Switzerland" without suggesting hidden money, "Austria" calls up thoughts of rich pastries and old-world culture. Receiving mail from Austria doesn't hint at your interest in financial privacy, as receiving mail from Switzerland might.

Austrian banks do not provide the wide range of services available in Switzerland, but they do offer deposit accounts in Austrian schillings (a currency with a history of low inflation), U.S. dollars, and other currencies. The withholding rate on bank interest is 10%—which, under the U.S.-Austrian tax treaty, you can recover by applying to the Austrian government.

Names and addresses of Austrian banks that welcome U.S. investors and that will accept accounts by mail can be found in Chapter 35, "Where to Get Help."

ATLANTIC AND CARIBBEAN AREA

Three tax and privacy havens lie closer to home. They are tax havens because they have no income taxes and no estate taxes that apply to nonresidents. Names and addresses of haven banks appear in Chapter 35.

Bermuda

Bermuda is a two-hour plane ride from Atlanta, Baltimore, or New York. There is no tax or withholding on the income of individuals, corporations or trusts in Bermuda. The estate tax applies only to Bermuda residents.

The banking system in Bermuda is a closed shop. There are only three banks, and new ones are not welcome. Bermudian banks provide all the services of a Swiss bank, but their specialties are corporate and trust services. If you want to establish a foreign trust, the bank will be your trustee. If you want to set up a foreign corporation, the bank will handle the legal formalities and even provide local directors.

Of all the pure tax havens, Bermuda has the highest reputation for honesty and fair dealing. And Bermudian banks are somewhat fussy about whom they do business with. If you want to do anything more than open a small account, the bank will want to know who you are. The banks are scrupulous about avoiding drug dealers, embezzlers and other types you would want to keep out of your own neighborhood.

Bermuda's "clean hands" policy is to your advantage. If your tax haven dealings come to light, they are less likely to raise a suspicion of illegality if they are tied to Bermuda than if tied to certain other havens.

While there is no bank secrecy statute in Bermuda, there is in fact bank secrecy. It is enforced by common law, by long tradition and by the desire of the government and the banks to maintain Bermuda as a financial center.

Bermuda law has a narrow doctrine of fraudulent transfer. A creditor frustrated by your gifts or other transfers of property will get little help from a Bermuda court unless your debt was clearly in existence or foreseeable at the time of the transfers he is seeking to set aside. This makes Bermuda an attractive place for a trust.

And if you enjoy tennis, golf, boating, fishing, clean air, clear water, pink sand, white roofs, floral abundance or good manners, Bermuda is an excellent place to visit.

Bahamas

The Bahamas are the closest tax haven—just 50 miles off the coast of Florida and a 35-minute plane ride from Miami. The Bahamas impose no tax or withholding on any type of income.

The banking industry is highly competitive. Many international banks have offices in the Bahamas, and they offer a wide range of investment, corporate and trust services.

Because it's so close to the United States, the Bahamas are an especially desirable base for an international business or for any investment activity that requires frequent visits from the United States. An international bank with an office in the Bahamas can transmit your money privately to a bank in Switzerland or elsewhere.

Cayman Islands

The Cayman Islands are located in the Caribbean, about 450 miles south of Florida. They are a one-and-one-half-hour plane ride from Miami and a two-hour plane ride from Atlanta. As with Bermuda and the Bahamas, there is no tax or withholding on any kind of income. Bank secrecy is observed both by law and in practice.

The Cayman Islands are an attractive location for a protective trust. To attack a transfer to a trust, a creditor must prove you knew of his claim when you made the transfer and that you *intended* to defraud him. In addition, there is a six-year statute of limitations. A legal action to set aside a transfer for the benefit of a creditor *must* begin within six years following the transfer.

The Cayman government welcomes new banks. Many international banks, including some with no offices in the United States, have set up shop there. A full array of banking and other financial services is available, and vigorous competition keeps the costs of forming and maintaining trusts and corporations lower than in Bermuda.

The atmosphere in the Caymans is less formal than in Bermuda, and, depending on where you live, airline connections can be easier. ⚷

23

FOREIGN TRUSTS— A QUICK TOUR OF THE KING'S CASTLE

Foreign trusts are the king's castle of financial safety—stronger than family limited partnerships and stronger than any trust you can set up at your local bank.

In the right circumstances, and used properly, a foreign trust gives you:

- *Asset protection.* A foreign trust lawfully places assets beyond the reach of all potential creditors—even beyond the reach of government agencies. No matter what happens at home, trust assets will be available for you and your family. Withdrawing money when you need it can be as simple and private as using a credit card or getting tax-free cash from an ATM. The level of safety is very high, and it is not difficult to achieve.

- *Financial privacy.* If you set up the trust in a privacy haven, no unauthorized person will be able to get information from the trustee. A zone of privacy will surround the trust—a zone you can extend anywhere in the world, even into the United States.

- *Income tax savings.* If you select a trustee that will manage the trust with an eye to tax consequences, the trust can reduce your income tax liability.

- *Estate-planning advantages.* The safety and income tax advantages free you to make lifetime gifts to family members and to make wealth-shifting transactions that chip away at your *taxable* estate. And you can put your foreign trust on the receiving end of those transactions.

- *Big income tax savings for generations to come.*   After your lifetime, the trust automatically disconnects from the U.S. tax system. Your beneficiaries have no tax liability for earnings the trust
  accumulates.

- *Financial-planning advantages for your heirs.*   The trust itself
  (apart from the assets it contains) can be a financial-planning
  instrument of incomparable power for future generations—none of
  whom will have any obligation to file tax returns or other reports on
  the trust's activities. They can use it to protect their own assets and
  reduce their own tax bills. And, unlike property you leave in your
  will, property you leave in the trust need never again be subject to
  estate tax.

- *A friend in need.*   Whenever called for, the trust can use its accumulated assets to help you and your family—perhaps sending
  money tax free or as a long-term capital gain. It is an "International
  Red Cross" dedicated to the security and welfare of you and yours.

A foreign trust can be a king's castle of protection precisely because it
is *foreign.* The money you send to a properly structured foreign trust leaves
"the system" that governs all your other assets.

Perfect Companion

A foreign trust works smoothly with other financial-planning devices—
and even increases their effectiveness.

If you have a *family limited partnership,* a foreign trust can be a limited
partner or own a corporation that serves as a general partner.

If you have a *family business* corporation, a foreign trust can protect it by
owning some or all of the stock.

If you have a *living trust,* it can receive money from the foreign trust
when you need it or send money to the foreign trust after your lifetime.

If your will calls for property to be held in *trust for your heirs,* a foreign
trust will give them the greatest benefit.

Your foreign trust can collect any portion of your qualified *pension plan
or IRA* you don't spend in your lifetime—and rescue the money from income
taxation.

You can leave the trust any *assets you have held privately* outside the
United States without compromising that privacy.

PROTECTIVE FOREIGN TRUST

Foreign trust is a broad umbrella. It covers any kind of trust established outside the United States for any purpose. However, our concerns are narrower—safety and tax savings. So, from here on, we'll assume the following about your trust—which we'll call a *Protective Foreign Trust.*

■ *Governing law.* The Trust is governed by the laws of a particular foreign country—one that does not tax income.

■ *Trustee.* The trustee is a bank or trust company located in the same foreign country, where it administers the Trust. The trustee is independent—that is, not under your control.

■ *Grantor.* You are the grantor—the person who transfers property to the Trust.

■ *Beneficiaries.* The beneficiaries are you and anyone else you care to provide for, such as your children and further descendants—including, if you want, descendants not yet born. You also can include charitable beneficiaries.

■ *Discretionary (sprinkle) trust.* No beneficiary has a fixed interest in the Trust, such as the right to receive a fixed share of its income or capital. Instead, the trustee—in consultation with the Protector (see below)—has wide discretion in apportioning benefits among the beneficiaries. With the advice of the Protector, the trustee determines who gets what and when. However, the trustee in any event must give preference to your personal financial needs, to whatever extent you cannot satisfy them from other sources.

■ *Divisible trust.* After your lifetime, the trustee can set aside portions of the Trust for particular groups of beneficiaries. For example, if you have included your three children and all further descendants as beneficiaries, the trustee could split the Trust into three parts—each part for a particular child and all his or her descendants.

■ *Indirect benefits.* The trustee can help the beneficiaries by indirect means, not just by distributing money to them. The trustee can, for example, have the trust buy a house for a beneficiary to live in, hire a doctor or a lawyer for a beneficiary, or pay a beneficiary's credit card or other bills. And the trustee can lend Trust money to a beneficiary or invest in a beneficiary's business.

- *Protector.* You are Protector of the Trust for life or until you resign. You may name a successor, who will serve on the same terms.

   As Protector, you can consult with the trustee on all Trust affairs, including investments, distributions, indirect benefits and dividing the Trust. The trustee is authorized to rely upon the information you give to it. And as Protector you can fire and replace the trustee if you aren't satisfied with its performance.

- *Retained powers.* As grantor, you retain the power to remove beneficiaries and to add charitable beneficiaries.

- *Term.* The trust is irrevocable, and it can continue for many years beyond your lifetime.

Giving extensive discretion to the trustee may seem hazardous—like handing money to a stranger and hoping for the best. But, as we'll see, that isn't what discretion means. Instead, the trustee's discretionary authority enhances the Trust's power to protect your assets and reduce taxes for succeeding generations.

U.S. TAX RULES

We'll examine the relevant U.S. tax rules in chapters 25 and 26. Here is a brief preview.

Income Tax

Trust's Income. During your lifetime, the Trust is a grantor trust. *You,* not it, are taxed on its income—as though you still own the Trust's investments. This seems to make income tax savings impossible—but it doesn't, as Chapter 25 will make clear.

After your lifetime, the Trust still will be free of U.S. tax, provided it avoids certain types of investments tied to the United States, and no one will be taxable on income the Trust accumulates.

Trust Distributions. During your lifetime, distributions from the Trust are tax free for you and other beneficiaries.

A distribution will be taxable to a beneficiary only if it represents income the Trust earned after your lifetime. Any other distribution—from assets you originally placed in trust, trust earnings during your lifetime or tax-exempt income—will be tax free. Certain benefits the trustee confers on beneficiaries indirectly, without making a distribution, also will be tax free.

If a distribution to a beneficiary is taxable, the tax will carry an "interest" charge of 6% per year, based on the number of years after your lifetime that the Trust held on to the money before distributing it. The interest charge can be avoided with simple planning.

Gift and Estate Tax

Transfers you make to the Trust during your lifetime are "incomplete" for gift tax purposes. You pay no gift tax on the transfer. Distributions the Trust makes during your lifetime to beneficiaries other than you or your spouse are subject to gift tax to the same extent as if you had made the gifts directly.

The Trust's assets will be included in your taxable estate, just as though you still owned them. Thus establishing the Trust, as described so far, has no gift or estate tax consequences for you.

However, you can take certain steps (explained in Chapter 26) to make a small portion of what you transfer to the Trust a completed, taxable gift. Doing so would push that portion out of your taxable estate and turn it into a powerful estate-planning tool.

Excise Tax

When you die, your estate *may* have to pay an excise tax if you have transferred a deferred annuity, deferred-payment contract or other asset representing deferred income to the Trust. But no such tax is due during your lifetime.

WEALTH EXITS HERE

A Protective Foreign Trust lets your wealth emigrate, while you stay home. By transferring assets to the Trust, you place them under the laws and the courts of the country you choose—and remove them from the laws and the courts of the United States. Thus a Protective Foreign Trust enhances

LIVING TRUSTS

A living trust is a popular way to shelter assets from the cost and publicity of probate court and authorize someone close to you to manage your personal affairs if you become incapacitated. But it doesn't provide the tax-planning advantages or asset protection of a Protective Foreign Trust. On the other hand, a Protective Foreign Trust doesn't allow a friend, relative or local bank to act as trustee.

Fortunately, you don't have to choose between a living trust and a Protective Foreign Trust. You can easily coordinate the two and have the advantages of both.

Step 1. Include yourself as a beneficiary of the Protective Foreign Trust and authorize the trustee to distribute money to your living trust—to be used for your benefit. Then, if you ever become incapacitated, the trustee of your living trust can request transfers from the Protective Foreign Trust and use the funds for your support.

Step 2. Make the Protective Foreign Trust a beneficiary of your living trust. You can do this when you establish the living trust, or you can amend the living trust you already have. At the end of your lifetime, the assets of the living trust will pour into the Protective Foreign Trust.

your freedom as well as your safety. Every dollar you send to the Trust is a dollar that cannot be taken hostage by any agency of your home government to compel your obedience.

To be free, read on. 🔑

24

ASSET PROTECTION WITH A FOREIGN TRUST

A Protective Foreign Trust has all the protective power of a domestic trust—and much more.

By selecting the right country for your Trust, you embrace laws that are friendly to people who want to keep what they earn. You adopt a legal system that is hostile to adventurous litigants. And you place your property under the jurisdiction of courts that revere the stability of the law, thereby escaping courts that delight in testing novel legal theories. In other words, you get what no longer is assured in the United States.

And with a Protective Foreign Trust, you get a foreign trustee. It can do what no domestic trustee would dare: it can say "No" to the demands of U.S. courts and agencies.

Using a Protective Foreign Trust to shield assets from lawsuits is wonderfully straightforward. There are no complicated tricks to learn. All that's needed is to notice the obvious: the Trust is *foreign*. It is subject to the courts of the country *you* choose, not to U.S. courts.

EASY REQUIREMENTS

For full protection, your Protective Foreign Trust should:

- Be located in a country that welcomes investors who want to safeguard their assets
- Be governed by a trust declaration that frustrates potential creditors
- Avoid holding assets in its name in the United States

If you satisfy these conditions—which isn't difficult—no potential future creditor can ever get its hands on Trust assets.

You also can achieve important tax advantages with a Protective Foreign Trust, as discussed in the next three chapters. But, if you want to, you can set the complexities of tax planning aside and use a Protective Foreign Trust simply for asset safety.

COUNTRY

The Trust should be organized in a country with a well-established body of trust law. In practice, that means a country with a common-law (English) legal system. And the country should have a strong sense of territoriality, so that its courts will not automatically accept the findings and enforce the judgments of courts outside the country.

The country's fraudulent transfer laws should be limited both in principle and in fact. Where a trust is involved, they should protect only creditors whose claims arise from events or circumstances preceding the grantor's transfer to the trust.

Chapter 22, "Foreign Financial Services," offered some suggestions for choosing a country. Chapter 35, "Where to Get Help," identifies specific trust companies.

LOCATION OF ASSETS

The safety of Trust assets depends on where they are located. The trustee's stomach for the job of protecting them may depend on where the trustee's own assets are located.

Trust Assets

A U.S. court might permit your creditor to seize the Trust's U.S. assets—if he can find any. To reduce this threat:

■ The Trust shouldn't hold anything in the United States that it can easily hold elsewhere. Precious metals, foreign currency investments and foreign stocks are conveniently acquired and held outside the United States.

■ The Trust shouldn't register publicly traded investments in the United States in its own name. Instead, stocks and bonds of U.S.

issuers should be registered in the name of the trustee—or, better yet, the trustee should hold them through another foreign bank.

- If the Trust owns real estate or a business in the United States, it should do so through a limited partnership or other company. If the Trust ever comes under attack in the United States, the holding company can liquidate the real estate or business and distribute the proceeds to the Trust.

Trustee's Assets

A creditor might ask a U.S. court to pressure the trustee by threatening to seize assets of the trustee's U.S. subsidiary or other related U.S. company. U.S. courts almost always say "No" to such requests, since saying "Yes" in any but the most extraordinary situations would disqualify the United States as an international financial center. But the risk of indirect pressure on the trustee is worth considering, especially since a Protective Foreign Trust is intended to continue for many years.

Your trustee may be conscientious, but it does not want to be a martyr. You should assume that if your trustee were squeezed by the U.S. government, it might want to abandon you. It may be tempted to look for some grounds, acceptable under the law of its own country, to wriggle out of its obligations to your Trust. If it doesn't find a way out for itself, you are safe. But it may try, in order to save its sister company's U.S. assets.

The possibility, however remote, that your foreign trustee someday might yield to pressure from the U.S. government is an additional reason to include a flight clause (allowing the trust to move to another country) in the trust declaration. And when you are selecting a trustee, you should favor institutions that do most of their business outside the United States.

TRUST DECLARATION

The standard provisions of a Protective Foreign Trust were explained in the preceding chapter. The provisions that are important for protecting against lawsuits are:

- The Trust is governed by the laws of a specific foreign country.

- The Trust is discretionary, i.e., the trustee decides which beneficiaries get what, and when—although your personal needs come first.

- The trustee has the authority to confer benefits indirectly—for example, by investing in a beneficiary's business.

- You (or your successor as Protector) have the right to monitor the trustee and to replace it.

TRUSTEE'S DISCRETION

It is essential that you not possess any power over the Trust that a court or anyone else could force you to use against your will. If, for example, you had the right to demand a distribution from the Trust, a court could compel you to exercise that right—and then order you to pay the money to a judgment creditor.

The trustee's discretion closes the door on such coercion. If a court subjects you to an onerous judgment, the trustee can suspend direct distributions to you (money that might be seized) until the judgment ceases to be a threat.

In the meantime, the trustee still can help you—by, for example, paying your credit card and other bills. And the trustee could make distributions to other beneficiaries, such as your spouse, who could spend the money for your benefit.

The trustee's authority to suspend distributions, and its authority to benefit you indirectly, would help you wait out any judgment creditor who hopes to get paid from Trust assets. Sooner or later, the judgment creditor probably would be willing to accept a modest settlement. And knowing in advance that only a modest reward is possible, anyone contemplating a lawsuit would wonder whether it was worth the effort.

The trustee's discretionary power also protects the other beneficiaries. Since no beneficiary owns an ascertainable interest in the Trust, no beneficiary can be forced to assign his interest to a creditor—whether a creditor who has won a lawsuit against him, a tax collector or someone threatening to break his legs.

Meaning of Discretion

The trustee's discretionary power doesn't allow it to act at its own pleasure or convenience or for its own profit or other advantage. The trustee's discretion is *only* the authority to do things for the purposes of the trust—i.e., for the welfare of the beneficiaries. It is not a license to act arbitrarily or out of whim. On the contrary, the trustee is obligated to use its discretion responsibly, and it *must* exercise its discretion when it would be unreasonable not to. Thus for a trustee, discretion is duty. And the duty is enforceable by law.

Reinforcement

The trustee's discretionary authority is the heart of the Trust's power to protect. Additional provisions in the trust declaration can reinforce that power.

Postponement.   The trustee should be allowed to delay payments that otherwise would be due to a beneficiary to prevent the beneficiary's creditors from seizing the money. If the trustee knows your creditors are waiting at your mailbox for a check from the Trust, they will have a long wait.

Spendthrift Clause.   The trust declaration should contain a *spendthrift clause,* which obligates the trustee to disregard any instruction from a beneficiary to pay money due him to a third party. The clause is so named because it protects imprudent beneficiaries from squandering future benefits. It also protects beneficiaries from being forced to transfer their rights to creditors.

Flight Clause.   The trust declaration should contain a *flight clause* that permits the Trust to move to another country. There the Trust would be administered by a new trustee and governed by the laws of its new country. Authority to trigger the flight clause could be held by the trustee and/or by you as Protector.

A flight clause protects the Trust against unforeseeable changes in the country where the Trust is established. It also discourages any creditor of the grantor or of a beneficiary from attacking the Trust. A creditor would know that if he approached success—perhaps after years of expensive litigation—the Trust could disappear to another haven in an instant.

PROTECTOR'S POWER

It is the trustee's discretion that keeps the Trust safe. But it is the Protector's powers that make it safe to give the trustee so much discretion.

You, as Protector, can consult with the trustee on *any* matter relating to the Trust, including investment decisions and distributions to beneficiaries.

The trustee is authorized to rely upon the information and advice you give it. Thus following your advice is the trustee's easiest and safest path—provided, of course, you don't suggest anything unreasonable or that otherwise would violate the trust declaration.

As Protector, you can force the trustee to resign in favor of another trustee if you ever find its performance unsatisfactory. Since the trustee's business is to earn trustee fees, it ordinarily wants to avoid being replaced. Thus you can expect the trustee to weigh your advice carefully and give full consideration to your recommendations.

You have the power to appoint your own successor as Protector—who in turn will have the power to appoint his own successor.

Protecting the Protector

Your powers as Protector should be carefully crafted to insulate you from pressure or coercion—especially from court orders.

The trust declaration should authorize the Protector to act *only* out of his own free will, so that any action he attempts to take while under duress would be void. Thus you could not be forced to appoint a new trustee, such as a bank in the United States, that would follow the orders of a U.S. court.

PRIVACY

A Protective Foreign Trust establishes a zone of privacy—but during your lifetime the zone will have some leaks.

Income Tax Reporting

When you set up the Trust, you are required to file IRS Form 3520, reporting the creation of the Trust and the assets you transfer to it. And you must report the Trust's income each year by filing Form 3520-A at the same time as your personal tax return.

Inquisitive Creditors

In some states, in certain narrow circumstances, a judgment creditor can compel you to provide copies of your federal income tax return, which would reveal information about your Trust. But, of course, this wouldn't happen until you had fought and lost a lawsuit. And you might decide early in a lawsuit that revealing the Trust's existence would discourage the plaintiff from continuing.

Apart from the information you must submit to the IRS and that a state court might order you to give to a creditor, the Trust's affairs can be private. If the Trust is established in a country that respects privacy—and all the jurisdictions that invite protective trusts at least pay lip service to privacy—the trustee won't volunteer information to anyone. And you will have no power as grantor or Protector that a court could compel you to use to obtain documents from the trustee.

Credit Card

At your request, the trustee can extend the zone of privacy into the United States or anywhere else in the world by obtaining a confidential VISA card or MasterCard.

You can use the card to make purchases or draw cash anywhere in the world. All the account records are offshore, so your purchases and cash withdrawals are completely private. Charges to the card would be paid by your Trust.

The confidential card would not be a convenient or economical replacement for the credit cards you have now. But if you ever want to make a particular purchase privately or need to tap your trust quickly or quietly, your confidential card permits you to do so.

The card's credit limit should be high enough to give you the sense of comfort you want—but not too high, since a court can compel you to use every available source of credit to pay a judgment. As a practical matter, a court is unlikely to grab a credit card. But, in principle, the card's available credit could be lost to a judgment creditor—until the trustee has the card canceled.

The card can show your name or the name of any company you are associated with (such as a corporate name or doing-business-as name). You will, of course, need to sign a credit card voucher each time you use the card for a purchase. But the VISA or other system that processes the transaction will note only the card's account number, not your name. You also can use the confidential card to make a cash withdrawal from an ATM without signing anything.

If privacy is especially important, request two cards: one just for purchases (which require a signature) and one just for cash withdrawals (which don't require a signature).

Using such a card creates no income tax liability and requires no income tax reporting.

APPLICATION

It may be difficult at first to appreciate how simple it is to exploit the protective power of a Protective Foreign Trust. If all you want from a foreign trust is to protect assets from potential creditors, you can have that protection now—without satisfying any special conditions and without any complex tax considerations.

Money you validly transfer to a Protective Foreign Trust disappears until you or another beneficiary needs it. It's gone. No one can seize the money and no one can make you call it back. You win. The predators lose. ⚷

25

INCOME TAX SAVINGS WITH A FOREIGN TRUST

Your Protective Foreign Trust's income will be taxable to *you*. Deductions for Trust expenses or losses also will flow to you. Thus, at first glance, the Trust offers no income tax advantages or disadvantages. But look closer.

FOREIGN GRANTOR TRUST RULE

Under the grantor trust rules (explained in Chapter 16, "Trusts"), you are deemed to own whatever you transfer to a trust from which you can benefit—in which case you must include *all* the trust's income and deductions in your own tax return.

The *foreign* grantor trust rule casts an even wider net. It treats you (the grantor) as the owner of trust assets even if you retain no interest in the trust at all. The essence of the rule is that if:

- you are a U.S. citizen or resident,
- you transfer property to a foreign trust (except at your death or in a sale at full value), and
- the trust has any U.S. beneficiaries,

then you must pay tax on whatever income the trust earns on the transferred property.

Your tax obligation doesn't depend on your financial interest in the trust. Even if you never receive income from the trust, have no right to receive anything from it, and have no power to influence who does receive benefits or how the trust is managed, you still must pay U.S. tax on the trust's income.

If the trust keeps the property you gave it, your taxable income includes the interest, dividends, rents, royalties, etc. from the property itself and from reinvesting the income. If the trust sells the property, any profit is taxable to you, as is income from reinvesting the proceeds of the sale.[1]

SECOND LOOK

The foreign grantor trust rule will apply to your Protective Foreign Trust for as long as you live. Thus you will have to include the Trust's income and deductions in your own tax return year after year. Nonetheless, the Trust can result in substantial income tax savings for you.

The general tax strategy is for the Trust to defer recognition of its taxable income during your lifetime—using some of the same techniques you'd use for your own portfolio. Then, after your lifetime, the Trust, being foreign, can recognize income without anyone paying U.S. tax.

A strategy of deferral won't prevent the Trust from making good investments, and it won't stop the trustee from making cash distributions to you or other beneficiaries. Deferral simply keeps profits off your tax return.

Trustee's Advantages

In principle the trustee has the same deferral opportunities as you—no more and not much less.[2] But in practice the trustee may have much greater success in deferring taxable income than you would.

Expertise. Tax planning is (or should be) part of the trustee's business. It is practical for the trustee to spend more time and attention, and incur greater cost, to investigate tax-planning strategies than almost any individual investor—since what the trustee learns or devises it can use for many clients, not just one.

More Alternatives. The trustee has a greater range of investment choices. Beyond our borders is a rich world of investment alternatives U.S.

---

[1] If more than one person transfers property to the same foreign trust, the IRS will link a portion of the trust's entire income to each of those transfers. In some cases, this may leave room to argue over how much of a trust's income should be attributed to a particular transferor.

[2] The Trust cannot use a qualified pension plan.

investors seldom see—for a simple reason. Most foreign financial institutions don't offer investment services in the United States—because they don't want to be subject to U.S. tax laws, U.S. securities laws, U.S. reporting laws and other complex and costly regimes of regulation. Some of the investment alternatives blacked out in the United States are ideal for deferring taxable income.

Efficient Shopping. The trustee has buying power. When you look for ways to defer income on your own, high fees or substandard returns may eat up much of the tax benefit. The tax advantages of life insurance sold in the United States, for example, are enormous, but fees or low returns may offset the lion's share of the tax savings. Because the assets under the trustee's management are so great, it is practical for the trustee to search extensively for the right investments—and to exact favorable terms from sellers.

Matchmaking. The trustee manages many separate pools of capital, including pools not subject to U.S. taxation. It is relatively simple and inexpensive for the trustee to arrange a tax-planning transaction between one pool of capital and another. If you are acting on your own, on the other hand, sophisticated tax-planning transactions can be expensive in time, effort and legal fees—and may involve complex and hazardous negotiation.

Specialization. It may be easier operationally for the trustee to defer taxable income than it is for you. All the pools of capital the trustee manages are earmarked for long-term or other specific investing purposes. But as a practical matter you may find it difficult to isolate a definite part of your capital for long-term planning.

Trump Card

The trustee of a Protective Trust has one further, very important advantage in carrying out a strategy of tax deferral. It knows that after your lifetime your Trust will no longer be a grantor trust, so that eventually no one at all will have a tax liability for the Trust's income. It knows that inevitably the horse will speak. ☞

26

FOREIGN TRUSTS AND YOUR ESTATE

Your transfers to a Protective Foreign Trust are "incomplete" gifts for tax purposes. There's no gift tax to pay. Instead, the Trust will be included in your taxable estate. Thus a Protective Foreign Trust, as described so far, has no direct bearing on gift and estate tax planning.

Indirect Advantages

Your Trust nonetheless will help you *indirectly* to reduce estate tax.

First, knowing the Trust is protected against lawsuits and seizures frees you to exploit the opportunities for tax-free wealth-shifting explained in Chapters 20 and 32. You can prudently dispose of non-Trust assets because the wealth safely housed in the Trust will be available to satisfy your personal financial needs.

Second, if you expect your spouse to survive you, the Trust lets you take greater advantage of the spousal exemption (tax-free gifts to your spouse). Such gifts enlarge your spouse's taxable estate while shrinking yours. But your spouse eventually can use the Trust for estate planning in ways you cannot, since your spouse will not be taxable as the grantor. (Opportunities for your surviving spouse to use the Trust to reduce estate tax are explained in Appendix A.)

GREATER ADVANTAGE

But you can do much more. You can turn your Protective Foreign Trust into a powerful tool for cutting your own estate tax.

Non-estate Portion

A single feature of the Trust, as described so far, keeps it in your taxable estate: your power to remove beneficiaries.

Of course, you probably want to keep that power. But giving it up for a *small portion* of the Trust would push that portion out of your taxable estate.

This small, "non-estate" portion then can serve as a peg on which to hang tax-free, wealth-shifting transactions such as those described in Chapters 20 and 32. Any wealth you transmit to the non-estate portion leaves your taxable estate.

The gift with which you establish the non-estate portion would be taxable. But it needn't be much—perhaps only $10,000 to $20,000. And there may not be any actual tax to pay, since your first $600,000 of "taxable" gifts is in fact tax free.

No Hurry

You can designate a non-estate portion when you establish the Trust.

Or you can do it later. Merely advise the trustee to separate a portion of the Trust and begin accounting for it separately. Then renounce your power to remove beneficiaries for that portion.

EXCISE TAX

Depending on the kinds of property you transfer to your Trust and on whether the property goes to the Trust's non-estate portion, your estate might have to pay an excise tax on past appreciation. But if you avoid transferring the "wrong" kinds of investments to the "wrong" portion of the Trust, no tax will be due.

The story of the excise tax is a story of zigs and zags.

Zig 1. An excise tax of 35% is imposed on transfers of appreciated property to a foreign trust. The tax applies to the property's appreciation at the time of the transfer.[1] Alternatively, you may include the appreciation in your own income tax return, as though you had sold the property.

Zag 1. However, the excise tax doesn't apply to transfers to a Protective Foreign Trust during your lifetime, since the grantor trust rules pretend you still own the property.

---

[1] For most types of investments, the "income" would be capital gain.

Zig 2. When you die, the grantor trust rules cease to apply to the trust. In the imagination of the IRS, as your soul leaves your body, your Protective Foreign Trust is transfigured into a new, nongrantor trust. It is then that the excise tax applies.[2]

Zag 2. However, on the date of your death, the cost basis of most types of property in your taxable estate will be reset to equal the property's current fair market value. In other words, the taxable appreciation will disappear—so there's no tax. Notable exceptions are assets that don't qualify for the automatic resetting of cost basis, such as deferred annuities and deferred-payment contracts (about which, see box on page 240).

Investing the Non-estate Portion

Only assets in your taxable estate will have their cost basis reset. The cost basis of investments in the non-estate portion of the Trust won't change—and hence the excise tax will apply to all the appreciation in all its investments, including appreciation that occurred when you still owned the property.

Nonetheless, even the non-estate portion of the Trust can avoid the bite of the excise tax. Three strategies are available.

1. Investment Selection

Some investments elude the excise tax no matter who owns them.

Life Insurance. Life insurance has a unique ability to avoid the excise tax. At the moment the excise tax would apply (your death), the value of the policy itself evaporates, so there's no appreciation to be taxed. In its place is the policy's death benefit, which is tax-exempt income. Thus a cash-value policy on your life is the obvious first-choice investment for the non-estate portion.

Depreciated Assets. An asset that, at the time of your death, is worth less than you paid for it attracts no excise tax. So a depreciated asset is suitable for transferring to the non-estate portion of the Trust.

If your investment plan calls for holding life insurance or depreciated assets, the non-estate portion of the Trust is a good place to put them.

---

[2] The excise tax would apply in the same way to property you transfer to the Trust through your will.

DEFERRED INCOME

You may be able to transfer the value of a foreign deferred annuity to a Protective Trust without incurring the excise tax.

Irrevocably name the Trust as the beneficiary of the annuity and also give the Trust ownership of the contract itself. Then advise the trustee to make an irrevocable declaration that upon your death the annuity contract shall immediately become the property of a particular beneficiary.

The excise tax shouldn't apply, because at your death the annuity is not being transferred to a foreign trust. And because the annuity payments will come to the trust from a source outside the United States, no U.S. withholding or other U.S. income tax would be due.

2. Culling

The excise tax applies at the time of your death. While you are alive, the non-estate portion can invest in anything without triggering the tax.

But you should monitor the investments (other than life insurance). From time to time buy the biggest winners from the Trust. This won't generate any income tax liability, since under the grantor trust rules you are selling to yourself. And it won't increase your taxable estate, since you'll be paying full market value. But, as part of your estate, the appreciated assets will receive an adjustment in cost basis and so escape the excise tax—even if your will leaves them to the Trust.

3. Calculation

Even if you throw up your hands and let the excise tax dine on your estate, shifting wealth to the non-estate portion of the Trust still can reduce taxes overall.

Suppose, for example, that you shift $1 of appreciation to the non-estate portion and that your estate is in the 55% estate tax bracket. The estate could satisfy the excise tax rule by paying 28¢ in capital gain tax. But the shift reduces the taxable estate by $1.28 ($1 of appreciation plus the 28¢ of capital gain tax). Thus the estate would save 70¢ in estate tax, for a net savings of 42¢.

THE NEXT PROTECTOR

A Protective Foreign Trust is a long-term arrangement. It will survive you, assuming the trustee doesn't distribute all the money during your lifetime.

For your heirs to receive the maximum advantage from the Trust, you must name someone to succeed you as Protector. It should be an individual whom you can rely upon to influence the trustee wisely.

Your selection depends, first of all, upon how you want the Trust to be managed. It depends also on circumstances, especially the character and aptitude of your prospective heirs and the size of your Trust. Some examples are:

If you have only one child, you can simply appoint the child to succeed you as Protector. Or you can make your spouse the first in the line of succession and your child the second in line. Assuming you don't empower your spouse to appoint successors, your surviving child eventually will become the Protector.

If you have more than one child, you can recommend to the trustee (or specify in the trust declaration) that it divide the Trust into separate Trusts (either now or upon your death or resignation as Protector) and make each child the Protector of one of those Trusts, one Trust per child. Or you can place each child second in the line of succession for one of the Trusts (a different Trust for each child) and name your spouse as Protector of all the Trusts.

If you have more than one child and one of them is not suited to be a Protector, you can name his sibling, your spouse or your attorney or other trusted advisor as Protector of a separate Trust for the benefit of that child and his descendants.

The trust declaration should let you change your designation of a successor Protector at any time. ⚷

27

THE PEARL
BEYOND PRICE

Dollar for dollar, your Protective Foreign Trust will be the most precious gift you leave. Whether the Trust assets are great or small, the legal packaging that surrounds them will enable your heirs to live as much of their financial life outside the United States as they ever need or want to.

When you "disconnect" from this world, the Trust will automatically disconnect from the U.S. tax system. It will become truly foreign—as foreign as a monk in Tibet. Unless it earns certain types of income in the United States, it will pay no U.S. tax and have no occasion to file reports with the U.S. government.

And the Trust will be legally separate from the beneficiaries. Income the Trust accumulates won't be taxable to them, and no part of the Trust will be includable in any beneficiary's taxable estate.

For tax purposes, a beneficiary's dealings with the Trust will be dealings with an unrelated party—a stranger. Yet, for a beneficiary, the Trust will be the friendliest of strangers.

As an unrelated, tax-free, foreign friend, the Trust will be a financial-planning instrument of unsurpassed power for your heirs. With it they can perfect their own financial privacy and protect their own assets from lawsuits and taxes.

PROTECTOR'S ALTER EGO

Consider the extraordinary position the Protector will be in.

On the one hand, the Trust will operate outside the U.S. tax system, and any dealings the Protector has with it will escape numerous rules that disallow tax advantages on transactions between related parties. On the other hand, the Protector, being a beneficiary, will be eligible to receive distributions and other benefits from the Trust.

It is almost as though the Protector had a foreign, tax-free pocket he could put money into, or take money out of, at his convenience—while telling the tax collector the pocket belongs to someone else. Putting money into the pocket might generate income tax deductions and certainly would reduce his taxable estate. Taking money out of the pocket might be tax free. Until the day money does come out:

- It can be invested and reinvested tax free.

- It avoids all estate taxes.

- It's protected from all creditors.

How the Protector can exploit his position is a somewhat complex, but happy, topic and is covered in Appendix A. This is information you don't need for yourself, since the strategies will work only after your lifetime. But you may want to investigate the topic anyway, to gain a better understanding of the marvel you create for your family when you establish a Protective Foreign Trust.

Appendix A also explains how any beneficiary—not just the Protector—can use the Trust in his own financial planning.

TAXABILITY OF DISTRIBUTIONS

While the Trust itself will not be subject to U.S. tax, beneficiaries may have to pay tax on distributions—depending on when and how the Trust received the money and on how the trust manages its affair after your lifetime.

Principal. The Trust's principal will include everything you transfer to the Trust (including transfers through your will) and everything the Trust earns during your lifetime. It also would include any money the Trust borrows. Distributions of principal are tax free to the beneficiaries. Beneficiaries will have no obligation to report them.

Income. Direct distributions of income the Trust earns after your lifetime are taxable to the beneficiaries. And the beneficiaries are potentially liable for an interest charge on distributions made after the year the money was earned. However, the interest charge is easy to avoid.

Indirect benefits.   There are numerous ways for the Trust to help the beneficiaries without directly distributing money to them—by making loans to them or by purchasing long-term call options on their property, for example. Indirect benefits can be tax free and nonreportable.

Strategies for getting money out of the Trust and into the hands of beneficiaries with a minimum of tax and reporting is a topic also covered in Appendix A.

NOT YOUR ORDINARY PEARL

Any foreign trust your beneficiaries might create would fall under the grantor trust rules, and so would be entangled in the U.S. tax system. Thus your Trust gives them advantages they cannot possibly buy for themselves— advantages that can come to them only as a gift. For your beneficiaries, the Trust you create is a pearl *literally* beyond price. ⌇

PART SEVEN

YOUR OWN PLAN

If you wish, you can treat this book as a smorgasbord. Take some of each method and strategy you like and leave the rest.

That wouldn't be a bad way to proceed. But you can do far better by identifying all the methods and strategies that seem right for you and then assembling them into a coherent plan. You'll avoid redundancies, you'll reconcile competing goals, and, in the long run, you'll go to less trouble.

The next two chapters show you, step by step, how to construct an overall financial plan. The plan will give you as much investment safety as you want and protect your assets from lawsuits and taxes. Because these goals are intertwined in so many ways, you probably will have to work through the steps at least twice—the first time to make provisional decisions and a second time to make adjustments.

28

CHOOSING INVESTMENTS

All the methods for protecting your property are secondary to the property itself. Pension plans, trusts and partnerships will do nothing to protect *you* if their investments are losing value. So the first step in developing a financial plan is to decide what to own.

Before the plan is finished, you'll need to reconcile your investment decisions with your desire to avoid taxes and lawsuits. But that's the business of the next chapter. For now, pretend you are exempt from taxes and immune to litigation. In that case, your life is simple; your only chore is to select the right investments.

FRESH START

An investor's portfolio usually is the residue of years of unconnected decisions. Like a dirtball, it is simply an amalgam of whatever stuck. Your personal dirtball may be quite different from the portfolio you would choose if you were starting from scratch today.

So make a fresh start. Draw up a list of everything you own and a list of everything you owe. Exclude your home, if you own one, and any debt associated with it. And exclude the operating assets and the associated debt of your business, if you own one. But list everything else, including pension plans, trusts and any investments held by your business.[1]

---

[1] If you are receiving a fixed income from an annuity or pension, you can estimate its investment value by asking an insurance company the cost of a lifetime annuity paying the same annual amount. Multiply the insurance company's quote by 80%.

Estimate the current market value of each item, then subtract the total debt from the total value. This is your investment net worth.

Now forget your present holdings. Imagine you have a pile of cash equal to your investment net worth. How would you invest the pile of cash? You might want to take some risks with part of it, to shoot for high profits. But you almost certainly won't want to risk losing everything.

The Division

So divide your investment net worth into two parts. The first is the money you want to protect from risk. We'll call it the *Conservative Portfolio*. The other part is the money you're willing to take some chances with, to try for big profits. We'll call it the *Speculative Portfolio*.

Write down the two amounts.

The division between the two Portfolios is a necessary barrier to unacceptable losses. There's nothing else you can count on to work. Unless you rope off part of your investment net worth as the Conservative Portfolio, everything you own will always be available for gambling on any investment that incites your enthusiasm.

No rule can tell you how much to devote to each Portfolio. You must decide for yourself, based on your own circumstances and disposition. Some investors will want to put all their investment net worth in the Conservative Portfolio. But most will want to reserve at least a small budget for the Speculative Portfolio, so they can answer the door when they think they hear opportunity knocking.

Think Again

Did you divide your investment net worth between the two Portfolios correctly? Here's one way to judge.

Ask yourself how you would feel if you lost the entire Speculative Portfolio. Of course you wouldn't be happy, but would the loss upset your life? Would you feel foolish for having risked so much? If the answer to either question is "Yes," then your Speculative Portfolio is too big.

On the other hand, will you find it easy to be faithful to a Conservative Portfolio as large as you've written down? Will you be able to leave it alone when you read a convincing article on "Three Stocks Likely to Double in Six Months," or when you hear about an incredible trading system that has called every major turn in the gold market for 20 years, or when the investment expert you most respect decides that foreign stocks have nowhere to go but up or that it's time to get out of stocks altogether? And when you learn of a big-profit idea that seems immune to failure, will you be satisfied committing only the Speculative Portfolio? Unless the answer is "Yes," you have allocated too much to the Conservative Portfolio.

There is nothing imprudent about speculating, if you are risking only the money you can afford to lose. But it is foolish to label something a Conservative Portfolio and then take unnecessary chances with it.

Don't be surprised if you find it hard to decide on the split between a Conservative Portfolio, for protection of wealth, and a Speculative Portfolio, for a chance at big profits. This may be the first time you've thought about segregating funds for long-term conservation and identifying other funds for eyes-open exposure to speculative risk.

CONSERVATIVE PORTFOLIO

Having decided, at least provisionally, how much to devote to the Conservative Portfolio, you must devise a prudent strategy for handling it.

Facts of Life

Reflect on what you probably already know.

- Stocks being cheered on by the biggest, most prominent brokerage firms sometimes lose half or more of their value in six months.
- The entire stock market can move in one direction while most advisers are pointing the other way.
- Prices of precious metals sometimes sag miserably at the very time that analysts with the best records have picked for a bull market.
- Interest rates can rise even when it seems obvious the Federal Reserve will use its vast power to keep them low.
- The financial expert on *Wall Street Week* or CNBC, who speaks with such an air of shrewdness and conviction, has made a hundred predictions he dreads being reminded of.

No matter how strong the evidence at the moment, and no matter who supports your opinion, every time you decide what a particular investment is going to do, you take a chance.

Possibilities

The simple truth is that no one knows what the future holds. That is why competent, intelligent, well-informed decisions about particular investments can so easily go wrong. Moving your money from time to time into the investment that seems to have the best prospects won't shield your Conservative Portfolio from risk. On the contrary, it invites risk.

To be safe, your Conservative Portfolio must allow for *all* the possibilities the future might hold—not just the possibilities you judge likely. Thus, no matter what you or your favorite forecaster believes about tomorrow, your Conservative Portfolio should *at all times* include:

- Investments that profit from prosperity and growth in the U.S. economy

- Investments that profit in an environment of rising inflation

- Investments that profit if the economy sinks into stagnation or depression

- Investments that hold their value during periods of tight money

One Strategy for Uncertainty

Chapter 6 explained one strategy for a Conservative Portfolio—the *permanent portfolio.* If you want to apply that strategy, divide your Conservative Portfolio equally among the following four basic investment categories, 25% in each.

- *Stocks:* marketable common stocks, especially issues with above-average volatility—to profit during good times.

- *Gold:* gold bullion and gold coins—to profit from severe inflation.

- *Bonds:* long-term, fixed-dollar investments with fixed interest rates, such as long-term U.S. Treasury bonds—to profit when inflation is declining, especially if it declines rapidly.[2]

---

[2] Treat the investment value of a fixed annuity or pension, if you are receiving one, as though it were a bond. See the preceding footnote.

■ *Cash:* short-term, fixed-dollar investments or fixed-dollar investments with floating interest rates—such as U.S. Treasury bills, short-term corporate bonds, mutual funds that invest in such securities, cash-value life insurance, deferred annuities and deferred-payment contracts. Cash adds stability to the portfolio and lets you buy when investment prices are depressed.

The permanent portfolio strategy is a model of simplicity. Its four investment categories neatly match the economy's four perennial possibilities.[3]

You may decide to modify the simple permanent portfolio strategy in some way. For example, you might allocate different amounts to the four categories, or you might add other categories, such as real estate, foreign currencies or foreign stocks. Doing so wouldn't poison the strategy. But you can't get the safety of a permanent portfolio without following certain rules.

Credit Risk. For the bond and cash categories, don't buy anything with substantial credit risk—such as junk bonds, money market funds investing in Eurodollar CDs or other risky assets, or life insurance or annuities from companies with low credit ratings. Such investments are vulnerable to the very circumstances they are supposed to protect you against—periods of tight money or even depression.

Diversity. If you buy corporate bonds, invest no more than 5% of the portfolio in the bonds of any one company. If this isn't practical, use mutual funds—or buy U.S. Treasury bonds.

Within the stock category, make sure no individual stock represents more than 2% of the Portfolio, or use one or more mutual funds.

Minimums. Assign a fixed share—at least 15%—of the Portfolio to each of the four basic categories.

Monitoring. Examine the portfolio at least once a year. Buy and sell investments as needed to restore the actual value in each category to the percentage you decided upon.

---

[3] Investors who want even more simplicity in applying the permanent portfolio concept should consider using the Permanent Portfolio Fund, which is a mutual fund. See page 302 for information.

Constancy.   After you have decided on the portfolio's composition, stick to your plan. Don't change it because you believe you've identified the next hot investment or the next sure loser.

Other Strategies

You may choose some other strategy for protecting your Conservative Portfolio from the uncertainties of the marketplace. But before you adopt any program, make sure it is simple enough for you to manage. It will be useless if it becomes a chore to carry out. And don't expose your Conservative Portfolio to any plan that:

- depends on you to correctly forecast changes in investment prices or trends,

- depends on someone else to correctly forecast changes in investment prices or trends,

- requires you to buy—or do—anything you don't understand clearly and thoroughly,

- requires frequent decisions, or constant monitoring, by you or someone else,

- depends on the economy to behave a certain way,

- assumes history will repeat itself,

- promises exceptionally high returns,

- asks you to close your eyes and rely on the judgment of a professional with the best credentials, highest-level personal contacts and a documented record of proven success,

- makes you feel clever, or

- cannot withstand surprises.

SPECULATIVE PORTFOLIO

You should commit your Speculative Portfolio as you judge best at any moment—because that is what speculating means. If you don't have a speculation in mind right now, keep the Speculative Portfolio in cash until you do.

Notice how brief this section is. There is little that most advisors can tell you about succeeding as a speculator, although many advisors will try.

Some speculations succeed. And a few succeed spectacularly—usually when they're a bet against what most other investors believe.

Good luck.

THINK YET AGAIN

Are you truly willing to buy and hold all the investments needed for the Conservative Portfolio you have designed? If you want to hold back on any of them because you think their current prospects are poor, then what you really want to do is speculate on price changes. This is a sign you should reduce the budget for the Conservative Portfolio and add to the budget for speculating.

It would be far better—far safer—to be generous now with the Speculative Portfolio than to make compromises with your Conservative Portfolio later. Investors seldom suffer catastrophic losses from investments they admit are speculative. The tragedies come from programs that let investors pretend to be conservative when in fact they are placing bets.

THREE LISTS

Compare your ideal holdings (what you want in your Conservative Portfolio and in your Speculative Portfolio) with what you have now. From that comparison, draw up one list of things to sell and two lists of things to buy. The first buy list is for the Conservative Portfolio; the second is for the Speculative Portfolio. 🔑

29

A PLAN FOR ASSET PROTECTION AND TAX SAVINGS

Devising an overall financial plan is tricky. What seems to solve one problem so nicely often makes another problem worse. Here are some of the conflicts you may encounter.

- *Investment safety versus tax avoidance.* You can avoid tax on investment income by limiting your holdings to raw land, growth stocks, precious metals and other assets focused on appreciation—if you're not troubled by an investment program that might lose half its value in a bad year. To be safe from such drops, part of your wealth must be in fixed-dollar assets. But the interest earnings generally will be taxable.

- *Asset safety versus income tax planning.* Earnings of a deferred annuity you own directly are tax deferred. And you can protect an annuity from lawsuits by putting it into a family limited partnership—but doing so would poison the annuity's tax-deferral power.

- *Estate planning versus income tax planning.* Some steps that reduce estate tax increase income tax. A properly structured gift to a child might save estate taxes—but add to the family's income tax bill if the child invests the money differently than you would.

- *Personal budget versus estate plan.* Well-planned gifts reduce estate tax. But giving too much too soon could undermine your personal financial security.

- *Perfection versus simplicity.* Protecting assets and avoiding taxes are worth some effort. But you don't want a plan that's too complicated to carry out.

A Way Out

This chapter guides you away from such conflicts. By considering financial techniques *in the order in which they appear in this chapter,* you can devise a plan that avoids income tax, eliminates estate tax and throws up powerful barriers to lawsuits—no matter what kind of investment program you want.

Every financial-planning device in this chapter has already been explained fully. The page numbers in parentheses refer to those explanations.

INCOME TAX PLAN

The investment program you decided on in the preceding chapter may require you to sell some of your present holdings. Consider whether one or more of the following methods would help to avoid or defer capital gain tax on those sales.

- *Tax-free switching zones.* If you already have a self-directed pension plan, variable annuity or variable life insurance, use it as a tax-free switching zone. For example, if you want to reduce your exposure to the stock market, sell stock from your pension plan rather than stock you own directly.

- *Call options.* Rather than sell an investment, sell a call option against it—to raise cash and reduce risk. Your profit will go untaxed as long as the option remains outstanding.

- *Forward sales of precious metals.* Make sales of gold or other precious metals in the forward market, to defer tax on your capital gain until you deliver the metal—which needn't be for many years.

- *Short sale against the box.* If you are selling stocks, precious metals or other property traded in a public market, make a short sale against the box, to defer tax on your capital gain for a year or two.

- *Installment sales.* If you are selling real estate, collectibles, or other property not traded in a public market, make a deferred-

payment sale, to postpone tax on your capital gain for many
years.

■ *Capital losses.*   Sell depreciated assets, to recognize losses that
offset your capital gains.

Tough Decisions

If making *all* the sales would mean a large capital gain tax, reconsider
the most highly appreciated assets on your sell list. For each one, weigh the
desirability of selling against the tax you'll pay. But sell at least part of any
asset, tax or no, that prevents your Conservative Portfolio from being truly
diversified.

Old age argues against selling any asset with high appreciation, since
the potential for capital gain tax will disappear when the asset passes to your
heirs. But the risk of holding on to an unwanted or oversized asset, if great
enough, should carry the argument for selling at least part of it now.

Continuing Tax Problem

Whatever your investment program, most of its *taxable* return is likely to
come from just two sources: (1) fixed-dollar assets, such as bonds and money
market instruments, and (2) speculative investments, if they are successful.
Control those two sources, and you avoid most income tax.

The three best tools for the job are:

1. *A self-directed pension plan—for speculative investments and
   fixed-dollar investments.*   A qualified pension plan that lets
   you choose investments is the best home for your Speculative Portfolio. With it, you can trade bonds, currencies, stocks
   and stock options.[1] An IRA, unlike other self-directed pension
   plans, also can invest in gold, by buying American Eagle gold
   coins.

   Use any remaining space in your pension plan for your Conservative Portfolio's fixed-dollar investments.

---

[1] Using a pension plan to speculate may seem like turning the plan on its head. But recognize your pension plan for what it is, not for what it is called. It is an account with a special
ability to shelter investment income from taxation. You don't need to use it for retirement if
you are accumulating assets safely elsewhere.

If there still is room in the plan, fill it with some of every type of Conservative Portfolio investment, so that the plan can be a tax-free switching zone.

2. *Variable annuities, for speculative investments.*   If your pension plan isn't big enough for your entire Speculative Portfolio, consider placing the rest in a variable annuity. However, shop carefully, to avoid unnecessary fees and expenses.

3. *Tax-planning mutual funds—for fixed-dollar investments.*   If your pension plan isn't big enough for all the Conservative Portfolio's fixed-dollar investments, use a tax-planning mutual fund for what's left.

   A tax-planning mutual fund is the easiest way to shelter interest income. A large part of the return comes as tax-deferred appreciation. When you redeem shares, only the appreciation on those particular shares will be taxed. For the shares you don't redeem in your lifetime, the appreciation escapes income tax altogether. And the costs (fund expenses) are low.

Other Devices for Sheltering Interest

Each of the following fixed-dollar investments has important drawbacks, but is a good choice in certain circumstances.

1. A *deferred annuity* postpones tax on *all* earnings until age 80 or beyond. However, before-tax returns generally are not as good as with a tax-planning mutual fund. And the income, when received, will be taxable as ordinary income—even for your heirs. Nonetheless, a deferred annuity from a U.S. company may be a good choice if *all* the following are true:

   ■ You are sure you won't need to make withdrawals during the next 15 years, and not before you reach age 59½.

   ■ You expect to spend most of the annuity's earnings during your lifetime.

   ■ You don't intend to leave the annuity's remaining value to a Protective Foreign Trust.

2. *Cash-value life insurance* is income tax exempt,—not just tax deferred. But you have to bear the cost of mortality coverage

(the cost of a chance to earn a bonus for dying early).[2] If you don't expect to need the money during your own lifetime, a single-premium policy is the best choice. Otherwise, a seven-pay policy (which would permit tax-free borrowing) is a better choice—especially if you want mortality coverage. Shop carefully.

3. A *deferred-payment contract* may be a good choice for sheltering interest income if you need to sell highly appreciated real estate, collectibles or privately issued securities—or if it's too late to use a trust or family limited partnership for asset protection. But the sale must be negotiated privately, requires some time and effort on your part, and usually isn't practical for amounts under $400,000.

Sheltering Other Investments

Much of the return on stocks is tax-deferred appreciation, which reduces the need to shelter long-term stock holdings. But if you own high-yield stocks that could be sold without a stiff capital gain tax, switch to lower-yielding issues with more potential for appreciation.

If you invest in stocks through mutual funds, choose a tax-managed fund.

For a long-term investment in a foreign currency, buy a deferred annuity issued by a foreign insurance company. Such annuities are tax deferred, just as annuities issued by U.S. companies are, so there's nothing to report until you make a withdrawal. And there is no withholding on withdrawals from annuities issued in Switzerland and certain other countries. Anything you don't collect during your lifetime can be paid to your Protective Foreign Trust without U.S. withholding.

Gold and other precious metals produce no taxable income until sold. Of all investments, they are the least in need of sheltering.

Amend Investment Plan

Review the investment plan you decided upon in the preceding chapter. Adjust it, as needed, to reduce your tax burden. For example, if your Con-

---

[2] The cost of mortality coverage is the cost of a risk contract, as explained in Chapter 12.

servative Portfolio needs a certain amount in cash, replace "cash" with "tax-planning money market fund." Or you may want to assign a part of the bond budget to a deferred annuity.

ASSET PROTECTION PLAN

Whatever the assets your investment plan calls for, they need to be protected. The best protection is to get them out of your hands.

Protective Foreign Trust

No asset protection device is more powerful than a Protective Foreign Trust. If you are concerned about asset protection, get one. A Protective Foreign Trust is a grantor trust, so income tax considerations shouldn't limit the amount you transfer to it.

A Protective Foreign Trust is the first choice for holding liquid investments—such as stocks, bonds, mutual fund shares, precious metals and cash-value life insurance. And even if the Trust starts out small, it can protect the rest of your property through partnership transactions and other dealings.

Chapter 35, "Where to Get Help," provides information on an easy and inexpensive way to establish a Protective Foreign Trust (pages 305–306).

Family Limited Partnership

A family limited partnership is the first choice for protecting real estate or an unincorporated business from litigation. It also is a good, but second-best, choice for protecting liquid assets if you decide not to establish a Protective Foreign Trust. You can control the partnership by being the general partner.

Transfers to Partnership. A partnership can hold stocks, bonds, mutual fund shares, gold, life insurance and most other investments without special tax consequences. You generally can transfer investments to, or distribute them out of, a partnership tax free. But there are a few exceptions related to: (1) real estate that generates net tax deductions, (2) deferred-payment contracts, (3) deferred annuities, and (4) securities, unless substantially all the partnership's capital is coming from one person.

Multiple Partnerships.   If a partnership is sued, all its assets are at risk. So if you own property that might attract litigation—such as rental real estate where someone could be injured—put each potentially troublemaking property into its own partnership. Don't mix "accident-prone" assets in the same partnership with passive, "worry-free" investments such as stocks, bonds and life insurance.

Domestic Trusts

If you decide not to establish a Protective Foreign Trust, use a domestic trust to protect gifts for children or others. You must not be even a discretionary beneficiary.

Crummey Trust.   A gift in trust can qualify for the $10,000-per-year-per-donee exemption from gift tax if the beneficiary is given even a brief opportunity to withdraw it. The income from such a Crummey trust will be taxable to the beneficiary, as though he were the grantor. Thus the trust might not be *your* grantor trust.

Use a Crummey trust if the following both apply:

- Your estate plan calls for making tax-exempt gifts (see below) during your lifetime.

- The property you are putting in trust is not a deferred annuity or deferred-payment contract with substantial accumulated income (tax on which would be triggered by a gift to a Crummey trust).

Grantor Trust.   You should structure a domestic trust as your own grantor trust, rather than as a Crummey trust—so that you are taxable on the trust's income and so that transactions between you and the trust are tax free—if *either* of the following applies:

- You want to give away a deferred annuity or a deferred-payment contract with substantial accumulated income.

- You want to make indirect, tax-free gifts to the beneficiaries by paying the income tax on what the trust earns for them.

Make it a grantor trust by authorizing the trustee to buy insurance on your life. But retain the right to revoke that authority, in case you ever want to transform the trust into a nongrantor trust, to escape liability for tax on its income.

Deferred-Payment Sales

If it's too late to use a trust or family limited partnership for asset protection, you still might be able to strengthen your position in dealing with potential creditors by making deferred-payment sales.

Write down the asset protection devices you plan to use.

ESTATE TAX PLAN

Calculate the approximate size of your taxable estate, including any nonexempt gifts you have made. The amount over $600,000, for an individual, or $1.2 million, for a married couple, is the size of your estate-planning problem—the amount of wealth you need to shift to future generations.

Personal Reserve

Before giving anything away, reserve enough to provide for yourself for the rest of your life. To do so:

- Make a generous estimate of your yearly living expense.
- Subtract whatever you receive each year from outside sources of lifetime income, such as pensions from former employers and lifetime annuities from insurance companies. But don't subtract any income paid by your self-directed pension plan.
- Multiply the result by 16.
- Reduce the result by 2% for every year your age (or the age of your spouse, if younger) exceeds 60 years, or by 4% for every year you intend to support yourself by working.

This is what you need to set aside as a *Personal Reserve*—the amount you should not give away. But setting it aside doesn't necessarily mean owning it directly. Parts of your Personal Reserve can be owned by trusts or partnerships, provided the money will be available for you to spend when you need it.

Write down the amount needed for your Personal Reserve.

Estate-Planning Devices

You can drastically reduce estate tax by giving away only small amounts.

Estate-planning devices are listed here in order of their thriftiness. Those involving the smallest actual gift come first. They shrink your taxable estate even if you need to keep nearly everything for your Personal Reserve. Appearing last are devices that work only to the extent you actually give assets away.

Family Limited Partnership.   Transferring assets to a family limited partnership can instantly cut their estate tax value by one third.

If you haven't already done so, draw up a list of assets to transfer to a family limited partnership. Now recalculate your estate's taxable value, assuming that the partnership is worth only two thirds of what you put into it.

Count the full market value of your share of the partnership's assets toward your Personal Reserve.

Exempt Gifts.   The simplest way to reduce your taxable estate is to make exempt gifts to individuals—up to $10,000 per year per recipient. The gifts can be cash, interests in a family limited partnership or other investments. Don't give away a deferred annuity, deferred-payment contract or the note arising from a bargain loan.

You can make exempt gifts to a Crummey trust, as explained earlier in the chapter.

Your payments of tuition and medical expenses for your children and grandchildren also are tax free.

The money or other property you give away cannot, of course, be recaptured for your Personal Reserve. But if you can make exempt gifts without jeopardizing your own financial security, start giving now. Every year that passes is a wasted opportunity.

Estimate what you can eventually achieve through exempt giving. What is the *minimum* number of years you are likely to live, barring a catastrophe? What is the *minimum* amount you will be willing and able to transfer as exempt gifts each year? Multiple the number of years by the annual amount. The result is a cautious estimate of your future exempt gifts.

Taxable Gifts.   You can make "taxable" gifts up to $600,000 ($1.2 million for a married couple) without actually paying gift tax. If such gifts won't compromise your ability to make exempt gifts every year in the future, give now. Otherwise, wait—except, perhaps, for small gifts of limited partnership interest.

Planning for Your Beneficiaries

If you don't need a Protective Foreign Trust for any other reason, set one up now with at least a token amount—to give your descendants the machinery to protect themselves.

A Protective Foreign Trust also is the ideal "landing spot" for your assets after your lifetime. Make the Trust the a beneficiary of your will and your life insurance.

And if you own a foreign annuity, name the Trust as the secondary beneficiary. Then, after your lifetime, the annuity's remaining value will be paid by the insurance company directly to the Trust. The money will not pass through the U.S. income tax system.

You also can use a foreign annuity to leave the unused portion of your pension plan to a Protective Foreign Trust and protect it from U.S. income tax. To do so:

1. Apply the pension plan assets to purchase a foreign annuity.

2. Have the pension plan distribute the annuity contract to you.

3. Name the Trust as the secondary beneficiary of the annuity.

For this to work, it is essential that the foreign annuity contract include certain technical provisions required by U.S. tax rules—otherwise the annuity's full value would be taxable when the pension plan distributes the contract to you. So this is not a do-it-yourself project. You will need the help of a tax attorney or other qualified advisor.

Living Trust

You may already have a *revocable living trust.* None of the planning devices discussed in this book will conflict with it. It is a grantor trust, so it can hold any investment, including a deferred annuity or a limited partnership interest, without special income tax consequences.

Any trust of which you are a beneficiary can be authorized to transfer money to your living trust if and when you need it. And any trust that you establish for your prospective heirs can be a beneficiary of your living trust, receiving the living trust's assets at the end of your lifetime.

ASSEMBLE AND REVIEW

Once you have decided how best to protect your property against lawsuits and taxes, return to your amended investment plan. Exactly which assets go where?

Make up a planning sheet modeled after the form on page 265, but include only the particular entities—pension plan, family limited partnership or whatever—you intend to use. Then assign each asset to one of the entities. (For greater safety, don't concentrate all of any one investment category in a single entity.)

If an interest in one entity is to be owned by another, draw a box around that interest. For example, if a share in a family limited partnership is to be owned by a Trust, list that share in the Trust's holdings and draw a box around the entry.

In the "Value" column, for any investment you own directly, show its fair market value—what you could sell it for. For an interest in a trust or family limited partnership, show the fair market value of the underlying assets— not the discounted value that would apply for gift and estate tax purposes.

Estate-Planning Calculations

Add up the amounts that count toward your Personal Reserve. Is the total large enough? If not, eliminate one or more wealth-shifting transactions from your plan.

Determine what the taxable value of your estate would be. If it is less than $600,000 (or $1.2 million), your estate-planning work is finished. You won't need to read Part 8, "Planning for Large Estates."

But if, even after applying the devices reviewed in this chapter, your taxable estate would be substantially greater than $600,000, put the book down for a minute. Listen carefully. Can you hear them? They're saying, "Grandma! Grandpa! Read Part 8!"

Portfolio Review

Return to your planning sheet. Mark each investment with a C if it belongs in the Conservative Portfolio or with an S if it belongs in the Specu-

Planning Sheet

Entity	Asset or Debt	Value	Total Value
Personal			
Family limited partnership #1			
Family limited partnership #2			
Pension plan #1			
Pension plan #2			
Domestic grantor trust			
Nongrantor trust			
Protective foreign trust			

lative Portfolio. Add up the value for each. Do the two totals match what you decided upon in the preceding chapter? If not, you need to shift some assets from one Portfolio to the other.

Examine the composition of the Conservative Portfolio. Does it match the Conservative Portfolio you decided on in the preceding chapter? If not, you need to make further adjustments to your investment choices.

MAKING DECISIONS

Now do you know exactly what you should do to protect your assets and avoid income and estate tax? Probably not. Go back through this chapter once or twice to review your tentative decisions and to make them more definite and specific. Record the changes on your planning sheet.

Then, unless you need to read Part 8, "Planning for Large Estates," go directly to Part 9, "Action." You'll like it. It's easy. ☞

PART EIGHT

PLANNING FOR LARGE ESTATES

If your net worth exceeds $1 million or so (or $2 million for a married couple), the plan you devised in the preceding chapter may not be enough to reduce your taxable estate to $600,000. In that case, you should read this part. It covers additional estate tax rules—and powerful estate-planning strategies—to help you eliminate estate tax and generation-skipping tax.

Chronic Burden

Combined with income taxes and even low inflation, gift and estate tax is a chronic and debilitating burden for large estates and a handicap for any generation trying to conserve assets for its descendants.

Assuming that a pool of family wealth passes from one generation to the next every 25 years, an estate tax of 55% drains family wealth at an average rate of 3.2% per year, year after year. For example, if a pool of family wealth earns, say, 6% per year after income tax, the first 3.2% earned each year must be set aside to pay the eventual estate tax—leaving a net return of only 2.8% per year for the family to enjoy. And that would allow nothing to offset inflation. If the inflation rate exceeds 2.8%, the family will be losing wealth—even if it spends nothing at all from its investments.

30

MORE ESTATE TAX RULES

Attention coffee drinkers! It's time for that second cup. To protect a large estate from ruinous taxation, it is necessary to slog through a few more rules.

DIVIDED INTERESTS

The rules for gift tax and estate tax give special treatment to transfers of *divided interests,* which occur when you chop up an asset in certain ways and give or bequeath just some of the parts. Divided interests may be a new topic for you, since you're not likely to encounter it outside of estate planning. Within estate planning it is difficult to avoid. The most important types of divided interests are the following.

- An *income interest* is the right to receive the income from a pool of assets for a limited time. The time could be a fixed number of years or someone's lifetime. For example, the right to receive the dividends (however little or much they might be) from a portfolio of stocks for 15 years would be an income interest.

- An *annuity interest* is the right to receive a fixed amount of money each year for a limited time. The money is payable out of a pool of assets and their earnings, but the amount doesn't vary with the earnings.

- A *uni-interest* is the right to receive a fixed percentage of a pool of assets each year for a limited time. If the assets earn more than is due in any year, the surplus is added to the pool. If the assets earn less than is due, part of the assets are sold to cover the shortfall.

■ A *remainder interest* is the right to receive a pool of assets upon the expiration of an income interest, annuity interest, or uni-interest.

Pools

The pool of assets underlying a divided interest might contain just one asset. Thus, for example, you could create an income interest in a single block of stock.

Most commonly, divided interests are created through a trust. Some beneficiaries are given an income, annuity or uni-interest, and so receive payments for a number of years. Other beneficiaries are given a remainder interest, and so eventually receive what is left after the other interests have run their course.

U.S. Treasury Regulations provide tables for valuing divided interests. Each table applies to a particular type of interest and assigns a value (as a fraction of the value of the asset pool) based on current interest rates and the actual or expected number of years until payments begin or end.

AMAZING GIFTS

It's possible to do something that looks nothing like a gift and find out later that, in the eyes of the IRS, you have made a taxable gift.

Bargain Loans

Lending money at an interest rate that is too low (a *bargain loan*) may involve a taxable gift.

The bargain loan rules are tied to three interest rates published monthly by the IRS and called the *Applicable Federal Rates*, or AFRs. Each AFR is an index of current interest rates on U.S. Treasury securities of a particular maturity range—short-term, medium-term (3 to 9 years) and long-term.

If you lend money at an interest rate below the AFR, the *uncharged* interest—the difference between the AFR and what you actually charge—is considered a gift to the borrower. And the gift is taxable.[1]

In the case of a demand loan (for which you can demand repayment at any time), there's a taxable gift each year, equal to that year's uncharged interest.

In the case of a term loan (requiring payments on a fixed schedule), there's only one gift, in the year you make the loan. The gift is the difference between the loan's face value and the present value of all the future payments due under the loan, using the AFR to determine the present value.

A loan made exactly *at* the AFR does not involve a taxable gift, even though the loan would in fact be a bargain for the borrower.

Disproportionate Sales and Gifts

Selling stock or other interests in a closely held business to a family member may involve a taxable gift, even if the price is 100% of fair market value. Such a phantom gift occurs if you sell a larger share in the business's appreciation potential than in its income. And if you give away a larger share in the business's appreciation potential than in its income, the income rights you keep also may be a phantom gift.

Family Corporations. Suppose you own *all* the common and preferred stock in a corporation. If you sell to your granddaughter 40% of the common stock but only 30% of the preferred stock, you are taxed as though the matching 10% of preferred stock you are keeping is really a gift. Or if you give away proportionately more of the common stock than of the preferred stock, the "extra" preferred stock you keep is counted as a gift.

Family Partnerships. The rule applies also to transfers of family limited partnership interests, if you sell or give to a family member more of your interest in appreciation than of your interest in current income.

Trusts. A similar rule applies to intrafamily sales or gifts of interests in a trust, if the rights transferred are weighted more toward appreciation

---

[1] A bargain loan has income tax consequences as well. The IRS pretends that you earn the AFR and then give the borrower the difference between the AFR and the loan's actual interest rate. Each year's uncharged interest is taxable income for you and potentially a deductible expense for the borrower. There are some exceptions to the bargain loan rules for small transactions.

than income. For example, suppose you transfer an apartment house to a trust for eventual distribution to your children, but retain an income interest (the right to receive the rents) for the rest of your life. You have given away an interest in appreciation. But the taxable gift will include the value of the income interest you are keeping—not just the value of the interest in appreciation you actually are giving away. In other words, you will owe as much gift tax as if you had simply given the apartment house to your children.

Exceptions.   In the case of a trust, the rule on disproportionate transfers does not apply if *what you retain* is limited to one of the following:

- The right to receive a fixed dollar amount each year (an annuity interest)
- The right to receive a fixed percentage of the value of the trust's assets each year (a uni-interest)
- The right to use your primary residence for a period of years or for the rest of your life, if the trust holds nothing but the residence and small amounts of cash

For example, suppose you transfer $500,000 worth of stock to a trust for eventual distribution to your children and retain the right to receive $30,000 per year for ten years. This gift of a remainder interest is disproportionate, since you are giving *all* the stock's appreciation potential but not *all* the stock's income. But the gift would not be taxed as a disproportionate transfer, since what you are keeping is an annuity interest. Only the remainder interest itself—valued by an IRS table at just a fraction of $500,000—would be subject to gift tax.

Amazing Assets

Other assets are included in your taxable estate, in addition to what the estate actually owns. They are:

Incomplete Gifts.   Any incomplete gift you make during your lifetime is included in your taxable estate. The property is valued at the same time as the rest of the estate–not when you gave it away. Thus making an incomplete gift postpones payment of tax, but might lead to a much larger tax.

Retained Interests.   If you give away a remainder interest and retain an income, annuity or uni-interest that continues for the rest of your life, the asset pool's full value will be included in your taxable estate. This rule also applies if you sell a remainder interest for even slightly less than its fair market value.

The property would be valued at the same time as the rest of your estate. If you had sold the remainder interest, the value would be reduced by the price you received.

Short Story

The gift and estate tax rules contain so many twists and turns, and so much that is surprising and implausible, that at first it is not obvious what, taken as a whole, the rules mean. Their overall significance is this:

1. All the wealth you accumulate during your lifetime is taxed when you give or bequeath it *except:*

   ■ Wealth you give or bequeath to your spouse or to charities

   ■ Wealth you give away under annual exemptions or by paying medical or tuition bills for another person

   ■ Up to an additional $600,000 of gifts or bequests

2. Your spouse's opportunities for giving or bequeathing wealth without tax are the same as yours, and they are in addition to yours. While both of you live, any opportunity one of you doesn't use can be made available to the other.

3. For a given amount of wealth, the tax is the same whether you transfer it through a taxable gift or through your estate—but the timing of the tax could be very different.

4. The rules on incomplete gifts, disproportionate transfers and retained interests give the tax collector a second chance to value property you have transferred, and they may require you to pay tax sooner than if you had left the property in your estate. But the same value isn't taxed more than once.

GENERATION-SKIPPING TAX

Hoping to lessen your family's overall liability for estate tax, you might give or bequeath assets to your grandchildren—so that the assets won't be taxed a second time, as part of the children's estates.

EXPENSIVE FUNERAL

It is possible for your taxable estate to exceed the value of what the estate actually owns.

In fact, estate *tax* can exceed the estate's real value—in effect delivering everything to the government. Such a catastrophe might occur through any of the following.

- The value of the estate's assets collapses after the valuation day (normally, the date of death) but before the estate sells the assets.

- You made "incomplete" gifts of property that appreciated substantially.

- You sold a remainder interest for less than full value (retaining an income, annuity or uni-interest), and the underlying asset appreciated substantially.

- A combination of such factors.

It is a cautionary thought—the government hauling off your entire estate. For a big estate, because the top rates are so high, inept estate planning can be worse than no estate planning at all.

To discourage this, Congress imposed a tax on "generation-skipping" transfers—in addition to the regular gift and estate tax. It applies to gifts and bequests you make to persons more than one generation below you. The tax rate is a flat 55% (the same as the maximum gift and estate tax rate).[2]

---

[2] The generation-skipping tax is imposed on the *first* of three possible occasions.

1. When you make a generation-skipping gift or bequest directly to a beneficiary or to a trust in which a generation-skipping beneficiary has a fixed interest, you or your estate pays the tax.

2. When a trust you have established distributes assets to a generation-skipping beneficiary, the trust pays the tax.

EVAPORATING PENSION VALUE

Tax on your estate and income tax on your heirs can soak up the lion's share of a pension plan or other uncollected income.

Suppose, for example, that you leave an estate with stocks and bonds worth $3 million, an IRA worth $100,000, and (for the sake of simplicity) no debts or other deductions. The estate will pay a tax of $1,153,000, or an average tax rate of 37%. But the marginal tax rate will be 55%, meaning that if the estate were $100 smaller, the estate tax would be $55 less—and that if the IRA were not in the estate, the estate tax would be $55,000 less.

The heir who collects the IRA will receive taxable income of $100,000 and a deduction of $37,000 for the portion of the estate tax allocable to the IRA. If he's in a 31% tax bracket, his income tax bill will be $19,500. So, after income and estate taxes, the $100,000 IRA adds only $25,500 to the total wealth available to your heirs.

Excess Accumulations

Or your heirs may receive even less from your $100,000 IRA.

Your estate may be subject to an additional tax on your qualified pension plan. The tax rate is 15%, and it applies to "excess" accumulations.

Generation-Skipping Exemptions

Payments of medical expenses and tuition and *direct* gifts up to $10,000 per year that are exempt from gift tax also are exempt from generation-skipping tax.[3] In addition, your first $1 million of generation-skipping gifts

---

3. When a beneficiary's interest in a trust expires (because the beneficiary has died, or because a period of years has passed, or for any other reason), if all the remaining beneficiaries are more than one generation below you, the trust pays the tax, based on the value of its assets at the time.

[3] To be exempt from generation-skipping tax, the gift must go directly to the recipient and not to a trust (not even if the trust has a Crummy provision permitting the beneficiary to withdraw the gift).

and bequests is exempt from the tax. You can share your $1 million exemption with your spouse, so that either of you can make generation-skipping gifts of $2 million without incurring the tax.

Two Big Bites

If your estate is large but not well planned, the combination of estate tax and generation-skipping tax can eat up most of what you intend to give to your grandchildren. For example, if you were to make taxable gifts of $3 million, including gifts of $1 million to grandchildren, a subsequent nonexempt gift of $100 to a grandchild would attract a regular gift tax of $55 and a generation-skipping tax of $25 (55% of the after-tax $45), for a total tax of $80. Your grandchild would receive only $20, or 20% of the gift. ⚊

31

ELEMENTS OF ESTATE PLANNING

The complex rules explained in Chapters 19 and 30 boil down to just 12 simple elements. Some of them increase gift and estate tax, and others reduce it—as shown in the following ledger.

Elements That Increase Gift and Estate Tax	*Elements That Reduce Gift and Estate Tax*
1. Earnings from your business, profession or employment	1. Money you spend on the necessities of life for yourself and your dependents
2. Earnings from successful investments, and appreciation in your house and personal property	2. Money you spend on luxuries for yourself
3. Wealth you receive through gifts and bequests	3. Money you pay in income tax
	4. Wealth you lose on bad investments
	5. Gifts that qualify for a $10,000-per-year exemption
	6. Gratuitous payments of medical and educational expenses
	7. Gifts and bequests to charities
	8. Gifts and bequests to your spouse
	9. The lifetime credit (permitting the tax-free transfer of up to $600,000)

USEFUL LEDGER

You can use the ledger as a checklist, to discover how any estate-tax-cutting strategy works. And the ledger may help you see how steps taken to reduce income tax or protect assets might affect your estate plan.

The ledger also helps you spot bad ideas quickly. Any proposal for reducing estate tax that doesn't operate on at least one of the ledger's 12 elements probably won't work.

GENERAL STRATEGY

The general strategy for cutting gift and estate tax is to shrink the elements on the left side of the ledger and expand the elements on the right side. If you examine the elements one by one, looking for ways to make them bigger or smaller, you may turn up some surprises.

Shrinking the Left Side

Earnings from Business, Profession or Employment.   The more you earn, the greater the eventual bill for gift and estate tax—all other things being equal. Of course, earning less seems like the dumbest possible estate plan. But earning less *for yourself* could be smart—if it enriches someone to whom you otherwise would make a taxable gift or bequest.

Wealth from Investments.   A similar logic applies to your investments. It's foolish to forgo profits in order to avoid gift and estate tax—unless the profits you forgo somehow go to your heirs.

Wealth from Gifts and Bequests.   The wealth that has (or will) come to you through gifts and bequests may represent a parent's or grandparent's lifetime of hard work and thrift. It may even reflect careful estate planning. But did your forebear think about *your* potential estate-planning problems? Probably not. But you can adjust your own affairs to give enormous estate-planning advantages to *your* heirs.

Expanding the Right Side

Necessities of Life.   Necessity speaks for itself.

Luxuries.   Champagne and skiing at St. Moritz are wonderful tools for cutting estate tax. If you are in a 55% estate tax bracket, every $100 you spend on them reduces your estate tax bill by $55. But empty bottles of Roederer Crystal won't put your grandchildren through college.

Income Tax.   In one respect, paying income tax is like spending money on champagne and Alpine holidays. It reduces your estate; hence it reduces the bill for estate tax. But it isn't nearly as much fun. So paying income tax looks like another bad strategy—unless it's income tax your heirs would have to pay if you didn't.

Wealth Lost on Bad Investments.   The story for bad investments is the same as for good investments, but in reverse. You wouldn't want to lose money just to cut estate tax—unless your losses somehow could turn into profits for your heirs.

Gifts and Bequests to Charities.   Every $100 you donate to charity reduces your estate tax bill by up to $55.

Exempt Gifts.   Gifts that qualify for the $10,000 annual exemption and qualifying gifts of tuition and medical expenses represent a free ride in the estate tax system—provided you are willing and able to let go of the money now.

Spousal Gifts and Bequests.   Such transfers are an easy—but temporary—solution. They get wealth out of your estate without tax, but they add to your spouse's estate-planning problem. A temporary solution may be good enough, however, if it buys time for your spouse to carry out a low-tax plan for transferring family wealth to the next generation.

Lifetime Credit.   How much real wealth can you stuff into $600,000 of tax-free gifts? Ask yourself this: how many suits can you stuff into a two-suiter suitcase if you really need to? Three? Four? Or perhaps a closetful? ⚷

32

MORE ESTATE
TAX STRATEGIES

With the techniques explained in this chapter, even a very large estate can be whittled away. None of the techniques will do the job overnight. They need time. But given enough time, they can transmit an unlimited amount of wealth from your estate to your intended beneficiaries—without gift or estate tax.

BARGAIN LOANS

You can transfer wealth without attracting gift tax, and you can drastically cut the value of your taxable estate, by lending money at low rates—but not *too* low.

Make an unsecured, long-term loan (no longer than 30 years) to one or more of your children at an interest rate equal to the Applicable Federal Rate (AFRs are explained in Chapter 30). The loan should be no bigger than seven times the recipient's net worth.

Advise the recipient to use the loan to purchase fixed-dollar assets, such as high-grade bonds. Without taking on any substantial risks, he will be able to earn more on the bonds than the interest he pays you on the loan. The difference is, in effect, a gift. But it isn't a *taxable* gift under the bargain loan rules explained in Chapter 30, since the interest rate matches the AFR.

If the loan is not repaid during your lifetime, its value for estate tax purposes will be less than its face value—perhaps 50 to 75% less, if many years remain until it matures. The large discount would apply because the estate would have a hard time selling an unsecured note for which there is no public market.

As time passes and the loan's remaining term diminishes, the discount also will diminish. However, if you wish, you can periodically extend the term of the loan, and thereby restore the high discount. Or you can let the loan mature if you need the money.[1]

If interest rates decline, invite the recipient to prepay the loan. Then give him a new loan at a new, lower interest rate.

Fluctuations

The power of bargain loans to transfer wealth depends largely on fluctuations in interest rates. If rates rise, the borrower may earn much more by investing the money than he pays in interest. If rates decline, the borrower can replace the loan with a new one at a lower rate. Heads he wins; tails he doesn't lose, and he gets to play again.

Bargain loans are especially effective at transferring wealth during periods of volatile interest rates. The more rates jump around, the better.

You can reasonably expect a program of bargain loans to transfer wealth to the borrower at an *average* rate per year of 6% or so of the loan balance. But that's only an average. Most years will be substantially better or worse than average. So will many decades.

Bargain Loan Trust

A bargain loan to an individual reduces gift and estate tax, but it seems to conflict with other objectives. It forces you to earn taxable interest. And it may leave you with too little influence over how the borrower uses the money. You can eliminate these drawbacks by making the loan to a properly structured trust.

Establish a trust for the benefit of your prospective heirs, and transfer a modest amount of money to it as a nonexempt gift. The trustee should:

- be prohibited from making any distributions during your lifetime,
- have the power to borrow,
- be required to favor investments that defer taxable income and profits, and

---

[1] If you extend the loan, you must adjust the interest rate to the current AFR.

■ be held harmless for any investment transaction it makes with
your consent.

Retain no rights in the trust, so that it stays out of your estate. But
include provisions, such as permitting the trustee to purchase insurance on
your life, that make it a grantor trust.

Then make a loan to the trust, at the long-term AFR, of no more than
seven times the trust's net worth.

Since you are dealing with your own grantor trust, the loan is a nonevent
for income tax purposes. Interest on the loan is not taxable for you, nor is it
deductible for the trust. Instead, you are taxed on the trust's investment
income. So advise the trustee to buy whatever tax-deferred fixed-dollar
investments or other investments you would buy if you were investing for
yourself.

The trust's net worth should grow, since the trust is financing its investments at an extremely favorable rate. And as the trust's net worth grows, it
can accept additional bargain loans if you wish to offer them.

ANNUITY TRUST

Any annuity helps you satisfy your budget constraint because it
promises you an income for as long as you live. An *annuity trust* does so
while avoiding the disadvantages of an annuity purchased from an insurance
company.

To begin, organize a trust with the same provisions as a bargain loan
trust. Thus it will be a grantor trust, with no income tax consequences.
Make a nonexempt gift to it. Then purchase an annuity from the trust, and
advise the trustee to invest the purchase price primarily in fixed-dollar
investments.

Because you are dealing with your own grantor trust, the annuity transaction has no income tax consequences. Instead, you pay tax on the trust's
income—which shouldn't be much, since the trust can use most of the same
tax-deferral devices you can.

An annuity trust should be handled carefully, to make sure it doesn't
get dragged back into your taxable estate. Select an independent trustee.
Wait at least one year between establishing the trust and purchasing the
annuity. Match the terms of the annuity (the ratio of the annuity payments
to the purchase price) to the terms available from a commercial insurance

company. And give the trust enough capital at the outset to assure its ability to make the promised annuity payments even if you live longer than expected.

GRANTOR-RETAINED ANNUITY TRUST

A *grantor-retained annuity trust* (GRAT) can shift wealth to your children or prospective heirs without gift tax.

To establish a GRAT, transfer assets to a trust for the eventual benefit of your prospective heirs, but retain the right to an annual payment of a fixed dollar amount for a fixed number of years—i.e., retain an annuity interest (but not a *lifetime* annuity interest). The payments will be made out of the trust's income and by distributing trust assets back to you.

The trust represents a gift of a remainder interest to the beneficiaries. The gift tax value of the remainder is the difference between the value of the assets you put into the trust and the value of the annuity you keep.

If the annual income you select is big enough, the annuity (as measured by the IRS valuation tables) will be worth nearly as much as the trust's initial assets—and so the remainder's gift tax value will be only a token amount.

Assuming you outlive the annuity, the trust's remaining assets will fall outside your taxable estate, for a savings in estate tax. On the other hand, if you die while the annuity is still running, the trust will be part of your estate—in which case no tax is saved. But even then nothing will have been lost, since the underlying assets would have been in your estate if you hadn't established the trust.

Stacking the Deck

If you have a feel for financial arithmetic, you may wonder how much there is to win with a GRAT, even if there is nothing to lose. For the annuity's value (as measured by IRS tables) to match the original assets, doesn't the annuity have to be so generous that everything in the trust eventually comes back to you?

GRATs can shift wealth because the IRS annuity valuation tables are flawed. The tables disregard the makeup of the assets that finance an annuity, and thus fail to allow for the risk that the annuity will not be paid in full. You can exploit this weakness by setting up a series of GRATs, each with a short term and each holding a portfolio of investments selected for price volatility.

For example, suppose your holdings include $100,000 worth of stocks in companies in a particular industry. Transfer the stocks to a GRAT, retaining an annuity for just two years. To avoid substantial gift tax, select an annuity payment size that, by the IRS tables, makes the annuity worth $100,000. (If the AFR were, say, 5%, the annual annuity payment would be $53,800.)

If the stocks do well, substantial assets will be left in the trust at the end of the two years—assets that will have escaped from your taxable estate and will land in the pockets of your beneficiaries.

If the stocks do poorly, the trust will exhaust itself paying your annuity. Everything will come back to you, leaving nothing for the beneficiaries. In that case, no tax is saved, and the investment loss is the same as from holding the stocks yourself.

So, heads, you win; tails, you don't lose.

Deal Again

Next year, establish a second trust, with a different type of investment—say, bonds denominated in Swiss francs. Reserve an annuity for a term of two years or so with a nominal (IRS-table) value nearly equal to the value of the bonds. If the franc appreciates, the profit will go to your beneficiaries. If the franc declines, the trust leaves you where you would have been without it.

Other GRATs can use other investments. One might invest in long-term bonds, another in gold stocks. Each trust should be *un*diversifed, holding just one kind of investment, so that its performance is volatile. For estate tax purposes, some of the trusts will be big winners, and none will be a loser.

Use only investments you want to include in your overall portfolio, which can remain fully diversified even though each GRAT is invested narrowly.

The wealth that escapes your taxable estate through GRATs doesn't have to go directly to your intended beneficiaries. The legal beneficiaries of the GRAT could be a family limited partnership (in which you hold no more than a small interest) or another trust. Or, after your annuity expires, the GRAT could continue to hold the assets for many years before distributing them to your beneficiaries.

A GRAT's efficiency in transferring wealth depends on the volatility of the underlying investments, in much the same way that a bargain loan pumps wealth faster when interest rates are volatile.

You can reasonably expect GRATs to transfer wealth to the beneficiary at an *average* rate per year of 10% or so of the trust's assets, depending on the type of assets. But that's only an average.

FAMILY BUSINESS

As explained in Chapter 30, "More Estate Tax Rules," selling a greater share in the potential appreciation of your family business than in its income may involve a taxable gift—even if the sale is at fair market value.

Despite this rule on disproportionate transfers to family members, there are two ways to get growth in the value of your business out of your taxable estate and still keep as big a share of the business's income as you wish. In both cases, the trick is for your children or other prospective heirs to be among the corporation's early shareholders.

Early Plan

Estate planning is easier if you plan early, before your business has grown.

Suppose you are about to start a new, incorporated business that needs only modest equity capital—either because of the type of business or because it can lease equipment or operate on borrowed money. Before starting, set a target. At what point will the business's income be enough for you personally, so that you would want your children to receive any additional profits?

If, for example, $200,000 per year would be enough, organize the company with preferred stock entitled to the first $200,000 of dividends paid each year. Also issue common stock, which would benefit from any growth in the business's profits beyond $200,000 per year.

Give the common stock to your children or to a trust for their benefit. The taxable value of the gift will be no more than the corporation's small initial capital, which would be much less than the stock's eventual value if the business is successful.

The preferred stock's voting rights can give you effective control of the company. This lets you run the business as you judge best, and allows you to determine when your children receive dividends.

Late Plan

If you already operate a business, it's not too late to transfer further appreciation, or even past appreciation, to your children or other prospective heirs. But it will take a little more effort.

To begin, advise your prospective heirs (or the trustee of a trust for their benefit) to organize a new corporation. If you wish, buy preferred stock entitling you to a certain dividend each year dividends are paid.

Then let the new corporation undertake some of the activities your established business otherwise would handle. Precisely how this would be done depends on the nature of your business. So I can only give you examples.

If you plan to add a new product or service, let the new corporation handle it. If not, let the new corporation take on an existing product or service, but with some modifications.

Or let the new corporation take on a particular function—such as marketing, advertising, purchasing or selling. Or let the new corporation service customers in a particular territory.

The new corporation's operations may be closely intertwined with those of the established business. But the new corporation should have a life of its own—features that distinguish it from your existing business. For example:

- If the new corporation shares facilities with the established business, it should have the exclusive use of certain rooms or areas.

- It should hire some employees or outside contractors the established business doesn't use.

- The new corporation's profit-sharing or other incentive program should cover one or more employees who aren't in the established business's incentive program.

- The new corporation should have some officers and directors who are not affiliated with the established business.

You might want to shift profits (and hence appreciation) from one business to the other by controlling the prices they charge each other. Sometimes there are opportunities to do just that—but the opportunities are limited. Because the possibility is so obvious, an IRS auditor will scrutinize transactions between related companies, looking for rigged pricing.

The real power of the new corporation is its ability to absorb opportunities. Every business—even the most staid—operates in a world of change. It succeeds and grows only if its management makes correct decisions about new opportunities and new problems. Every successful business is a somewhat new business every year.

The new corporation should gradually take on everything new—whether it be new products, new processes, new functions, new customers, new territories or new employees. Thus the growth and change in your business will enhance the value of the new corporation—but not the value of your taxable estate. 🔑

33

A STRONGER PLAN

This chapter explains how to incorporate the estate-planning techniques just discussed into your overall financial plan. It also shows how to adapt estate-planning techniques to avoid the generation-skipping tax.

The steps suggested here are *in addition* to those covered in Chapter 29, "A Plan for Asset Protection and Tax Savings." They're not replacements for those earlier measures.

ANNUITY TRUST

If the need to retain enough wealth to assure your own financial security (your budget constraint) is interfering with your desire to reduce your taxable estate, establish an annuity trust. It gets assets of your estate even though they still are available to pay you a lifetime income.

Establish a trust for the benefit of your eventual heirs. Exclude yourself as a beneficiary, so that the trust can be a completed gift. And include a provision, such as the right to purchase insurance on your life, that makes it a grantor trust.

Some gift tax may be due if creation of the trust pushes your total lifetime gifts over $600,000. But since the trust is a completed gift, the trust will be outside your taxable estate. And, being a grantor trust, it will have no income tax consequences for you.

Then purchase a lifetime annuity from the trust. The trust should use the money to purchase the investments you want to have in your overall portfolio. All of the trust's assets will be available to pay you an income for as long as you live. But if you die early, there will be no estate tax on the assets you transferred to the trust.

BARGAIN LOAN TRUST

By making a loan at the Applicable Federal Rate (AFR), you immediately reduce the taxable value of your estate and begin gradually shifting wealth to the borrower.

The loan's term should be for as long as you are confident you won't need the money (but not more than 30 years). When the loan comes due, you can decide whether to renew it.

Make the bargain loan to a grantor trust for your prospective heirs— either a domestic trust or the nonestate portion of a Protective Foreign Trust. The loan generally should not exceed seven times the trust's net capital.[1]

The trust can use the loan to buy investments you want to have in your Conservative Portfolio. If you already own the investments, the trust can purchase them from you. Because it is a grantor trust, there's no income tax on the transactions. The trust also can invest in your family limited partnership.

To protect the note (that represents the loan) from your potential creditors, pledge it to secure your promise to contribute additional capital if and when the partnership demands it. Or transfer the note to a protective foreign trust—although this will provide maximum protection only if the bargain loan trust is itself foreign.

Decide how much to lend, and write down the amount. Recalculate the value of your taxable estate with the note discounted by 10% plus 2% per year. Include the note at its full face value, as part of your personal reserve.

GRANTOR-RETAINED ANNUITY TRUSTS (GRATs)

You can whittle down your holdings of marketable investments year by year by establishing a series of GRATs. Being a grantor trust, a GRAT has no income tax consequences.

Each year (or more often) transfer a volatile investment to a two-year trust. Retain a fixed annual income for yourself, and let whatever remains go

---

[1] The initial gift (but not the loan) will be taxable. However, gift tax actually will be due only if the transfer pushes your lifetime total of nonexempt gifts beyond $600,000.

to your prospective heirs. Make the annual income so high that the IRS tables value the remainder at close to zero.

If the investment enjoys above-average profitability during the two years, the trust will have a large remainder, which will go to your prospective heirs. Otherwise, everything you put into the trust will come back to you. The remainder can be paid out to the beneficiaries at the end of the two years, it can remain in the GRAT for a number of years longer, or it can go to the nonestate portion of your Protective Foreign Trust.

GRAT VERSUS BARGAIN LOAN

The investment you might place in a GRAT could instead be sold to a bargain loan trust. Which is better?

In the long run, GRATs are more powerful, but they're also more complicated. And the result for any one GRAT is very uncertain; it may transfer a large portion of the wealth you put into it or none at all. Generally, GRATs are preferable to bargain loans if you expect to use GRATs for at least ten years and your estate-planning problem is large enough to warrant their complexity, or if you are reluctant to tie up capital in a bargain loan for an extended period.

Write down the investment(s) you will transfer to a GRAT. Include their full value as part of your Personal Reserve.

Parallel Corporation. If you own a business, you can reduce estate tax by fostering a *parallel corporation*, owned by your prospective heirs, by a domestic trust for their benefit or by the nonestate portion of a Protective Foreign Trust.

Do not include the value of the parallel corporation in your Personal Reserve.

Generation-Skipping Tax

Gifts and bequests to grandchildren or other persons more than one generation younger than yourself are subject to a generation-skipping tax of 55%. Your first $1 million ($2 million for a married couple) of generation-skipping transfers is exempt.

If you intend to leave more than $1 million for your grandchildren, make them the recipients of the wealth-shifting mechanisms just discussed. Allocate a portion of your $1-million exemption to a gift in trust for them, so that all subsequent buildup of the trust's value will occur outside the ambit of the generation-skipping tax. Then let the trust benefit from a bargain loan or a GRAT, or own a parallel corporation.

Any step that reduces the estate tax value of your property also reduces the potential liability for generation-skipping tax.[2]

TIDYING UP

You now may have more trusts than children, grandchildren, friends, neighbors and pets. Are they all really necessary? No. Only the things they do are important.

You can use a single trust for more than one purpose. A bargain loan trust can also hold the stock of a parallel corporation and receive the remainder of a GRAT.

Do you want to establish a Protective Foreign Trust? It's nonestate portion can also be a bargain loan trust, receive GRAT remainders and own a parallel corporation.

PASSAGE OF TIME

Even if your plan, as revised in this chapter, still leaves some potential liability for estate tax, time may eliminate it.

Wealth-shifting devices such as bargain loans, GRATs and parallel corporations do their work gradually. They don't cart away your taxable estate all at once. They erode it.

Tax-exempt giving also works gradually. Even if today's tax-exempt gifts don't eliminate estate tax, the gifts you make over the next ten or twenty years might. And the pace at which you can deplete your taxable estate may increase with time, as new grandchildren or other beneficiaries appear.

By the formula explained in Chapter 29, after you reach age 60, the amount needed for your Personal Reserve also will decline year by year. ⌇

---

[2] Gifts eligible for the $10,000-per-year-per-donee exemption from gift and estate tax are exempt from generation-skipping tax only if you make them directly to the beneficiary (not through a trust).

PART NINE

ACTION

Now you have a plan for financial sovereignty—or at least a plan for getting closer to it.

If you act, your plan will save you money in income tax, save your heirs the painful experience of paying estate tax, let you stop worrying about lawsuits and put frosted glass in the windows of your financial life. If you don't act, your plan won't accomplish anything.

Don't feel discouraged if, on reflection, your plan seems too ambitious, too complex or too fraught with the unfamiliar for you to carry it out. Don't throw your plan away because you wonder whether some of its elements are too daring. And don't be paralyzed by the thought that the government is too powerful to let you achieve financial sovereignty. The government is busy with those other 280,000,000 people who want to live their own life.

You can succeed—if only you will begin.

34

GETTING STARTED

It is one thing to hear about clever strategies and to imagine using them. It is something quite different to *act* on the ideas—to plunge into what may be novel and unfamiliar, and to wrestle with all the messy details and the need for definite, unambiguous decisions.

Of all the things your financial plan requires you to do, the most difficult is getting started. If, having devised a plan, you hesitate to put it into effect, there are three avenues you can take.

AVENUE 1—PROFESSIONAL HELP

You will need the help of your lawyer if you are going to use a partnership or trust. And you may need to confer with your accountant, to estimate the estate tax savings from a family limited partnership, bargain loan or other arrangement you have in mind.

While you are getting that help, ask your lawyer or accountant to review your overall plan. His advice may give you the confidence to act. However, don't expect him to recommend specific investments.

Another source of guidance is an internationally minded investment advisor. He can help by evaluating and refining your overall plan and by defining the concrete steps needed to carry it out.

A small sampling of lawyers and other professionals who can help with one or more aspects of your financial plan appear in the next chapter, "Where to Get Help."

AVENUE 2—DARE TO BE STRANGE

Your financial plan may involve investments or techniques that seem exotic or out of the mainstream—ideas you won't find in *Business Week* or *Money* magazine.

Here are some easy things you can do to become more at home with the unfamiliar. Each is a simple, warming-up exercise for the bigger steps your plan may call for.

Foreign Account.   Open a foreign bank account with $5,000. You may be astounded at how simple and prosaic this turns out to be, but you will have accomplished a great deal.

Even the smallest foreign account is a valuable asset. It will be ready and waiting, if you ever want to move more money out of the country quickly. And opening the account will remove much of the sense of mystery from the other, more ambitious uses of foreign financial institutions discussed in Part 6. (See pages 303– 305 for information on specific foreign banks.)

Tax-Planning Fund.   Open a small account (say, $1,000) with a tax-planning mutual fund. When you have seen its tax-saving power, you probably will want to move more money to the fund, to shelter your return from taxation. (See page 302 for information on specific tax-planning mutual funds.)

Small Gifts.   Make small gifts (not more than $10,000) to each of your children, grandchildren or other prospective heirs, or to a trust (with a Crummey provision) for their benefit. The modest gifts will flush out all the questions about how your prospective heirs are going to use the wealth you expect to leave for them. This prepares the way mentally, both for you and for them, for more elaborate plans for tax-free wealth transfers.

Foreign Trust Information.   Purchase a Passport Financial "Off-shore Trust Information and Action Package." This package is complete. It explains exactly how to establish and use a protective foreign trust to repel lawsuits and reduce taxes. Its specific information and ready-to-use forms eliminate much of the effort and cost of establishing a protective foreign trust. (See page 306 for ordering details.)

Swiss Annuities.   Send for information on Swiss annuities. The information is free—and valuable. (The name and address of a Swiss insurance agency appear on page 301.)

Tax Haven Telephone Directory.   Buy a telephone directory for a tax haven. The Yellow Pages will introduce you to institutions that may offer exactly what you need and show you how any institution you are considering wants to appear to locals. (A convenient source of foreign telephone directories appears on page 301.)

AVENUE 3—DON'T JUST STAND THERE

Do *something.*

Even if you find it hard to devise a comprehensive plan, with every question answered, you probably can identify steps that clearly are beneficial—things that will improve your situation no matter what else you do. Take those steps—at least one of them—*now,* without waiting for your plan to be complete. Then, having done what's obvious, it will be easier to see what else you should do.

Or perhaps you've devised a comprehensive financial plan, but you hesitate to carry it out because it requires so many big steps.

Don't wait until you're ready to take all of them. Identify one or more easy steps that will improve your situation—even if you never carry out the rest of the plan—and take those easy steps now. Afterward, you'll find the others are far less difficult than they seemed. ⌐

35

WHERE TO GET
HELP

Since the problem of keeping what you earn has to do with money, you won't have trouble finding people willing to help. This chapter identifies a few of them.

NEWSLETTERS

If your mailbox bears the same curse as mine, you frequently receive solicitations for financial newsletters. Most are preposterous, filled with claims no advisor could live up to. While the newsletters themselves generally are more sensible than their advertisements, many do not deserve to be taken seriously.

Listed here are a few newsletters I've found particularly useful, intelligent and interesting.

Harry Browne's Special Reports

Harry Browne is one of the authors of the permanent portfolio concept. His newsletter reports on Swiss and other foreign banks, provides continuous coverage of permanent portfolio topics and also makes recommendations for speculative trading. *Special Reports* includes extensive analysis of political and economic topics. I occasionally contribute to this newsletter, and I've been Mr. Browne's editor since 1974.

Mr. Browne is an independent and original thinker whose newsletter serves its readers as vaccine against the fads that periodically sweep through masses of investors. An unusually large portion of the readership are long-term subscribers—a strong sign this newsletter really does provide something special.

The newsletter isn't published on a calendar schedule, but only as Mr. Browne has something to say—which usually turns out to be 8 to 10 issues per year, each issue running 16 to 20 pages. A subscription is for 10 issues and costs $225. You can purchase the current issue for $10 (one time only). Write to Harry Browne's Special Reports, Box 5586, Austin, Texas 78763, or call 1-512-453-7313.

Adrian Day Investment Analyst

Adrian Day's newsletter is a clearly written monthly publication emphasizing the international elements in successful investing. The approach is conservative, with a sprinkling of speculative opportunities. It always is a pleasure to read, and it always contains something fresh. The cost is $49 per year. Order from *Adrian Day Investment Analyst,* Box 6644, Annapolis, Maryland 21401. For a free sample issue, call 1-410-224-8885.

Crisis Investing

Written by Douglas Casey, this newsletter is rich in independent political and economic analysis. It can show you what faithful readers of *The Wall Street Journal, The New York Times* and *Newsweek* will never know. *Crisis Investing* also is a fertile source of ideas for high-risk, high-potential speculation. A one-year subscription (12 issues) costs $195. You can purchase a sample issue for $15. Write to *Crisis Investing,* 1217 St. Paul Street, Baltimore, Maryland 21202, or call 1-410-234-0691.

John Pugsley's Journal

Mr. Pugsley has spent years and years trying to identify *something* the government does that is more useful than mischievous. He hasn't found it yet—a fact from which he draws important conclusions for managing and protecting capital. Issued monthly. The cost is $95 for the first year. Order from Marketing and Publishing Associates, Ltd., 23-00 Route 208, Fair Lawn, New Jersey 07410, or call 1-201-794-8886.

Financial Privacy Report

The emphasis of this publication is on the practical—what you can actually do to protect your privacy. It also serves up wonderful horror stories of innocent people who have been crushed by government regulators and run-away juries. A subscription for 12 monthly issues costs $156, $15 for a sample issue. Write to Financial Privacy Report, Inc., P.O. Box 1277, Burnsville, Minnesota 55337, or call 1-612-895-8757.

BOOKS

Following is information on a few volumes I believe are worth your attention, although I don't endorse everything said in every one of them.

Escape the Pension Trap, by Ron Holland. Explains the danger of keeping "too much" in a qualified pension plan and identifies some practical alternatives. $20.00. Order from Offshore Publications, P.O. Box 1201, Skyland, North Carolina 28776. Telephone 1-800-256-7296.

Freedom, Asset Protection and You, by William Comer. Available for $69.95 from Financial Freedom Publishers, Ltd., P.O. Box 268, 9260 Colonville Road, Clare, Michigan 48617. Telephone 1-517-386-7720.

All You Need to Know About the IRS, by Paul N. Strassels, published by Random House. This book is out of print, but you can find it in most large libraries.

Simple Ways to Protect Yourself from Lawsuits, by Mark Warda. Available for $24.95 from Sphinx Publishing, P.O. Box 25, Clearwater, Florida 34617. Telephone 1-800-226-5291.

Internal Revenue Code. Available for $39.00 from Research Institute of America, 117 East Stevens Avenue, Valhalla, New York 10595. Telephone 1-800-431-9025.

Telephone Directories

You can purchase a telephone directory for any place in the world from U.S. West Direct. Call or write to order a directory or request a catalog: U.S. West Direct, c/o PDC, 13100 East 39th Avenue, Unit U, Denver Colorado 80239. Telephone 1-800-422-8793, ext. 100.

MAGAZINE

Offshore Investment reports on tax and privacy havens around the world. A few issues of this publication will remove much of the aura of mystery from the idea of using havens. A one-year subscription is for 10 issues and costs $378, $50 for a sample issue. Write to Subscription Department, Offshore Investment, 62 Brompton Road, Knightsbridge, London SW3 1BW, or call 011-44-171-225-0550. Fax 011-44-171-584-1093.

LIFE INSURANCE AND ANNUITIES

Direct Insurance Services is a discount insurance brokerage for investors. DIS will give you a short list of recommended insurance companies and policies, selected for high rates of return, which it believes best fit your purpose. They handle fixed-dollar and variable life insurance and annuities. They will rebate to you one half of the commissions they earn on your business. Write to Jack White & Co., Insurance Department, 9191 Town Center Drive, Suite 220, San Diego, California 92122, or telephone 1-800-622-3699 or 1-619-552-2000.

JML is a Swiss brokerage company that specializes in Swiss-franc annuities for American investors. To obtain information, write to JML, Baarerstrasse 53, Suite 471, 6304 Zug, Switzerland. They will respond with a brochure on the types of policies available and a form for you to use if you wish to purchase a policy.

Vanguard variable annuities beat most of the competition in keeping expenses low. Write to Vanguard Annuity Center, P.O. Box 1103, Valley Forge, Pennsylvania 19482, or telephone 1-800-522-5555.

Bests Reviews is the standard reporting service on the financial soundness of insurance companies. It is available at most public libraries.

Weiss Reports will give you an evaluation of the financial condition of any U.S. insurance company. The service is available by mail or by telephone, at a price of $25 per evaluation. Write to P.O. Box 109665, Palm Beach Gardens, Florida 33410, or telephone 1-800-289-9222.

TAX-PLANNING FUNDS

The Treasury Bill Portfolio is a money market fund that invests exclusively in short-term U.S. Treasury securities. It is a no-load fund (no commissions) and allows redemption by check. Instead of paying *all* its income in taxable daily dividends, the fund pays an annual dividend in the smallest amount sufficient for the fund itself to avoid income tax. The rest of an investor's return is added to the redemption value of his shares, for long-term tax deferral.

The Versatile Bond Portfolio is a similar fund that invests in short-term corporate bonds (maturing in two years or less) rated A or higher by Standard & Poor's.

The Permanent Portfolio is a highly diversified fund that makes it easy and convenient to apply a permanent portfolio strategy for long-term investment protection and profit. It too pays the smallest dividend possible each year, so that more of an investor's total return comes as tax-deferred appreciation in the redemption value of his shares.

All three funds belong to the Permanent Portfolio Family of Funds, of which I am the president. To obtain a prospectus (which you should review carefully before investing), write to Permanent Portfolio Family of Funds, Box 5847, Austin, Texas 78763, or call 1-800-531-5142. Fax 1-512-453-2015.

LEGAL

Your own lawyer may be the best source of legal advice in devising and carrying out your financial plan. But if he is not expert in tax-planning matters, he probably can refer you to someone who is.

If you are not satisfied with the expertise available to you locally, contact the Law Office of Robert B. Martin, Jr. They specialize in tax law and are knowledgeable about the legal aspects of all the topics covered in this book. Write to Robert B. Martin, Jr., Attorney at Law, 350 West Colorado Boulevard, Suite 320, Pasadena, California 91105, or call 1-818-793-8500. Fax 1-818-793-8779.

PLANNING

Private Investors—I provide a consulting service for investors who want to keep what they earn. The service covers portfolio planning, tax planning, and asset protection and foreign trusts. When appropriate, the service includes referrals to other professionals and to domestic and offshore financial institutions. You can contact my office by writing to Private Investors, P.O. Box 2657, Petaluma, California 94953, or telephone 1-707-778-1000. Fax 1-707-778-8804.

International Retirement Consultants advises on global investing and protection strategies for Individual Retirement Accounts and other pension plans. Their specialty is a Swiss franc annuity program for IRAs that insulates your retirement funds from inflation and protects against sudden changes in U.S. tax rules. For information, write to Ron Holland, International Retirement Consultants, P.O. Box 167, Asheville, North Carolina 28802, or call 1-800-467-5214. Fax 1-704-285-0414.

SWISS BANKS

The three Swiss banks listed here specialize in serving U.S. investors. They provide all the services a stockbroker would provide in the United States—and more. You can use an account at any one of them for simple deposits denominated in Swiss francs, U.S. dollars, or other currencies, or to purchase gold or securities in any market around the world. They welcome accounts opened by mail.

Anker Bank S.A.
Case Postale 127
50 Avenue de la Gare
CH-1001 Lausanne
Switzerland
Telephone: 011-4121-321-0707
Fax: 011-4121-323-9767
(Minimum account: $5,000)

Banca Unione di Credito
Bellariastrasse 82
CH-8038 Zurich
Switzerland
Telephone: 011-411-482-6688
Fax: 011-411-482-2884
(Minimum account: $20,000)

Union Bancaire Privee
Bahnhofstrasse 20
CH-8022 Zurich
Switzerland
Telephone 011-411-219-6111
Fax: 011-411-211-3928
(Minimum account: $100,000)

AUSTRIAN BANK

Anglo Irish Bank (Austria) actively solicits business from North Americans. It can provide all the benefit of Austria's strong secrecy laws while giving you the convenience of dealing with an institution that understands the attitudes and assumptions of U.S. investors. For information, write to Anglo Irish Bank (Austria), Rathausstrasse 20, P.O. Box 306, A-1011, Vienna, Austria. Telephone 011-431-405-8166. Fax 011-431-405-8142.

TAX HAVEN BANKS AND TRUSTEES

Bermuda

Bank of Bermuda is the largest and most sophisticated of Bermuda's three banks. It offers a complete range of deposit, investment and credit card services. Its affiliate, Bermuda Trust Company, can provide trustee services of the highest quality and reliability for personal trusts. Write to Bank of Bermuda, Front Street, Hamilton, Bermuda. Telephone 1-441-295-4000.

Bank of Butterfield is Bermuda's oldest bank. It provides a complete range of banking and trust services. Write to Bank of Butterfield, 65 Front Street, Hamilton, Bermuda. Telephone 1-441-295-1111.

Grosvenor Trust Company is an independent trust company established by former senior trust officers from Bermuda Trust Company (a subsidiary of Bank of Bermuda). It is now the third-largest trust company in Bermuda.

Grosvenor is more flexible than most large institutions, and it has no offices in the United States. Unlike most offshore institutions, Grosvenor is alert to the importance of getting favorable tax results for U.S. investors. And its trustee fees may be less than you would pay elsewhere. Write to Grosvenor Trust Company, Airlie House, 33 Church Street, Hamilton, Bermuda. Telephone 1-441-292-7474. Fax 1-441-292-2668.

Cayman Islands

Royal Bank of Canada is the world's eighth-largest bank. Its Cayman Island office offers a full range of banking services. Write to Royal Bank of Canada, Royal Bank of Canada Building, George Town, Grand Cayman, British West Indies. Telephone 1-809-949-4600.

Royal Bank of Canada Trust Company (Cayman) Limited is an affiliate of Royal Bank of Canada. It provides trustee services for offshore trusts. Write to Royal Bank of Canada Trust Company (Cayman) Limited, Royal Bank of Canada Building, George Town, Grand Cayman, British West Indies. Telephone 1-809-949-8680.

Bermuda Trust (Cayman) is the Cayman Islands affiliate of Bank of Bermuda (see above). It provides trust services and company management. Write to Bermuda Trust (Cayman), British American Tower, Third Floor, George Town, Grand Cayman, British West Indies. Telephone 1-809-949-9898.

Bahamas

Coutts & Company is a 300-year-old English institution specializing in private banking and trust services. For large accounts, they will provide any service a customer might request. They are good at pampering their clients and good at charging for it. Write to Coutts & Company, West Bay Street, Nassau, Bahamas, or call 1-809-326-0404.

REPORTS

A Portfolio You Can Walk Away From. This is the classic telling of Harry Browne's easy-to-live-with formula for investment safety and profit. Available for $10 from Harry Browne's Special Reports, Inc., Box 5586, Austin, Texas 78763, or call 1-512-453-7313.

Passport Financial Offshore Trust Information and Action Package. This extraordinary package allows you to reach the benefits of a foreign trust easily and inexpensively. It contains:

- "Passport to Financial Safety," a technically precise, but very understandable, 36-page report on protective foreign trusts.

- "Protective Trust Guidebook," 67 pages of additional details and estate-planning suggestions.

- A ready-to-use form of trust declaration.

- An annotated trust declaration, explaining the workings of each key provision.

- Professional opinions from a U.S. tax attorney, a U.S. accountant (CPA) and an offshore attorney.

I was involved in preparing this material, so I won't feign objectivity, but I consider the Information and Action Package a masterpiece. For a wide range of investors, it opens the door and makes a foreign trust *practical*. Available for $145 (with a $145 money-back guarantee) from Passport Financial, Inc., P.O. Box 5586, Austin, Texas 78763, or call 1-800-531-5142. ⚷

36

FINANCIAL SOVEREIGNTY

You probably have complained about the government a hundred times—or was it a thousand? And almost everyone you know complains about the government, although the grievances vary from teller to teller.

NEW TIMES

Politics, like religion, once was considered an impolite topic. But today it is a staple of casual conversation—like the weather, the Dodgers and what's for dinner. Nearly anyone you encounter will listen at length to your complaints about government—although he's really waiting for a chance to tell you his.

Unlimited complaining about government has become the norm—the background music of almost every gathering. Don't overlook the significance of this. It means your complaints don't matter. Despite all the squawking, government rolls on—and over most of us.

I don't mean that the efforts you may make—supporting candidates, writing to your newspaper or showing up to vote—are wasted. Even if no one you vote for is ever elected, those who do win count the votes carefully, to figure how much they can get away with. So your efforts do impose a micromilligram of restraint on all those people from whom you wouldn't buy a used car.

But your political efforts won't help you keep what you earn. Instead they are a gift, a kindness you perform, for all the millions of Americans who benefit ever so slightly from the micromilligram of restraint your efforts generate.

Thank you for the gift. Now let's work on *your* problem.

STOP COMPLAINING

I suggest you swear off complaining about the government until you have devised a plan to protect yourself and have put it into effect. The complaints and your efforts to influence the government can easily distract you from the more practical work of protecting what you already control—your own wealth.

Knowledge

Keeping what you earn is a problem—but the problem is solvable. And you can solve it now, without waiting for the world to change. But you need information.

I hope this book has helped.

Chapter 35 will lead you to other sources of information. But don't try to read everything you encounter. Instead, try to digest thoroughly everything you do read. And when you find something you don't understand or that doesn't seem to fit something else you've been told, don't let go of it. Take your puzzles to your attorney, accountant or other advisor. Resolving apparent conflicts in the advice you receive is hard work. It often is frustrating. But it pays generously in deeper understanding.

Then begin to work out your plan. Chapters 29 and 33 give you a procedure to follow, but you may decide to use some other method.

Make your plan as complete as possible—so that you don't get trapped by conflicts between tax planning, asset protection and portfolio planning. But don't wait until you have devised the perfect plan. Perfect never works, because you never quite reach it.

When the plan is complete, put it into action. Most likely, you will start with the easy changes and then go on to the others.

Or if you can't settle on a complete plan, make the changes in your financial life that will help no matter what your final plan turns out to be.

THE STAKES

It may not be easy, but it's worth the effort. Financial planning isn't just about money.

For one thing, it's about your freedom. How free are you if you can lose everything to a clever lawsuit? Or if your business can be destroyed when an innocent jest is twisted into a multimillion-dollar complaint about racial discrimination or sexual harassment? Or if all your property can be seized because a government employee decides you violated Rule 47608362959562785? Not as free as an American colonist *before* the Revolution. Placing your wealth beyond the reach of grabby hands goes a long way toward restoring your freedom.

And money is more than champagne. There are circumstances when it is a matter of life and death.

You probably never have faced such circumstances and most likely never will. But you would be wise to make some allowance for how narrow our imaginations can be. The future surely holds unpleasant secrets we will wish we had known—and had prepared for—today. The best all-purpose preparation is money. And even if *you* never need it for survival, your children or grandchildren someday might.

By keeping what you earn, you perform a great public service—a far greater gift to your friends, neighbors and the millions of decent people you'll never meet than your few minutes in the voting booth. Government doesn't just waste money, its spends it on mischief. By keeping what you earn, you keep your money from being spent to ruin the life of some other alleged violator of Rule 47608362959562785—or from being spent to devise Rule 47608362959562786. Every dollar you save in taxes makes government less dangerous for all of us.

And for that kindness I will be sincerely grateful. ⚿

Terry Coxon
Petaluma, California
June 20, 1996

APPENDIX A

FOREIGN TRUST PLANNING FOR YOUR BENEFICIARIES

In the sections that follow, you'll see how the Protector of your Offshore Protective Trust can use the Trust in his own financial planning. Then we'll show how *any* beneficiary can be given the opportunity to do the same.

ASSET PROTECTION FOR THE PROTECTOR

Because the Trust is a discretionary trust, neither the Protector nor any other beneficiary has any rights he can assign to a creditor. Thus lawsuits aimed at beneficiaries can't reach Trust assets.

In addition, the Protector can use the Trust to protect his own assets through the kinds of transactions described in earlier chapters. He can:

- contribute his assets to a limited partnership (foreign or domestic) in which the Trust's holding company is a general partner.
- sell to the Trust stock representing voting control in his business.
- make long-term, deferred-payment sales to the Trust.

The trustee would have a duty to use its control of the partnership, corporation or property for the advantage of the beneficiaries, including the Protector.

These are the same asset-protection transactions you can use right now. But they will be even more effective for the Protector who succeeds you. For him, the Trust can't be attacked as a fraudulent transfer—because he didn't establish it.[1] And he will be dealing with a Trust that has become completely silent and invisible.

In practice, transactions "with the Trust" probably would be with the Trust's holding company—a foreign corporation owned by the Trust—rather than the Trust itself. This would protect the privacy of the Trust and the Protector, by keeping the Trust's name out of all documents related to the transaction. The same is true of all other transactions between the Protector or other beneficiary and the Trust.

TAX STATUS OF TRUST

To understand how the Protector and your other beneficiaries can best use the Trust, we'll first look at the income tax rules that will surround the Trust after your lifetime. Even though the Trust will be operating in a tax-free environment, the trustee's investment practices will have important income tax implications for the beneficiaries.

Income Tax Rules for the Trust

After your lifetime the Trust will no longer be covered by the grantor trust rules. Instead, it will be classified as a foreign person.

Being foreign, the Trust will have to file a return and pay tax only if it has income from a U.S. business (perhaps through a limited partnership) or from U.S. real estate. It will be subject to 30% withholding if it receives dividends, royalties, pensions or annuities from U.S. sources, although no tax return would be due.

The Trust will be *free* of U.S. tax on all other types of income, including:

- Business and investment profits earned outside the United States
- Life insurance and annuity proceeds from non-U.S. sources
- Capital gains earned in the United States on stocks, bonds, commodities, and almost anything else except real estate
- Interest earned in the United States on all bank deposits and money market instruments, and on bonds issued after July 18, 1984
- Life insurance proceeds from U.S. companies

---

[1] The doctrine of fraudulent transfer protects creditors only of the person who made the transfer. Thus, while *your* creditors might hope to attack your Trust as a fraudulent transfer, creditors of other beneficiaries could not.

In short, by avoiding certain U.S. investments, the Trust can collect and compound its investment returns tax free.

Tax Accounting for the Trust

Despite its freedom from U.S. taxation, the Trust should keep an accounting of its "taxable" income as though it were a U.S. taxpayer. Doing so will help the beneficiaries avoid unnecessary taxes on money the Trust gives them.

The Trust's account of "taxable" income begins as of the date of your death. (Under the grantor trust rules, earnings during your lifetime are *your* income, not the Trust's.) The account should include all interest, dividends, etc., and all capital gains and losses—but exclude any items that would be tax exempt for a U.S. taxpayer, such as life insurance proceeds.

The Trust also will keep a record of its distributions to beneficiaries. By comparing the cumulative distributions with its cumulative income, the Trust will be able to determine at any time whether, under U.S. tax rules, it is holding any undistributed income.

Income Tax Rules for Beneficiaries

Because the Trust is discretionary, no beneficiary can be taxed on "his share" of earnings the Trust accumulates for future use. The tax collector's only opportunity for taxing a beneficiary is when he receives a distribution.

Taxable Distributions.   A beneficiary is taxable only on distributions paid to him out of the Trust's income. A distribution is assumed to be drawn from Trust income unless, at the time it is made, the Trust has already distributed all its income, as measured by the income account described above.[2]

The tax a beneficiary pays on an income distribution is subject to an interest charge, based on the number of years the trust held the income before distributing it.[3] The interest charge is 6% per year of the regular tax, but it does not compound. Without proper planning (explained below), reg-

---

[2] An income distribution from a foreign trust is ordinary income for the beneficiary who receives it, even if the trust earned the money as a capital gain.

[3] Each distribution of income is considered to be drawn from the "oldest" money earned by the Trust and not yet distributed. The interest charge applies only to distributions from *foreign* trusts.

ular income tax plus the interest charge can consume every penny of a distribution.

Tax-Free Distributions. A distribution made when the trust has already paid out all its income is a distribution of capital and hence is tax free to the beneficiary.

Foreign Beneficiaries. A distribution to a beneficiary who is not a U.S. taxpayer (someone who is neither a citizen nor a resident of the United States) is free of U.S. tax. When you establish your Trust, all the beneficiaries then living probably will be U.S. taxpayers. But if *all* your descendants are to be beneficiaries, including those not yet born, someday one of them might be a foreigner.

Income Tax Planning by the Trust

The first goal of the Trust's tax planning should be to protect beneficiaries from the 6% interest charge.

The 6% Solution. The Trust can stifle the interest charge by deferring its income until it needs money for a distribution. It might use almost any device you would use to defer income, but a more sweeping solution is available to it.

Rather than hold all its assets directly, the Trust should transfer its income-producing investments to a tax haven corporation in which it owns all the stock. The holding company will serve as a reservoir, accumulating income until the Trust is ready to make a distribution.[4]

Eventually, when money is needed, the holding company can pay a dividend, which for the Trust would be "fresh" income, not accumulated income. The Trust then can distribute the money without subjecting the beneficiary to the 6% interest charge.

---

[4] The rules on foreign personal holding companies and controlled foreign corporations, and the tax penalties for investors in passive foreign investment companies, (all explained in Appendix B) should not apply, since the company would have no U.S. shareholders, all the stock being owned by the Trust, which will be a foreign person. Because the Trust is discretionary, the holding company would not even have *indirect* U.S. shareholders. While it probably is not necessary, you can erect a further barrier to the discovery of U.S. shareholders by including a foreign person (such as a foreign charity) in the beneficiary class of your Trust.

Distributions Without Tax. The steps the trustee takes to protect beneficiaries from the 6% interest charge come close to protecting them from regular income tax. If the Trust goes a step further and raises cash to pay distributions without first recognizing taxable income, the beneficiaries will receive the money tax free, as discussed more fully under "Tax-Free Distributions," later in this appendix.

TAX PLANNING *WITH* THE TRUST

In many dealings, tax advantages can be shifted from one party to another—for example, by making offsetting changes in price and interest rate; by making the transaction a lease rather than a purchase; or by characterizing an investment as a bond, a share of stock or an option. Tax benefits frequently are part of the bargaining: the party who gets them has to give up something in return.

But when your successor as Protector deals with the Trust, he can have the good without the bad. Being a foreigner, the Trust will have no need for U.S. tax advantages, so it will gladly tailor any transaction to his tax-planning convenience.

Shifting Wealth to the Trust

By shifting income and assets away from himself and toward the Trust (or its holding company), the Protector can cut his income tax bill and reduce his taxable estate. The Protector can be generous in such dealings because he needn't lose what the Trust gains. The Trust exists for his welfare and the welfare of the other beneficiaries—some of whom may be his dependents. What the Trust earns will come back to him and them—perhaps after a sojourn in the world of tax-free investing and perhaps as tax-free cash—when it is needed.

Transactions that feed the Trust and save taxes for the Protector or his estate include:

Sale of Call Options to the Trust. The Protector can sell to the Trust long-term options to purchase stocks, bonds, precious metals, collectibles, and other investments he owns (almost anything except U.S. real estate). Such options could run for very long periods, such as 20 or 30 years, or even beyond the Protector's life expectancy. As explained in Chapter 15, "Managing Capital Gains," selling a call option turns an investment's appreciation into spendable cash—without triggering capital gain tax or reporting obligations. But usually it's hard to find a buyer for a long-term call option, unless you are a Protector dealing with your own Trust.

Such long-term call options aren't traded in any public market, so there are no published prices or quotes. Thus the Protector has considerable leeway to offer attractive terms to the Trust without creating the appearance of a giveaway.

Deferred-Payment Sales to the Trust.   As explained in Chapter 14, some deferred-payment sales postpone tax on capital gain and interest earnings—if you are willing to tolerate a measure of illiquidity. But illiquidity isn't much of a problem when the Protector makes a deferred-payment sale to the Trust, since he always can ask the trustee for an early payoff.

To make the sale especially profitable to the Trust, the Protector can accept an interest rate as low as the Applicable Federal Rate.[5]

Loans.   The Protector can borrow from the Trust to finance his business or investment purchases. The interest he pays would be tax deductible, and if he pays an especially generous rate of interest, he gets an especially generous tax deduction.

U.S. Business.   The Trust can own all the stock in a U.S. corporation formed to gradually absorb the value of the Protector's U.S. business, as explained in Chapter 32, "More Estate Tax Strategies." This reduces the Protector's taxable estate and eventually allows the business to be sold to an outsider without capital gain tax. Depending on the nature of the business, the corporation may require only nominal initial capital, so that the cost of the Trust's investment would be small.

International Business.   If the Protector does business outside the United States, he can use the Trust to rescue a portion of his profits from income and estate tax. For example, if the Protector has an import or export business, the Trust can form an international sales corporation, in a tax haven, to act as a middleman. Its markup on the goods being traded would reduce the Protector's taxable income and estate—and would go untaxed.[6]

---

[5] The AFR, is explained in Chapter 30.

[6] Arrangements of this type are the primary target of the rules on Controlled Foreign Corporations (CFCs, discussed in Appendix B). You avoid those rules, however, because a corporation owned by a nongrantor, discretionary foreign trust has no U.S. stockholders and therefore is not a CFC.

Investment Opportunity.   From time to time, the Protector may encounter an unusually attractive business or investment opportunity—a
chance to make a large profit on a small outlay. Rather than pursue it himself, he can invite the Trust to do so, thereby avoiding growth in his taxable
estate.

Sales of Collectibles.   Collectibles of any kind—art works, gem-
stones, stamps, numismatics, antiques—are extremely difficult to appraise.
Similar items may vary greatly in price from dealer to dealer or from one
auction to the next. The broad uncertainty about value makes collectibles
ideal for selling to the Trust. If, for example, the Protector owns a stamp collection with an appraised value of $50,000 to $70,000, he can sell it to the
Trust for $55,000.

Annuities.   To reduce his taxable estate and to acquire an income he
cannot outlive, the Protector can buy an annuity from the Trust.

Other Transactions.   These are just some of the ways the Protector
can use the Trust to reduce his taxable income and estate, while building up
a fund of assets that can be invested and reinvested tax free until needed.
Your successor as protector probably will find other opportunities. Typically,
they will involve some unsettleable question about value that permits the
Protector to deal on terms that are profitable for the Trust.

ENJOYING THE FRUITS

Sooner or later, the Protector will want to draw on the Trust's assets for
his own comfort and enjoyment or will advise the trustee to assist other beneficiaries (such as the Protector's children or grandchildren). The Trustee
will have many avenues for doing so. Its choices will affect each recipient's
tax bill and privacy.

Taxable Distributions

When the time comes, the Protector can simply ask the trustee to
make a distribution—a gift. A distribution of income will be taxable, to the
extent explained on page 155. But the 6% interest charge won't apply,
assuming the Trust has used a holding company or other device to defer
income.

Tax-Free Distributions

A distribution will be tax free to the beneficiary if the Trust has already distributed all its income.

Using a holding company to accumulate income helps to keep distributions tax free, since it defers the Trust's receipt of the income. But if the holding company is not paying dividends to the Trust, where will the Trust get the money to distribute? Fortunately, there are a number of possible sources.

Investment Sales. If the Trust owns investments that have fallen in value, it can liquidate them without recognizing income.[7] Or it can sell investments that have appreciated, if it sells other investments with offsetting losses, without recognizing net income. In either case, the entire proceeds could be distributed to beneficiaries tax free.

Exempt Income. Income that would be tax exempt for a U.S. taxpayer is treated as capital, not as income, when the Trust collects it. Thus the Trust can distribute life insurance proceeds and interest on municipal bonds tax free to beneficiaries.

Borrowing. The Trust can borrow against its investments to raise cash and can distribute the proceeds to beneficiaries tax free.

Borrowing, however, is not as broad an opportunity for raising no-income cash as it might appear. Loans against precious metals and non-dividend-paying stocks, which the Trust might own directly, would be a workable source of no-income cash. But money borrowed against the stock of the Trust's holding company would not be. As explained in Appendix B, "Foreign Corporations," the Trust's holding company will be a Passive Foreign Investment Company, or PFIC. If PFIC stock is pledged for a loan, the loan proceeds are considered income and thus would be taxable when distributed.

Other Tax-Free Avenues

At some point it will become impractical for the Trust to raise cash without receiving income, such as a dividend from the holding company.

---

[7] If the Trust was included in your estate, gain or loss on a sale of Trust property is based on the property's value at the time of your death. If the Trust was not included in your estate, then gain or loss is based on the property's cost to you.

But there are other avenues for transferring money to a beneficiary without tax. Any transfer that is not a distribution (that is, not an outright gift) will do.

Lending.   The Trust's holding company can lend money to a beneficiary or guarantee a loan for him. Eventually the beneficiary (or his estate) will have to repay the loan, which may require a taxable distribution from the Trust. But the loan itself will be tax free. So in the worst case, lending money to the beneficiary rather than giving him a taxable distribution delays whatever tax might eventually be due.

The interest rate on the loan could be as low as the Applicable Federal Rate.

Long-term Options.   As explained earlier in the chapter, the holding company can buy long-term call options on investments owned by a beneficiary. Such a transaction would be tax free for the beneficiary until the option either expires or is exercised. The holding company can pay the highest reasonable price for the option.

INVISIBLE TRUST

What is impossible during your lifetime will be fairly simple afterwards. Once you're gone, the Trust can be lawfully invisible. But if your successor as Protector wants the Trust to remain invisible, he should advise the trustee to take some care in handling distributions. While no one has to file reports on the Trust itself, distributions could trigger reports that in turn point to the Trust.

Reporting Taxable Distributions

Taxable distributions are the biggest problem because they must be reported. To file a correct tax return, a beneficiary must identify the Trust as the source of the distribution. Because of the potential penalties, he would be foolish not to.

The Protector can advise the trustee to control this "leak" by postponing taxable distributions for as long as possible—perhaps for a generation. In the meantime, the Protector and other beneficiaries can receive cash through tax-free distributions, loans or option sales.

Exposing Tax-Free Distributions

Tax-free distributions also present a privacy problem, but a lesser one. Tax-free distributions are not reportable, so a beneficiary breaks no rules by keeping them secret. A beneficiary could, for example, use an ATM card to receive tax-free cash without making any reports.

However, in a thorough tax audit, a large distribution that a beneficiary has received in recent years might come to light. To prove the distribution was in fact not taxable, or at least to shift the burden of proof onto the IRS, the beneficiary would be forced to point to the Trust as the source of the money. And he would need to present at least a summary history of Trust income and distributions to show that his distribution was not taxable.

In short, while tax-free distributions are private in principle, in practice they may not be, especially if they are large. So if the Trust's privacy is important to the Protector, he should advise the trustee that loans and option transactions are preferable to large distributions of any kind.

Private Benefits

A further avenue (or, rather, an eight-lane highway) for providing cash privately is to reverse the direction of the Trust-feeding transactions described earlier. Instead of weighting a transaction in favor of the Trust, weight it in favor of the beneficiary. For example, you might *buy* an investment from the Trust at the lowest reasonable price.

A single transaction might not guarantee a profit to the beneficiary, but a series of them would stack the deck in his favor—he would be playing in a casino where the odds are tilted his way. This isn't as simple as receiving a distribution, but, in the long run, it's nearly as good. None of the transactions would trigger reports pointing to the Trust.[8]

PLANNING FOR OTHER BENEFICIARIES

Any beneficiary can use the Trust for his own tax planning and asset protection. But only the Protector is likely to use it to full advantage, because only he has the comfort of knowing he can, if necessary, pester the trustee or even fire it.

---

[8] Such transactions also could be used to milk value out of the Trust if the Trust had accumulated income that, if distributed, would trigger the 6% interest charge.

BE REAL

Dealings between the Trust and a beneficiary can be tilted in favor of one side or the other. But if tilted too far, they will fall over and hurt someone.

Feeding the Trust

The Protector can be generous in dealing with the Trust, but not to the point of making a gift to it. That would make the Protector, for U.S. income tax purposes, a *grantor*, and under the grantor trust rules he would be taxable on the Trust's income from the gift.

To put it differently, the Protector should not be so generous with the Trust that he seems to be dealing with his brother. For example, if he wants the Trust to profit from a deferred-payment sale, he can agree to an interest rate as low as the Applicable Federal Rate. Low as that is, it isn't unreasonable for a seller, perhaps wanting to defer taxes, to accept. But a lower rate would invite the IRS to say "giveaway."

Or if the Protector borrows from the Trust, he can reasonably pay interest at 4 or 5 percentage points over the prime rate. But paying 15 percentage points over the prime rate would be a poorly disguised gift.

Or if the Protector sells something to the Trust, the price can be low—but not so low that it would be easy to find a buyer willing to pay more.

For the Protector, the Trust can be the goose that sucks up golden eggs. But the Protector should not stuff the goose artlessly. As explained in Chapter 3, "Words at Play," you can't transform a gift into a sale or a loan just by calling it that.

The Protector can easily provide the same comfort to any other beneficiary who wants to use the Trust for his own financial planning. Only three steps are needed. The Protector:

1. advises the trustee to separate a portion of the Trust's assets and hold them for the exclusive benefit of certain beneficiaries;

2. names one of those beneficiaries as his successor for that portion of the Trust;

3. resigns as Protector with respect to that portion of the Trust.

FEEDING UPON THE TRUST

Beneficiaries must observe the same restraint in draining wealth from the Trust.

If a beneficiary sells something to the Trust, the price shouldn't be demonstrably higher than anyone else would be willing to pay. Or if he borrows from the Trust, he should pay at least the Applicable Federal Rate if the loan is secured, or a higher rate if the loan is unsecured.

Going beyond these limitations risks making the transaction partly a gift, or a distribution, from the Trust to the beneficiary—which, if the Trust has undistributed income, would be taxable. The beneficiary would need to report the distribution as income and pay tax, which would invite the IRS to argue about the size of the distribution.

The standard for transactions that drain the Trust is the same as for transactions that feed it. Whatever the transaction—loan, cash sale, installment sale, option or something else—the terms can be especially advantageous for one side or the other, but not so extreme that the transaction is a giveaway.

For example, suppose you have named all your descendants, including persons not yet born, as beneficiaries. Suppose further that you have named each of your three sons to succeed you as Protector of a separate portion of the Trust. Eventually, the adult daughter of your eldest son wants to use the Trust for her own financial planning. The trustee, with the advice of that son, can separate a further portion of the Trust for the exclusive benefit of his daughter and her descendants. Then your son can name his daughter as his successor, and resign, with respect to that portion of the Trust.

The daughter can deal with the Trust as she wants—for example, by selling a long-term call option to a holding company owned by "her" separate portion of the Trust.

APPENDIX B

FOREIGN CORPORATIONS

As you investigate tax havens, you may encounter offhand suggestions about using a foreign corporation to avoid tax. Or you may be advised to defer tax by investing through offshore mutual funds. Or you may receive cynical promotions for the tax magic of a foreign bank charter.

Don't bite. As a stand-alone device for income tax planning, foreign corporations simply don't work.

What It Is

A corporation is *foreign* if it is organized or chartered under the laws of a foreign country.

It's easy for a foreign corporation to invest tax free, provided it avoids certain types of U.S. investments subject to withholding (as explained in Chapter 21, "Introduction to Havens"). But arranging for the corporation to avoid U.S. tax does not *by itself* do you any good.

FOUR SNARES

Over the years, Congress has defined four special categories of foreign corporation, with special, sand-in-your-eyes tax treatment for their U.S. stockholders. The four categories are:

- Foreign Personal Holding Company
- Controlled Foreign Corporation

- Foreign Investment Company
- Passive Foreign Investment Company

Whether a foreign corporation falls into one of these categories depends on how much stock is owned by U.S. investors (especially by a small number of U.S. investors) and/or on whether most of the corporation's income is "passive income."

Passive income has a slightly different meaning for each special category, but generally includes:

- Dividends, interest, rents, royalties and annuities
- Gain from sales of securities
- Gain from commodity or commodity futures transactions
- Income from personal services if the customer may require an individual who owns 25% or more (by value) of the corporation's stock to perform the services

To close some obvious loopholes, a U.S. investor may be deemed to own stock in a foreign corporation "indirectly" or "constructively" if he spreads shares among family members or controlled partnerships, trusts or corporations, or if he owns options to buy stock in the foreign corporation.

Foreign Personal Holding Company

A corporation is a Foreign Personal Holding Company (FPHC) if it satisfies *both* of two tests:

FPHC income test—more than 50% of the corporation's gross income for the year is passive income.

FPHC ownership test—more than 50% of the *value* of the corporation's stock is owned by five or fewer individuals who are U.S. taxpayers.

If a corporation is an FPHC for the year, each U.S. stockholder must include his share of the company's net income in his own tax return, as though he had received a dividend.

Controlled Foreign Corporation

A foreign corporation's status as a Controlled Foreign Corporation (CFC) is based on how much stock is owned by U.S. stockholders who individually own 10% or more of the voting power in the corporation. If five or fewer such stockholders together own more than 50% of the voting power or more than 50% of the value of the stock, the corporation is a CFC.

Each 10%-or-more U.S. stockholder must include his share of the corporation's passive income in his tax return each year, regardless of whether the corporation pays it to him as a dividend. And when the shareholder sells his CFC stock, the profit is ordinary income, not capital gain. If the shareholder dies owning the stock, the basis of the stock is not reset to equal fair market value.

Foreign Investment Company

A foreign corporation is a Foreign Investment Company (FIC) if it passes *both* of two tests:

> *FIC ownership test*—more than 50% of the value of the stock, or more than 50% of the voting power of the stock, is owned by U.S. stockholders. Concentration of ownership doesn't matter; a foreign corporation can pass the FIC ownership test even if no one shareholder owns more than a few shares.

> *FIC activities test*—the corporation is engaged primarily in investing, reinvesting or trading in securities or commodities.

The penalty associated with an FIC is comparatively mild. When you sell or redeem your stock, the profit is taxed as ordinary income *to the extent* of your share of any income the corporation accumulated while you owned the stock. If you die owning the stock, its basis is not reset to fair market value.

Passive Foreign Investment Company

A foreign corporation is a Passive Foreign Investment Company (PFIC) for a given year if 75 or more of its gross income is passive income or if 50% or more of its assets (by value) are held for the production of passive income.

The tax penalties for PFIC investors are horrendous. You are not required to pay tax on phantom dividends, but when you do sell your shares:

- The profit is ordinary income.
- The profit is subject to tax at rates that may be higher than you pay on the rest of your income.
- You must pay compound interest on the tax, based on the number of years you held the shares.
- The basic tax and the interest together can exceed the value of the shares.

If the dividends you receive from a PFIC grow at a rate higher than approximately 8% per year, the "excess" is taxed as though it were profit on the sale of shares.

If you dispose of the shares in any way, such as by giving them away or by dying, you are taxed as though you had sold them. If you pledge the shares as collateral for a loan, the money is taxed as though it were the proceeds of a sale. If you die owning the stock, its basis is not reset to fair market value.

You can avoid this financial mutilation by electing to have your PFIC stock treated as stock in a *Qualified Electing Fund* (QEF). By making the election, you volunteer to be taxed currently on your share of the corporation's earnings and profits, much as though the corporation were a FPHC. For your QEF election to be valid, the corporation must agree to make its income and shareholder records available to the IRS.

REPORTS

If you own 5% or more of any class of stock in a foreign corporation, you are required to file special information returns. Your filing requirements depend on how much stock you own, the degree of control you have over the corporation, and whether the corporation is an FPHC, CFC, FIC or PFIC.

If you own any stock in a PFIC, you must file Form 8621 with your annual tax return. You do not need to disclose the size of your holdings until you dispose of stock or receive a dividend.

USE BY PROTECTIVE FOREIGN TRUST

Despite all the rules, your Protective Foreign Trust will be able to use a foreign corporation to accumulate income after your lifetime. Because the corporation will have no direct or indirect U.S. stockholders, it will not be an FPHC, CFC or FIC. It probably will be a PFIC. But because neither the trust nor the beneficiaries will be subject to tax on the trust's income, the corporation's status as a PFIC won't entail a tax liability for anyone.

APPENDIX C

TAX SHELTERS— WHAT'S LEFT

A tax shelter is an investment that lowers your tax bill by generating more deductions or credits than taxable income.

Before 1976 there was no limit to the deductions you could achieve fairly easily with tax shelters. If you needed more deductions, you got them by buying more shelters. The nation's investment dealers were well stocked, and they were waiting for you.

Even until 1986 it was possible to shelter an unlimited amount of income, although it had become more difficult. The trick also was becoming more expensive, as successive rule changes foreclosed many opportunities for deducting "expenses" you would never actually bear.

THREE CHANGES

Three radical revisions in the rules shrank the wide, wild world of tax shelters down to a tame hamlet.

At-Risk Rule

The first change was the *at-risk rule*, enacted in 1976. Under the at-risk rule, you can't deduct more on an investment than the amount you put "at risk"—the cash you invest plus any debt for which you are personally and unconditionally liable.

The at-risk rule ended many shelter schemes that paid for movies, industrial equipment or other business assets with a small amount of cash plus huge nonrecourse notes secured solely by the assets themselves (i.e., with no residual liability for the borrower). Nonrecourse debt made it painless for investors to "pay" extravagant prices for business assets and then claim large depreciation deductions.

Rental real estate originally was excluded from the at-risk rule, which accounted for real estate's increased importance in tax planning from 1976 onward. Real estate was brought under a modified at-risk rule in 1986.

Original Issue Discount

The second attack on tax shelters was the *original issue discount* (OID) rules enacted in 1984.

The OID rules made it impossible (or at least very difficult) to avoid the effect of the at-risk rule by financing tax shelter assets with low-interest, long-term promissory notes. Low-interest notes have a true economic value far below their face value. A promise to pay $10,000 in 20 years at an interest rate of 4%, for example, has much less economic value than a promise to pay $10,000 in 3 years at an interest rate of 12%. The at-risk rule doesn't distinguish between the two. The OID rules do.

Passive Loss Limitation

The third measure, the *passive loss limitation* enacted in 1986, struck at the heart of the tax shelter business.

Beneath all the hocus-pocus of a tax shelter, there usually was some fairly ordinary thing that made it work—the oil well, the apartment house, the leased-out computer. It was something that, in principle, you could buy on your own, provided your budget was large enough and you were prepared to manage the project.

What made tax shelters workable for most investors was the packaging that promoters wrapped around the underlying business—arrangements that freed investors from the cares of management and allowed them to buy in small increments. The packaging made it practical for many taxpayers to invest in businesses they otherwise would not have entered.

But with the passive loss limitation, a taxpayer can deduct tax losses from a "passive business activity" only to the extent he has income from the same or other passive business activities. Passive activity losses can't be deducted against income from salary, investments or active business interests.[1]

---

[1] Although it may in fact be utterly passive, investing in stocks, bonds or commodities is not a passive business activity. Hence interest and other expenses associated with such investments are not restricted by the limitation on passive losses.

What makes a business activity passive for a taxpayer is that he participates only as an investor. Thus the effect of the passive loss limitation is to make the packaging of tax shelters futile. Even if a business can be structured to show a tax loss, any arrangement that relieves an investor of the cares of management also blocks the business's tax deductions from reaching his tax return.

Because of the these three broad changes—the at-risk rule, the OID rules and the passive loss limitation—tax shelters no longer hold out the promise of sweeping away your tax bill. It won't do any good to tell a tax advisor the day after Christmas that you need some quick deductions. But there is still a little life left in shelters.

BASIC INGREDIENTS

Tax shelters operate by exaggerating and distilling the discrepancies between the tax rules and economic reality discussed in Chapter 2, "The Tax Collector's Puzzle." In working this magic, most shelters emphasize one or more of three elements the tax rules do a poor job of measuring: interest expense, capital recovery and capital expenditures.

Interest Expense

When inflation occurs, interest rates rise to allow for the rate at which money is losing value. When inflation is high, an interest payment is mostly a repayment of the loan's purchasing power, rather than a true expense.

But the tax rules ignore inflation. In determining profit, the tax rules say, "Subtract interest payments (but ignore the shrinkage in the debt's purchasing power)."

The high inflation of the 1970s, which coincided with the heyday of tax shelters, made the deductibility of interest more significant than it is today. But inflation is still high enough that a large part of any interest payment is in economic fact a repayment of principal and not a true expense.

Capital Recovery

The owner of a business may claim deductions—usually, depreciation or depletion—for the using up of long-lived assets.

Buildings and machines wear out with use and time. Their decline in value is a cost of doing business and should be subtracted in determining true net income. For many assets, the tax rules allow a fraction of the original cost to be deducted each year as depreciation. Eventually, over a period of years, the entire cost is deducted.

The rules for computing capital recovery deductions are far from perfect, sometimes overstating and sometimes understating the rate at which capital assets are deteriorating or being exhausted. Any asset for which the rules permit a substantial exaggeration or acceleration of capital recovery is potentially a tax shelter.

Capital Expenditures

Some tax shelters, especially oil- and gas-drilling programs (discussed below) let you deduct the cost of an investment—as though the money you spend were an expense of operating, rather than acquiring, a business asset.

RENTAL REAL ESTATE

Renting real estate is classified as a passive activity. But, despite the passive loss rule, an investor may deduct up to $25,000 per year of real estate tax losses against income from any source. However, the maximum allowable deduction is reduced by $500 for each $1,000 of the investor's adjusted gross income over $100,000, reaching zero when adjusted gross income equals $150,000.

To qualify for this limited exemption from the passive loss limitation, a real estate investor must own at least a 10% share in a property and must "actively participate" in managing it. Approving tenants and leases is sufficient to meet the test of active participation. (No one will hold it against you if you have trouble understanding how you can actively participate in a passive activity.)

Rental real estate became subject to the at-risk rule in 1987. Deductible losses may not exceed the amount you have at risk in a property, but the rules for computing that amount are friendlier to real estate than to other investments.

Initially, the amount at risk in a real estate investment is your cash down payment, plus any borrowings for which you are personally liable, plus any *nonrecourse* borrowings from a bank or other commercial lender that has no equity interest in your investment (but not from the seller). Thus if you purchase a $200,000 property with a $40,000 down payment, a $100,000 nonrecourse first mortgage from a bank and a $60,000 nonrecourse second mortgage from the seller, your amount at risk is $140,000.

The amount at risk decreases each year by your net tax loss on the property. It increases if you have net taxable income from the property, if you make principal payments on debt that was not originally included in the amount at risk, or if you make improvements that are not currently deductible.

In the usual circumstance, a real estate investment is financed by a cash down payment plus a mortgage from a commercial lender, both of which would count as at risk. And even if you finance a purchase partly with a nonrecourse mortgage granted by the seller, your principal payments to him will contribute to the amount at risk. Thus the at-risk limitation is not likely to get in the way of deducting losses on rental real estate.

Nature of Shelter

It is depreciation deductions and interest expense that make rental property a tax shelter.

Residential real property may be depreciated on a "straight line" over a period of 27½ years, or at a rate of 3.64% per year. Thus if you purchase a house for $100,000, you will receive depreciation deductions of $3,636 per year for as long as you own it, up to 27½ years. Of course, unless a house is very poorly constructed or very poorly maintained, its true economic life will be much greater than 27½ years, so depreciation deductions ordinarily will exceed the actual physical deterioration of the house.

Nonresidential real property is depreciated over a period of 31½ years, or at an annual rate of 3.17%.

Interest you pay to finance the property will be deductible. But, so long as inflation continues, the interest deduction will exceed your true interest expense. If you borrow $80,000 at a rate of 9% per year when inflation is running at 5%, the true borrowing cost is only 4% per year. You recover the other 5% indirectly, through a decline in the purchasing power of your debt.

OIL AND GAS

Oil- and gas-drilling programs receive unusual, and very generous, tax treatment.

"Intangible drilling costs," which usually amount to 60% or 70% or so of the cost of a successful well, are fully deductible in the year the well is drilled. The intangibles—things that get used up and become unsalvageable—include fees paid for drilling services (probably the largest single item), professional fees, drilling mud and other consumable materials, and fuel and labor.

If a well is not successful, all costs not already deducted are deductible in the year the well is abandoned.

Even after you have deducted the full amount of your investment, you continue to receive *percentage depletion* deductions equal to 15% of the gross value of the well's production—which may amount to much more than 15% of the well's *net* income. However, percentage depletion is limited to 50% of the well's net income (computed without regard to the percentage depletion deduction) and is further limited to 65% of your net income from all sources.

The passive loss limitation allows an exception for oil and gas drilling. Even though you do not participate in the drilling except as an investor, your interest is deemed to be an active interest if you own it through an arrangement that doesn't limit your legal liability for the debts of the project. Thus oil and gas drilling is one of the few avenues left for obtaining large deductions without getting your hands dirty. The type of entity ordinarily used is a *joint venture,* in which one venturer has all management responsibility and the investors agree to be liable for all the venture's debts.

If the managing joint venturer knows what he is doing, your apparently open-ended liability should in fact be nominal. Assuming that the venture doesn't borrow any money, the only potential for loss beyond your cash investment is from accidents at the well site. Unless the program is run recklessly, this risk will be covered by workers' compensation and casualty insurance.

Sleeping, Not Dead

Little has been heard from promoters of drilling programs since the collapse of oil prices in 1984. With oil at $15 or $18 per barrel, there are few practical opportunities for drilling in the United States. But drilling programs are likely to become prominent again if the price of oil gets over $30 a barrel or so. If and when that happens, should you invest?

I have had a considerable amount of experience with oil and gas drilling—mostly sad. The fundamental problem for an investor is the difficulty of determining whether or not he is being cheated—which inflates the probability that he is.

The drilling business is extremely complex. Even an honest, competently run program is subject to numerous hazards—including explosions above and below ground, equipment failures, accidents and injuries, encounters with unexpectedly hard rock, discovering an underground sea, encountering a cavity, bad weather, shortages of materials, strikes and disputes with landowners and local regulatory authorities. Another common hazard is drilling in a place where there is no oil and no gas.

And finding oil or gas is only one requirement for success. The well still must be "completed"—which means setting steel casing (pipe) to seal the wall of the shaft, cementing the casing into place, perforating the casing (with explosives or tools) at exactly the right depth to permit the oil or gas believed to be present to flow into the casing, and treating the geological formation at the selected depth (with more explosives or with air, nitrogen, water, acid or other chemicals) to stimulate the flow of petroleum.

Even if the well is successfully completed, it may produce abundantly for only a few months and then peter out. Or, in the case of a gas well, it may produce like a champion—until the local pipeline operator stops accepting delivery.

Everything has to go just right for a well to be profitable, and the work ordinarily will be done by numerous independent firms, many of whom draw comfort from the thought that any evidence of their negligence would lie thousands of feet below the ground. Any one of them can turn a project into a money loser by overcharging or underperforming—and no one but an attentive oil and gas professional would notice.

The drilling program salesman who one day may knock on your door probably won't be an oil and gas professional—he'll be a salesman. And there's a good chance the program's manager or other organizer will be a financial professional and only secondarily an oil and gas man. On the other hand, if the program manager is an astute oil and gas professional, you will be dealing with someone who knows all the tricks for milking investors.

THE FUTURE OF TAX SHELTERS

The tax shelter industry is quiet now, but I expect it to liven up.

Every industry requires raw materials of one kind or another. The tax shelter industry receives its essential raw materials from Congress, which impose high tax rates together with provisions for earning deductions and credits. Congress was paid well for turning out the raw materials for the golden age of tax shelters in the 1970s—paid with campaign contributions and political favors that added to the tenure and power of numerous Congressmen.

Through various tax reforms culminating with the Tax Reform Act of 1986, Congress confiscated most of the raw materials it had sold over the years. It did so to be able once again to sell the same materials, or workable substitutes, to the tax shelter industry—for more campaign contributions and more political favors.

Step by step the supply of raw materials will be restored to the tax shelter industry. You will hear elected officials announce almost tearfully that tax rates must be raised to save us from a deficit disaster and to pay for certain oh-so-worthy purposes. And the same officials will invite you to thank them for the deductions, credits, deferrals, accelerations and other tax gizmos they have bestowed upon investments for certain oh-so-very-worthy purposes—which purposes are thereby fostered without additional government spending, about which they wholeheartedly share your opinion that it is much, much too high and they have a plan to reduce it in five years. You can count on it. Tax shelters will return. Campaigns aren't getting any cheaper.

ACKNOWLEDGMENTS

What a pest I've been! Poking into this and that and asking long questions of nearly every attorney, accountant, investment advisor and international banker I've encountered since I began this book. Fortunately I have an excuse: the encouragement I received from everyone to whom I turned for help. I am particularly grateful to:

Leonard Radomile, who introduced me to international tax planning and who spent many hours over many years answering and discussing;

Bob Martin, that most skilled and passionate taxpayer advocate, who guided me through a thousand puzzles;

Rick Rolnick, who criticized and tuned large portions of the book;

John Chandler, who showed me the importance of showing benefits; and

Harry Browne, who taught me to be kind to the reader.

INDEX

Page numbers for definitions or overviews are in boldface type.
Page numbers for exhibits or text that is boxed and highlighted
for emphasis are in italic type.